Gary Siegel
The Rhinebeck Center
Progressive Psychotherapy
8 Garden Street
Rhinebeck, N.Y. 12572

Panic Disorder

Panic
Disorder

Assessment and Treatment
Through a Wide-Angle Lens

FRANK M. DATTILIO
JESUS A. SALAS-AUVERT

ZEIG, TUCKER & CO., INC.
PHOENIX, ARIZONA

Published by

ZEIG, TUCKER & CO., INC.
3618 North 24 Street
Phoenix, AZ 85016

Library of Congress Cataloging-in-Publicatiaon Data

Dattilio, Frank M.
Panic disorder : assessment and treatment through a wide-angle lens / Frank M. Dattilio, Jesus A. Salas-Auvert.
p.   cm.
Includes bibliographical references and index.
ISBN 1-891944-35-5
1. Panic disorders—Treatment.   2. Panic attacks—Treatment.
3. Anxiety—Prevention.   I. Salas-Auvert, Jesus A.
[DNLM: 1. Panic Disorder—therapy.   WM   172 D234p 1999]
RC535.D38   1999
DNLM/DLC
for Library of Congress   99-27032
CIP

Designed by Kathleen Lake, Neuwirth and Associates

Manufactured in the United States of America

10   9   8   7   6   5   4   3   2   1

Acknowledgments

As any scholar or researcher knows all too well, writing a book is much easier when little research or written material on the given topic exists. In such cases, there is plenty of time for composing and less time devoted to sifting through decades of literature and coordinating concepts and references. Unfortunately, panic is not one of those topics and consequently the time and coordination expended in preparing this text were exorbitant.

This work would not have been possible without the help of many people. We owe our gratitude to the hundreds of patients whom we have treated over the years who have helped to refine our understanding of what panic is truly about. If it were not for the many difficult or atypical cases that we treated, we would not have looked harder to find more effective treatment interventions.

We would also like to thank our doctoral-level research assistant, Gonzalo Vasquez of Lehigh University. He made the literature search a pleasure and provided helpful comments on the final draft of the manuscript. We would also like to thank our colleagues and mentors who were extremely helpful in providing references, information, and consultation in our search for the most current material on the treatment of panic, including David Barlow, Joseph Wolpe, Aaron T. Beck, Francine Shapiro, Roger Callahan, Fred Gallo, Peter Goldman, Clif-

Acknowledgments

ford Schilke, Edward Sweitzer, Robert M. Gordon, Dan Egli, Dianne Burg, Erik Von Kiel, Robert Roeshman, Steven Shore, Mirjami van Rijsoort, Barbara Olasov-Rothbaum, and Jim White. And very special thanks are extended to Donald Klein for his constructive criticisms on the final draft of this manuscript.

Many thanks also go to our expert typist, Carol Jaskolka, who invested a countless number of hours in preparing numerous drafts of this text. Her patience with this project is greatly appreciated.

Such a manuscript would not have been possible without the foresight of our editor, Suzi Tucker, at Zeig, Tucker & Co. Her patience and understanding were central factors in facilitating our production of a thorough and comprehensive text.

Last, we thank our families, Maryann and Michael Dattilio, and Carolina, Anna Carolina, and Monica Salas for being supportive and understanding in enduring our many hours of absence while preparing this manuscript. They are truly the backbones of our lives.

Contents

About the Authors

Frank M. Dattilio, Ph.D., ABPP, is a clinical associate in psychiatry at the Center for Cognitive Therapy, University of Pennsylvania School of Medicine, and the clinical director of the Center for Integrative Psychotherapy in Allentown, Pennsylvania. A clinical psychologist, he is listed in the National Register of Health Service Providers in Psychology. He is also a Diplomate in behavioral and clinical psychology of the American Board of Professional Psychology and serves as a full Professor (Adjunct) at Lehigh University in Bethlehem, Pennsylvania, as well as a visiting professor at several major universities throughout the world and as a guest lecturer at the Harvard School of Medicine.

Dr. Dattilio trained in behavior therapy in the Department of Psychiatry at Temple University School of Medicine under the direct supervision of the late Joseph Wolpe, and completed a postdoctoral fellowship at the Center for Cognitive Therapy, University of Pennsylvania School of Medicine under Aaron T. Beck. He has more than 100 professional publications to his credit in the areas of anxiety disorders, behavioral problems, and marital and family discord, and has also presented extensively on cognitive-behavior therapy for the treatment of anxiety disorders and marital and family discord throughout the United States, Canada, Africa, Europe, South America, Australia, Cuba, and Mexico. Dr. Dattilio's works have been translated into more than a dozen languages and are used as required reading worldwide. Among his many publications are *Cognitive Therapy with Couples* (1990), *Comprehensive Casebook of Cognitive Therapy* (1992), *Cognitive-Behavioral Strategies in Crisis Intervention* (1994, rev. ed., 2000), *Cognitive Therapy with Children and Adolescents: A Casebook for Clinical Practice* (1995), *Case Studies in Couple and Family Therapy: Systemic and Cognitive Perspectives* (1998), *The Family Psychotherapy Treatment Planner* (1999), and *Comparative Treatments of Couples Problems* (1999). He has also filmed several professional videotapes and audiotapes, including the popular series "Five Approaches to Linda" with M. Goldfried, A. A. Lazarus, W. Glasser, and J. F. Masterson (Lehigh University Media, 1996). He is on the board of several professional journals and has received a number of professional awards for outstanding achievement in the field of psychology.

Jesus A. Salas-Auvert, M.A., graduated from Universidad Catolica Andres Bello in Caracas, Venezuela, with a bachelor's degree and a license in psychology. He received his master's degree from Carleton University in Ottawa, Canada, where he studied under Nicholas P. Spanos. He is currently a doctoral student in clinical psychology at the Philadelphia College of Osteopathic Medicine under the direction of Arthur Freeman. Mr. Salas also trained in cognitive therapy at the Beck Institute for Cognitive Therapy and Research, directed by Aaron T. Beck and Judith S. Beck.

Mr. Salas conducted a private practice for eighteen years as a clinical psychologist in his native Venezuela, specializing in anxiety and stress-related disorders and couples therapy. He is currently a full-time clinical staff member and director of research at the Center for Integrative Psychotherapy in Allentown, Pennsylvania. Mr. Salas has also served as an Associate Professor of Clinical Psychology in the Master's Program in Clinical Psychology at the Universidad Rafael Urdaneta, Maracaibo, Venezuela, where he continues as a visiting faculty member. The recipient of several professional awards in Venezuela for outstanding achievement in the field of psychology, his research and publications have focused on anxiety, clinical and experimental hypnosis, and behavioral medicine. He is also the author of a book, *Inteligencia Social* (1997), and the coauthor of a number of papers for professional journals.

Foreword

No mental condition has affected human beings across all cultures more profoundly than that of anxiety. Whereas anxiety and its disorders have been noted to produce debilitating effects, panic has been recognized as one of the more paralyzing of the disorders because of its abrupt and intrusive effects. In the last 25 years, panic has gained increasing attention in the media, as well as in the professional literature. This emerging emphasis on the disorder can be attributed both to the refinement of the diagnostic criteria and to the recognition of its incidence in the general population.

Much of the professional literature has focused on various treatment approaches, including medication and the use of cognitive-behavior therapy (CBT). I, myself, have been fortunate in having introduced CBT as an alternative treatment for panic disorder and in having played an active role in conducting empirical outcome studies that have supported CBT alone as an effective treatment intervention. In addition, CBT has also proved effective when combined with pharmacotherapy. In fact, the most recent practice guidelines set forth by the American Psychiatric Association (APA, 1998) promote a combination of drug treatment and CBT. As a psychiatrist, I can appreciate the complementarity of CBT and pharmacotherapy in treating cases of panic.

I am pleased that two of my former students have embarked on a project that presents an overview of the multiple treatment approaches to panic. Frank M. Dattilio has worked with me as a member of the staff at the Center for Cognitive Therapy since 1985. His input has always been helpful in our weekly case conferences. Jesus A. Salas completed our extramural training program at the Beck Institute in 1995 and proved a knowledgeable clinician. He has also worked closely with Frank Dattilio in the past several years in clinical practice. Both men bring years of training and clinical experience to the treatment of anxiety and panic. Their text provides a compendium of treatment approaches to panic with an accurate and updated review of the professional literature. The authors have nicely addressed a range of approaches, including the psychodynamic, cognitive-behavioral, pharmacological, and many other modalities used in the treatment of panic. A number of case vignettes, along with a full-length case study that includes detailed explanations of the authors' rationale and strategies with a difficult case, illustrate each modality. The reader is given a balanced overview of treatment interventions that describes the most effective techniques for treating panic disorder.

As our world evolves toward a more complex society, so do its demands. Thus, clinicians as a whole are likely to encounter more complex cases that require expedient and effective treatment. This book provides its readers with an armamentarium of techniques and allows them to weigh the advantages and disadvantages of various treatment interventions.

—Aaron T. Beck, M.D.
University Professor of Psychiatry
University of Pennsylvania School of Medicine
Philadelphia

Preface

ew would argue with the fact that the professional literature is
inundated with information on panic disorder and its treatment.
During our preparation of this text, we uncovered more than
2,500 citations in just the last seven years on panic disorder alone. This
should be no surprise since research has demonstrated that anxiety disorders are the leading mental health problem among American women
and second only to alcohol and drug abuse among men. An early 1980s
study conducted by the National Institute of Mental Health found anxiety disorders to be the most prevalent of all emotional disorders, including depression (Myers, Weissman, Tischer, et al., 1982). Panic
disorder itself affects more than 4% of the U.S. population and is estimated to affect at least as many, if not more, in other parts of the
world (Von Korff, Shapiro, Burke, et al., 1987).

Why then another book on panic? What more could be offered other
than an update of the professional literature or a rehashing of old theories or techniques?

For one, despite the plethora of information, new discoveries are being made constantly regarding pharmacological as well as nonpharmacological interventions. Some of the most fascinating research ever
undertaken, in our opinion, was recently carried out at the National
Institutes of Health, Columbia University, and the New York State Psy-

chiatric Institute. Here, large-scale investigations were conducted on the use of DNA and genetic mapping among panic victims and the members of their families of origin. Researchers are attempting to identify a chromosomal linkage that may determine whether abnormal genes are predisposing individuals to panic attacks.

Likewise, there have been pharmacological breakthroughs with new classes of antidepressant compounds that remediate panic more effectively than ever before and with fewer side effects. Some of the more recent nonpharmacological techniques involve EMDR (Eye Movement Desensitization Reprocessing), TFT (Thought Field Therapy), PI (Paradoxical Intention), biofeedback, and a combination of stress-control techniques in large-group didactic training sessions. Although some of these interventions lack empirical support, they are, nonetheless, being implemented to treat panic and clinicians should become familiar with them.

We also know much more about some of the demographic variables involving panic sufferers, as well as predetermining characteristics in personality and relationships that render individuals more prone to panic attacks and more likely to respond positively to certain treatments.

As clinical psychologists, we were well trained in cognitive-behavior therapy (CBT). Both having studied with Aaron T. Beck and myself with Joseph Wolpe (FMD), our orientation has been focused away from psychoanalytic principles and more toward short-term nonpharmacological interventions. However, years of clinical experience in the field have taught us to be respectful of other approaches to treatment, especially with anxiety disorders. Thus, we remain open to perspectives that combine the use of more than one modality, especially when working with difficult cases. Consequently, we have attempted to address a broad range of treatment approaches with a greater emphasis on the use of CBT, because, when combined with pharmacotherapy, CBT has proved to be the most effective treatment for panic as compared with any other intervention alone. This is quite obvious from the professional literature, as well as from clinical experience.

Aside from treatment, assessment, and the specifics of multiple interventions, an overview of common medications prescribed, together with lists of proposed patient readings, as well as of annotated professional references for clinicians, are also included.

Preface

This book was designed for clinicians of diverse perspectives who treat anxiety and panic. Our philosophy contends that no one intervention has a patent on the remediation of panic. No particular treatment can be all things to all people and, therefore, clinicians must remain open to exploring various treatment options. Thus, an integrative approach may prove to be the most effective, particularly as it is tailored to the individual needs of a patient. As a result, this book considers a number of perspectives, including the biophysiological, psychopharmacological, CBT, psychodynamic, and homeopathic, as well as a host of other interventions, on the effective treatment of panic. In addition to a review of theory and techniques, a detailed history portrays the evolution of the concept of panic disorder. We also include a number of short case vignettes throughout the text, followed by a full-length case study that involves a combined approach to treating a woman with panic disorder with the onset of agoraphobia. Each case example includes comments on the conceptualization and treatment method and a rationale for the chosen intervention.

Also discussed in the text are atypical cases of panic and how to treat a dual diagnosis, as well as sundry complications that are frequently encountered with panic sufferers, including various physical disorders.

In view of the vastness of the literature available on the topic of panic, it was necessary to keep the information and references to a minimum. Therefore, only the highlights are included in this text. The reader is referred to the list of recommended professional readings in Appendix A.

It is our hope that this book will provide its readers with the essential tools and knowledge that will allow them to choose the most effective and most appropriate treatment for specific cases of panic disorder. A sample treatment plan is outlined in Appendix D.

—*Frank M. Dattilio*
—*Jesus A. Salas-Auvert*

Panic Disorder

1

The Nature and Definition of Panic

If a layperson were to consult Webster's Dictionary, he or she would find that the definition includes the phrases, "an intense irrational fear felt by an individual," "a sudden overpowering fear," or "a sudden unreasoning terror" (Lexicon, 1989). What is confusing about this definition is the word "unreasoning," suggesting that the sensation of panic is not based on reason or logic, but is "illogical." This is particularly intriguing since the term "panic" usually pertains to a heightened state of physiological arousal that by no means is illogical. In fact, the sensation experienced during any episode of panic involves the true activation of a survival mechanism, which dates back to a time when human beings first roamed the earth. Although the thought process that activates the autonomic arousal sometimes may be irrationally based, the symptoms are real, making the experience appear to the sufferer as a serious threat.

The definition of panic ascribed to by mental health professionals carries a bit more detail than that found in most dictionaries. It is also accompanied by certain conditions that are required to warrant a diagnosis of "panic" and qualify the experience's intensity. The fourth edition of the *Diagnostic and Statistical Manual of Mental Disorders* (DSM-IV) (American Psychiatric Association, 1994) outlines the following criteria for the formal diagnosis of panic disorders:

1. Shortness of breath or a sensation of smothering.
2. Dizziness, a feeling of unsteadiness, or faintness.
3. Palpitations or an accelerated heart rate.
4. Trembling or shaking.
5. Sweating.
6. Choking.
7. Nausea or abdominal distress.
8. Depersonalization or derealization—a feeling that the sufferer's body or the environment, respectively, is not real.
9. Numbness or tingling sensations in one or more parts of the body.
10. Hot flashes or chills.
11. Chest pain or discomfort.
12. Fear of dying.
13. Fear of going crazy or losing self-control and the inclusion of "unexpected attacks."

These criteria have become part of the diagnostic nomenclature only in recent decades, despite the potential for their recognition centuries ago. In the mid- to late 1960s, investigators and clinicians began to differentiate patients who reported unexpected anxiety attacks from those with other anxiety disorders.

Mental disorders with some form of anxiety as a predominant feature have been addressed in the professional literature for decades and first appeared formally in DSM-I in 1968. The process of grouping anxiety symptoms together into a single diagnostic class only occurred after the development of DSM-II in the 1970s. In this version, the anxiety disorders were classified under the term "anxiety neurosis," with much less specificity in the way of descriptive features and subclassification (Dattilio, 1986).

The diagnostic category of panic disorder was later officially recognized with the publication of the third edition of the *Diagnostic and Statistical Manual of Mental Disorders* (DSM-III) (American Psychiatric Association, 1980). The proposed criteria were later modified with the 1987 publication of the revised version, the DSM-III-R.

With the proliferation of research findings and clinical outcome studies, another modification, made with DSM-IV, required the unexpected development of symptoms reaching a crescendo within 10 minutes and lasting 10 minutes or more. For a more detailed outline of the evolution of the DSM and panic, see McNally (1994).

One of the enigmas that surround the notion of panic is: Why was it not recognized as a formal diagnosis much earlier? This is of particular interest since human beings undoubtedly always have experienced episodes of panic. It is likely that the significance of panic was ensconced in the various theories of physiology and psychopathology, where it was assigned various other labels. It was not until the past several decades that panic slowly evolved into a formal diagnosis, becoming distilled from what was described in the DSM-III in 1980.

Panic, Fear, and Anxiety

An important aspect to address when defining panic is the specific differences among panic, fear, and anxiety. These terms are frequently confused, not only by patients, but by clinicians treating anxiety as well. It is also important to specify how these states may be similar to or different from each other since there is much overlap. Barlow (1988) views anxiety or any anxious apprehension as a loosely defined, widespread effective network stored in memory. Anxiety is viewed as a future-oriented emotional state characterized by high negative affect and a sense that upcoming events are uncontrollable and unpredictable. Fear, on the other hand, is usually considered an alarm reaction that involves an intense push to escape from potential danger that is *known* and in which the organism is mobilized, both physically and cognitively, for action. Fear is viewed as a hard-wired, fight-or-flight response that is present across cultures and species and can vary in its intensity depending on the situation. When a very intense fear occurs in the absence of any real threat, the fear reaction is called a false alarm or "panic attack." Thus, in Barlow's model, "panic" is phenomenologically identical to the emotion of fear (Rapee, 1996).

Consequently, panic may be viewed as an acute reaction to perceived immediate danger, similar to the feeling that arises when one is surprised by another person abruptly or one momentarily loses one's balance on a narrow, high walkway and must quickly grab the railing. The reaction to such events must be immediate in order to allow for appropriate actions to be taken in time to remove oneself from the perceived danger.

In contrast, anxiety is future-oriented apprehension over some possible threat or perceived threat. A example is an individual who slips on a wet or icy sidewalk and is injured and subsequently develops anxiety over the possibility of encountering another such situation in the future. He or she may even be vigilant for early signs and signals that the path is unstable.

Barlow believes that many episodes of anxious apprehension may be misdiagnosed as panic (Barlow, 1988). According to the DSM-IV (American Psychiatric Association, 1994), a panic attack must reach a peak within 10 minutes.

The reader is directed to Barlow, Brown, and Craske (1994) for an excellent overview of this concept.

A History of Panic

Scientists now speculate that the earth is approximately four and a half billion years old and that some form of humanlike species most likely roamed the earth as early as five million years ago.

There is still some controversy over whether the first species of hominids, known as australopithecine (five million years B.C.) or homoerectus (a million and a half years B.C.), were our ancestors. Currently, homoerectus is regarded as the first "true man." More important, it is now known that Homo sapiens, a species that appeared about 500,000 years B.C., clearly exploited the environment systematically with the use of spears and other weapons. This indicates to modern anthropologists that Homo sapiens were consciously in tune with their survival mechanisms and felt the need to defend themselves in the face of any perceived or real threat. This being the case, it is very likely that the autonomic nervous system of these predecessors had advanced to a level where they experienced a "fight/flight syndrome." If this hypothesis is correct, than perhaps Homo sapiens were also capable of experiencing some form of physiological arousal, or possibly even panic, as far back as 500,000 years B.C.

Unfortunately, we have very few data to support any such hypothesis, but it is probably fair to assume that early humans at least had the potential to experience such sensations, since we know that many animals undergo similar sensations during fear reactions when confronted with a psychological threat or physical danger. This reaction prepares the animal for possible injury and automatically mobilizes the body for defense (Beck, Emery, & Greenberg, 1985, p. 107). Organisms ranging from protozoa to mammals have evolved defensive responses to external stimuli.

In some sense, the notion of arousal has always been a part of the human condition and probably always will be. According to the professional literature, the first reports of panic symptoms go back more than three centuries.

The term "panic" was derived from Pan, the name of the goat-legged Greek god of shepherds and hunters (D'Aulaire & D'Aulaire, 1962). Apparently, Pan was a jolly sort, but also was very lazy and whenever disturbed while napping, would emit a terrifying scream to scare anyone within earshot away. This reaction became known as "Pan-ic," with "ic" representing the sense of being inflicted.

Unfortunately, little seems to have been written describing anything about the term "panic" prior to the seventeenth century. If written accounts did exist, they probably were destroyed during the wars and natural disasters, that marked the passage of time. The earliest descriptions of "panic attacks" that still remain were provided by the English author Thomas Burton (1624) in his classic literary text, *The Anatomy of Melancholy*. Burton wrote:

> Many lamentable effects of this fear causeth in men, as to be red, pale, tremble, sweat, it makes sudden cold and heat to come over all the body, palpitations of the heart, syncope, dizziness, etc. It amazeth many men that are to speak or show themselves in public assemblies, or before some great personages . . .

Aside from Burton's mention, little is found in the subsequent literature until approximately the nineteenth century when physicians actually began to describe cardiac conditions that included chest pain, intercostal tightness, tachycardia, dyspnea, and a choking or smothering sensation. Physicians of that era had difficulty distinguishing these symptoms from organic heart disease and so many conditions were probably misdiagnosed.

One of the earliest reports regarding panic in the medical literature is that written by James A. Hope (1832), a British cardiologist. Hope described patients who were plagued with "nervous palpitations," a condition he termed as "an exaggerated idea exacting alarm and anxiety in the mind."

This was followed by another description several years later by an English physician who wrote about "nervous and sympathetic palpitations of the heart" (Williams, 1836).

Surprisingly, after Williams' article, little about panic appeared in the professional literature for almost 30 years. It was not until the 1870s that a surgeon in Britain's Coldstream Guards mentioned a syndrome he called "soldier's heart" (Myers, 1870). Later, J. M. DaCosta (1871), a Civil War physician, described a syndrome he termed "irritable heart disease." It appeared that the traumas of battles and military service precipitated atypical cardiac symptoms, including palpitations, tachycardia, dizziness, shortness of breath, chest pains, gastrointestinal distress, fever, enlarged heart, and "nervous symptoms," many of the symptoms that Thomas Burton first described in the seventeenth century. It is not surprising that war would evoke such symptoms in healthy young men, considering the obvious effects on the human condition and the general threat to life posed by combat. It is important to note that while the existence of such symptoms may not necessarily be unreasonable during wartime when a true threat exists, it is the fact that such symptoms have lingered well after the wars have ended that has intrigued researchers and clinicians.

In that same year, C. Westphal (1871), a German physician, used the term "agoraphobia" with regard to a woman who avoided venturing into the marketplace because of "spell-like symptoms" that fit Myers' and DaCosta's descriptions of "irritable heart." In his article, which goes into great detail about the woman's symptoms, Westphal discusses many of the symptoms that are constituted by the contemporary term "agoraphobia." Darwin (1872) also spoke about the "ancient alarm reaction of fear" in his early writings on evolution, and described many of the sensations of "panic." Later, Beard (1880) popularized the term "neurasthenia" for a cluster of illnesses long recognized by physicians as "nervous prostration," "nervous disability," or "nervous asthenia." Among a number of symptoms reported were headaches and other bodily pains; a lack of concentration; noises in the ears; pressure, and a heaviness in the head; morbid fears, including specific phobias; and diz-ziness, palpitations, insomnia, dyspnea, sweating, tremors, poor appe-tite, and exhaustion.

Around the same time, Sigmund Freud (1894), who had been refining his early theories of neurosis, identified a syndrome he called "neuras-thenia," which constituted a much smaller class of symptoms than those described by Beard. Freud attempted to differentiate anxiety neurosis from neurasthenia. This involved a description of free-floating anxiety or anxious expectation, as well as anxiety attacks with tachycardia, nervous dyspnea, sweating, tremor, diarrhea, dizziness or vertigo, pa-resthesia, and congestion (p. 82). Freud also described an "anxious ex-pectation" or what is referred to by modern clinicians as "anticipatory anxiety." This, he believed, was a precursor to common danger phobias (fear of snakes, thunderstorms, darkness, etc.) and to the agoraphobia described earlier by Westphal.

In England, during World War I, Lewis (1917) discussed a condition he referred to as "effort syndrome," which appeared to be remarkably similar to DaCosta's description, evolved more than four decades ear-lier, during the Civil War era. Lewis apparently coined the appelation "effort syndrome" because he noticed that the soldiers developed it dur-ing periods of physical exertion.

Oppenheimer (1918) proposed a slightly different slant on the situ-ation, referring to the same syndrome as "neurocirculatory asthenia," when the anxiety state was accompanied by cardiovascular features.

By the late 1930s, increasing reports of "cardiac neurosis" began to appear in the literature, which was principally defined as neurosis in which the circulatory manifestations were the main subjective and ob-jective partners of the clinical problem (Caughey, 1939). As a result of more emphasis on cardiac neurosis, the soldiers' heart phenomenon was now accounted for by involuntary hyperventilation and the resulting respiratory alkalosis. Moreover, observations made in the 1940s fo-cused on dyspnea and chronic hyperventilation (Wolf, 1947). Lewis (1940) also wrote about how the "effort syndrome" was becoming one of the most chronic afflictions of sedentary town dwellers.

Between the late 1940s and early 1950s, dyspnea associated with sighing respirations was also noted by several clinicians as a common manifestation of chronic hyperventilation (Wolf, 1947). Cohen and as-sociates (Cohen, Badal, Kilpatrick, et al., 1951) and Cohen and White

(1950) elaborated on the work of Oppenheimer (1918), conducting epidemiological studies in the 1940s and 1950s on neurocirculatory asthenia—namely, nervous tachycardia, nervous exhaustion, vasoregulatory asthenia, and vasomotor neurosis.

Unfortunately, very little is found in the literature on "panic" as such during the decades of the 1940s and 1950s. This is likely attributable to the fact that the fields of psychology, psychiatry, and medicine placed a greater emphasis on schizophrenia and depression since the demands had increased during this period. It wasn't until the 1960s that the term "panic" became more common among clinicians in the field. In England, Roth (1959) described the phobic-anxiety depersonalization syndrome that is characterized by panic sufferers, suggesting that the phenomenon of depersonalization and the underlying psychophysiology of the regulation awareness associated with depersonalization be identified as important keys to panic disorder.

One of the researchers who deserves major credit for laying the groundwork in defining panic is psychiatrist Donald Klein, who, in 1962, proposed the idea that panic might be qualitatively different from other states of anxiety (Klein & Fink, 1962). Klein later initiated a line of research that came to be known as "pharmacological dissection" (Klein, 1964). During his experimentation with the then-new compound imipramine, Klein administered the drug to a number of patients who were "panicking" in a desperate attempt to remediate their symptoms. After several weeks of imipramine treatment, he noticed significant improvement (Klein, 1981, p. 237). This subsequently sparked a line of empirical research that inspired Klein to "dissect" panic attacks from generalized chronic or anticipatory anxiety as a qualitatively different state (Klein & Fink, 1962; Klein, 1964). Klein's early work with imipramine not only prompted him to distinguish between spontaneous and other forms of anxiety, but also enabled him to develop the conceptualization of agoraphobia as an outcome of panic (McNally, 1994, p. 2).

As the distinctive presentation of panic became more pronounced to mental health professionals, more research and investigation were carried out in an effort to isolate the specific symptoms and properties that contributed to this phenomenon. Early research in the 1970s set off what became a literal explosion of theory and research on agoraphobia and panic.

In his popular book, *Fears and Phobias*, Isaac Marks (1969) described agoraphobia in great detail. To set the stage for a number of studies that dissected the term, agoraphobia splintered off the distinct category among phobias that would eventually be called panic disorder. The 1980s saw a revolution in classification with the publication of the third edition of the *Diagnostic and Statistical Manual of Mental Disorders* (DSM-III) (American Psychiatric Association, 1980) with the new diagnostic subcategory "agoraphobia with panic attacks." Such studies by Goldstein and Chambless (1978) had provided a reanalysis of the term "agoraphobia" by describing complex agoraphobia as a syndrome that includes fear of fear or fear of eventually cued panic attacks as a central phobic element. Other elements of the reconceptualization of agoraphobia syndrome were the initial onset of panic attacks in the context of interpersonal conflict, the client's tendency to misunderstand the source of anxiety episodes and other emotional states, and the low levels of autonomy and self-sufficiency witnessed in the typical agoraphobia patient. In the late 1980s, as a result of numerous studies focusing on agoraphobia and panic disorder, a revised classification of anxiety disorders was undertaken—making the typical agoraphobia syndrome a subcategory of panic disorder itself, or panic disorder with agoraphobia. This reclassification of terms follows from the view that it is the onset of panic attacks that explains clients' progressive avoidance of specific situations associated with panic. The latter part of the 1980s saw a redirection of theorists' interest toward eliminating the panic attacks themselves instead of addressing them indirectly by attacking the avoidance situations. Goldstein and Chambless' (1978) concept of fear of fear cycles elicited a great deal of research (e.g., Jacob & Rapport, 1984; Stampler, 1982). Also, the appearance of many fine researchers on panic and agoraphobia, such as Barlow (1988), Clark (1986, 1988), and Hibbert (1984), has contributed to the proliferation of articles in the professional literature.

In the 1990s, research has focused on the patient's thoughts and images of awareness that usually become catastrophically misinterpreted. Many of these studies have included pharmacological interventions (Klasko, Barlow, Tassinari, & Cerny, 1990; Clum, 1989; Sanderson & Wetzler, 1933) in order to provide an effective combined treatment approach.

Cued Versus Uncued Panic

There is considerable clinical evidence that psychological factors, particularly cognitions, can precipitate panic attacks. In the early 1980s, an interesting study was published that described 10 patients who had experienced panic attacks following a separation from or the loss of a "loved one" (Raskin, Peeke, Dickman, & Pinsker, 1982). The panic occurred as a result of the perceived effect that the absence of their significant others would have on their lives.

Beck and colleagues proposed that panic patients are characterized by "overactive cognitive patterns (schemata) that are relevant to dangers that are continually structuring external and/or internal experience as a sign of danger" (Beck, Emery, & Greenberg, 1985). The role of cognitions is strongly supported by retrospective interview studies in the professional literature (Beck, Laude, & Bohnert, 1974; Hibbert, 1984; Rapee, 1985a; Ottaviani & Beck, 1987).

It was Donald Klein who described three types of panic (Klein & Klein, 1989). The first one was spontaneous panic, which he describes as a sudden surprising, unexpected, spontaneous, swift crescendo of terror associated with a wide range of autonomic activity, in particular, cardiorespiratory syndromes. From the perspective of the panic victim, these attacks seem to appear out of the blue without any obvious external precipitant. Spontaneous attacks are the hallmark of panic disorder and presumably originate from the dysregulation of a primitive alarm system in the brain. "Spontaneous" does not mean "uncaused," but the absence of environmental precipitants as opposed to the absence of neurobiological etiology.

The second type of panic involves what Klein refers to as stimulus-bound panic, which is a sudden surge of fear triggered by exposure to a phobic stimulus or by anticipation of such exposure. According to Klein, these attacks are especially characteristic of specific phobias (e.g., fear of animals or of heights) and almost invariably occur when phobic individuals encounter their feared stimuli.

The third and last aspect of panic involves a situational predisposed state that tends to occur more in certain situations than in others. Although these provocative situations increase the probability of panic, they do not invariably trigger it. For example, whereas individuals diagnosed with agoraphobia typically experience panic more often in malls than at home, being in a mall need not provoke an attack on every shopping excursion. Situationally predisposed panic attacks may eventually dominate the clinical picture of agoraphobia (McNally, 1994).

In addition to the terms that Klein proposed, other terms utilized include such qualifiers as predicted, major, and minor. Barlow's view synthesizes categories by utilizing the terms "expected" and "cued" and their antonyms. He refers to a detailed table for delineating descriptors (Barlow, 1988, p. 105).

A cue may be best exemplified by a specific phobia, such as a fear of bridges (see Table 1, p. 12). For the bridge phobic, the sight of a bridge would be the reported cue for panic, a cue readily understood by the individual. But with another type of phobia, such as claustrophobia, the phobic individual may either expect or not expect to have a panic attack at any given time when entering a small enclosed place or any environment where the person may feel enclosed or restricted. Barlow and colleagues (Barlow, Vermilyea, DiNardo, et al., 1985) contend that the term "cued" seems preferable to situational in that these are identifiable cues preceding panic, and, in most cases, are cognitive. Barlow's thinking is that cued panic attacks can be either expected or unexpected. Similarly, uncued panic can also be expected or unexpected. The difference rests solely on the patient's perception of the presence of a discriminating cue and not on the actual presence of the cue in the environment. Therefore, in essence, the perception of a particular cue may be arbitrary and affected by specific cognitive distortions, an area highlighted in research by Ottaviana and Beck (1987), Rapee (1995b), and Clark and Ehlers (1993).

Since cues seem to precipitate or trigger panic symptoms, it is important for patients to become familiar with some of the internal as well as external cues.

Internal Cues

There are a number of internal physiological cues, such as changes in body rhythm or temperature, but there also may be more affective types of cues as well. One of the latter is anger. But whereas anger is essen-

Table 1. Panic Descriptors

Expected	Unexpected
Cued	Uncued

Reprinted with permission from Barlow, D. H. (1998). *Anxiety and its disorders* (p. 105). New York: Guilford.

tially a feeling or an affective state, it may vary in intensity from mild irritation to unfettered rage. Anger in its various forms may commonly trigger autonomic symptoms that facilitate panic. George and Anderson (1989) found that anger often served as a precipitant for panic patients, particularly when it was acted out.

In our clinical experience, we have found that the mere difficulty of expressing anger may also facilitate autonomic symptoms.

Another emotion involves feelings of shame, pity, or even guilt, which may be part of a larger underlying dynamic contributing to the cause of one's anxiety.

External Cues

Among the more common external cues described by panic sufferers; are warm, stuffy atmospheres; certain pungent or unpleasant odors (usually that make breathing difficult); photosensitivity, including fluorescent or flashing lights; and sometimes loud, piercing noises that may disturb one's sense of equilibrium.

Margraf and associates (Margraf, Taylor, Ehlers, et al., 1987) suggest that even when cues are obvious, panicking persons may fail to discriminate the cues and will report the panic episode as being "spontaneous." Most clinicians in the field agree that there are clear antecedents, whether biological or physiological, to all panic attacks. When an individual perceives a cue, whether or not it actually exists, the cue affects the development of symptoms, the cognitive and physiological responses, and, ultimately, the amount of avoidant behavior displayed. As with agoraphobics, panic victims may begin to avoid any cues perceived as being associated with panic.

For a more complete discussion of the specific differences between cued and uncued panic, the reader is referred to Barlow (1988, p. 107). The important aspect of both cued and uncued panic is that the cues serve as a primary defining characteristic of panic disorder. Whether a cue is perceived or not perceived by the individual has significant functional implications for the development of panic disorder and, more specifically, how the individual will respond to treatement. This is an area that will require further empirical investigation, particularly as treatment interventions become more refined.

Atypical Panic Attacks

As with any diagnosis, panic has atypical characteristics that need to be addressed. Following are some cases of panic in which the course and duration of symptoms either do not meet the general criteria for panic or occur in unusual circumstances.

Limited-Symptom Attacks

When fewer than four symptoms that meet the criteria of the DSM-IV are reported, these experiences are referred to as "limited-symptom attacks," or "minor" attacks (Taylor, Sheikh, Agras, et al., 1986). Although minor attacks are rated by patients as less intense then major attacks, they still involve the same distressing symptoms. It is also reported that patients who experience a major panic attack may have a number of minor attacks prior to their first major episode (Taylor, Sheikh, Agras, et al., 1986).

Overall, limited-symptom attacks seem to serve the same purpose as full panic attacks, specifically with regard to the consequences; however, the course and length of treatment may vary, depending on the circumstances and the individual.

Nocturnal Panic

Taylor, Sheikh, Agras, et al. (1986) found that panic attacks occur most frequently between 1:30 A.M. and 3:30 A.M. Aǧargün, Kara, Algün, Sekeroǧlu, and Tarakçioǧlu (1996) found that patients with recurrent sleep panic had significantly more panic attacks per week than did those without sleep panic. Barlow and Craske (1988) stated that 25% of all panickers and agoraphobics with panic attacks who presented with symptoms at his anxiety disorders clinic reportedly experience at least one nocturnal attack. Patients are often awakened in the middle of sleep by autonomic activity, such as increased heart rate or body temperature. Barlow and Craske (1988) further reported that of the 41 nocturnal panic patients they assessed, 43% reported their first symptom upon awakening as falling within the cognitive domain, for example, fear of losing control, of dying, or of going insane. They also reported, however, that 57% said that the initial symptom experienced upon awakening was somatic (e.g., a racing heart).

Several explanations for nocturnal panic have been advanced. For one, changes in internal body states take place during different phases of the sleep cycle and may serve as triggers for a panic-prone individual. These include reduced heart rate and respiration during slow-wave and deep sleep.

Another phenomenon is panic attacks preceded by states of diminished arousal. Recently, it was suggested that relaxation induces panic (Uhde & Mellman, 1987). Mellman and Uhde (1989a) suggested that there was a relationship between this phenomenon and sleep-related panic. Hauri et al. (1989) observed that sleep panic attacks occurred in the transition phase between stage 2 and stage 3 sleep. They suggested that nocturnal panic attacks are unique—different from stage 4 sleep terrors and different from dream anxiety attacks. A more analytic explanation involves the use of dream content that includes repressed material from daytime activity that may give rise to anxiety and, consequently, became manifest in autonomic activity during sleep hours. However, research has not supported such a hypothesis, since nocturnal panic occurs in deep sleep, not during dreams (Craske & Barlow, 1989; Mellman & Uhde, 1989, 1990).

A third possible explanation may be the use of benzodiazepines at bedtime, as these are often prescribed to help induce sleep. With an average half-life of four to six hours for benzodiazepines, panic-prone individuals who take them just before bedtime may find themselves abruptly awakened by autonomic activity as the effects of the drug wear off.

Another possibility is that nocturnal panic may result from a person's temporary inability to modulate bodily reactions according to the nature of the stressor. Such a condition results from a neurological hypersensitivity to arousal located in the subcortical limbic circuitry (Everly, 1989). This limbic hypersensitivity appears to develop as a consequence of an acute traumatic stimulation (e.g., a panic attack) or repeated excitation of the limbic system (e.g., chronic distress, anticipatory anxiety). Other subcortical structures (e.g., amygdala) may also develop hyperexcitability, contributing to the individual's predisposition for an exaggerated startle response (Adamec, 1978; Rosen, Hamerman, Sitcoske, et al., 1996). A reverberating circuit of neuroendocrine changes can be established, which can alter the balance of autonomic control. Such potentially self-perpetuating high neurological tone results in changes in the cardiovascular or respiratory systems (Lisander, 1979; Zegans, 1982; Everly, 1989). Hence it is our belief that even though the panic-disordered individual may be asleep, the neurophysiological components of his or her stress response remain active. Catastrophic misinterpretations of unexpected bodily changes (e.g., tachycardia) prompted by such neuroendocrine disregulations may spike a nocturnal panic attack.

A final consideration involves the notion of sleep apnea, which refers to a pause in or a complete cessation of breathing during the sleep cycle. This is another phenomenon that clinicians have linked to nocturnal panic attacks (Barlow, 1988). However, there is some controversy concerning the issue of sleep apnea and its role in panic. Since the concentration of nocturnal panic during the first four hours of sleep is not consistent with the repeated pattern of sleep apnea, the hypothesis remains questionable.

Panic During Pregnancy

Practitioners who specialize in panic disorder sometimes may be called upon to treat a pregnant woman who is struggling with panic. In most such cases, the woman becomes pregnant during the course of treatment or experiences panic during the postpartum period. This may present a problem, particularly if the patient is on medication. In most instances, physicians or gynecologists will recommend that the medication be discontinued immediately, although new research does indicate that some compounds are safe to take during pregnancy (Pastuszak, Schick, Boschetto, et al. (1997).

For many women who become pregnant during or after a phase of panic disorder, symptoms tend to reduce markedly (Altemus, 1997), as found in a retrospective study of 33 pregnant women diagnosed with panic disorder (Klein, Skrobala, & Garfinkel, 1995). Despite the reduction in symptomatology, however, avoidance behavior did not change. This appears to be consistent with previous studies that contend that exposure treatment is necessary to eliminate avoidant behaviors.

It is hypothesized that several of the hormonal and physiological changes that occur during pregnancy may play a role—specifically, the greatly increased levels of progesterone. Since progesterone enhances the (gamma-amino butyric acid (GABA) receptors, it is likely that progesterone may have an effect similar to that produced by benzodiazepine compounds (i.e., alprazolam and diazepam), which are designed to undulate the activity in the brain that causes panic. Furthermore, reactivity of the sympathetic nervous system is reduced during pregnancy. Since CO_2 levels in the bloodstream diminish, they lessen the likelihood of signaling a "suffocation alarm." There are exceptions, of course. Not all women with panic disorder improve during pregnancy, and a small percentage actually become worse (Villeponteaux, Lydiard, Laraia, et al., 1992).

It is generally agreed that at the completion of pregnancy, panic symptoms tend to worsen during the subsequent year (Sholomskas, Wickamartne, Dogolo, O'Brien, Leaf, & Woods, 1993; Cohen, Sichel, Faraone, et al., 1996). It is unclear, however, whether this is due to a hormonal change occurring subsequent to pregnancy or whether the return to a prepregnancy stage paves the way for preexisting sympto-matology or conditions to reappear.

It is suggested that women who enter treatment during any phase of their pregnancy be advised of the foregoing, and that treatment be geared toward avoiding medication if possible until pregnancy and the subsequent nursing period are over.

Unusual Situations

Panic attacks may occur as a result of unusual external situations, most of which fall under the rubric of traumatic experiences. These incidents may or may not meet the criteria for posttraumatic stress disorder, and at times may meet some of the criteria.

Case Example: Struck by Lightning—A Case of Atypical Panic Attacks
Rodney, a 36-year-old construction worker who suffered panic attacks, gave the following account of a traumatic event that he experienced prior to his having panic episodes.

"About a year and a half ago, I came home from work at approximately 5 P.M. and decided to work in my garage. It had been raining heavily that day and I was drying out the inside unit of my heat pump. Apparently the coil in the pump had collected dirt from sawdust and other debris in the garage. The heat pump is a dual unit that heats and cools the garage. I do quite a bit of woodwork in my garage, and when the unit is running, it tends to attract dirt and tiny debris that get stuck in the coil. Therefore, in the summer, when I run the air-conditioning unit, the condensation from the air handler tends to drip off the coil onto the floor. It's a lot easier to take a rag and clean up the water than to have the unit repaired.

"One night, I returned home as a thunderstorm was brewing. I had just finished drying out the bottom part of the unit and I was down on one knee, turning the thumbscrew that holds the cover onto the unit, when I heard a thunderclap and saw a streak of lightning. Within the instant that I heard it, I saw electricity dancing over the top of the pump in a blue light, and then gathering together at the bottom of the unit, some 18 inches off the floor. That blue light came together, turned into a white light, and jumped from the heat pump to my hand and threw me against my truck. I was stunned for about 15 to 30 seconds. My arm was buzzing like crazy and the only sound that I could utter was an unintelligible babbling. It all happened so quickly. It felt as though someone had hit me with a baseball bat. It was a remarkable thing—it really scared the hell out of me.

"I probably should have gone to the hospital when it happened, but I didn't. I felt confused for a while and was a bit anxious afterwards in the form of jitteriness. About a week later, I began to experience a tightness in my chest and difficulty in breathing. I went to my doctor, who thought that I might have had a heart attack.

"As it turned out, it wasn't a silent heart attack after all, but there was a change in my electrocardiogram from one taken two years earlier as part of a routine physical. The internist sent me to a cardiologist who said that my heart rhythm had changed because I was struck by lightning. Apparently, this, in turn, caused me to have symptoms of panic. It was only after I discovered what was happening to me that I learned not to overreact to my symptoms."

The above is probably among the more atypical types of panic disorder. Nonetheless, such cases are occasionally encountered in clinical practice and need to be considered. It is recommended that atypical cases be treated in the same manner as other panic cases, but at the same time addressing the trauma and/or unusual circumstances involved.

Epidemiology

Prevalence Rate in Clinical and Nonclinical Populations

In any epidemiological study involving anxiety disorders, the criteria typically are taken from the DSM.

The most recent data are prevalence studies. Individuals who qualify as experiencing a panic attack are subjected to endorsing at least four of the DSM panic symptoms, as noted in the 1987 study by Katon and colleagues (Katon, Vitaliano, Russo, et al. 1987). Intense symptoms were reported by 5.9% of the sample. Only 3.8% experienced panic attacks that were unrelated to response to medication, drugs, alcohol, or physical illness or injury. Furthermore, 1.7% of the sample experienced attacks at least three times during a three-week period.

Not surprisingly, in clinical samples, panic disorders are significantly more common in women than in men in a ratio of 2.5 and 3.1 to 1 (Sheehan, 1983). Thus, women experience panic disorder at approximately twice the rate of men. There are some variables that may affect this ratio, however. For one, it is hypothesized that women tend to seek health care more frequently than men do. It is also estimated that women tend to be more honest in reporting their symptoms than are men, who may feel pressured to hide their symptoms.

In general, clinical populations indicate that panic disorder generally appears between the ages of 17 and 30 years, with a mean of 22.5 years (Sheehan, Sheehan, & Minichiello, 1981). Panic disorder occurs frequently in the general population with estimates ranging from 1.6 to 2.9% for women and 0.4 to 1.7% for men (Crowe, Noyes, Pauls, & Slyman, 1983; Myers, Weissman, Tischler, et al., 1984).

Lower estimates of the prevalence of panic disorder were found by Von Korff and colleagues (Von Korff, Shapiro, Burke, et al., 1987) in a large, primary-care epidemiological study of predominately middle-aged to geriatric-aged internal medicine patients. These ratios determined that panic disorder occurred in approximately 1.4% of the patients sampled.

With the advent of increasing reports in the literature and greater attention to panic attacks and panic disorder, studies are beginning to suggest that occasional panic attacks are relatively frequent in the general population. A study reported by Rapee, Ancis, and Barlow (1987) suggested that approximately 14% of the general population has experienced uncued, unexpected, spontaneous panic attacks at one time or other.

In conclusion, panic attacks clearly are not limited to individuals with panic disorder. Panic symptoms may be found in a broad range of mental and physical disorders, as well as in the general population. What is important to note, however, is that the recovery rates for individuals in nonclinical populations may be greater depending on whether or not other psychopathology exists. It also has been observed that nonclinical panickers appear to experience fewer symptoms and less severe symptoms during their panic episodes than do those diagnosed with panic disorder (Norton, Harrison, Hauch, & Rhodes, 1985).

Panic Disorder in Special Populations

The Elderly

It is said that panic disorder is often an infliction of young women and is rarely seen before the age of 10 or after the age of 50.

An interesting study by the Epidemiological Catchment Area (ECA) that examined 18,571 people living in a community for the presence of psychiatric disorder indicated that, with the exception of cognitive impairment, the frequency of all psychiatric diagnoses declined with age (Weissman, Myers, Tischler, et al., 1985). Phobias as a group, however, continued to be the most frequent diagnosis in women and the second most frequent in men ages 65 and older.

Studies of panic disorder in geriatric clinical settings are lacking, however, clinicians now report seeing it more frequently in elderly patients.

The University of South Florida Psychiatric Center undertook a study that observed 540 patients seen in the clinic who met the DSM-III-R criteria for panic disorder with or without agoraphobia. Of these individuals, in 41%, the onset of panic disorder took place before the age of 60, and in 59%, it took place at age 60 or later.

During panic attacks, the elderly were found to be more likely to exhibit shortness of breath, dizziness, sweating, and depersonalization than other populations. They frequently report fatigue and levels of anxiety that are similar to those observed in young adult panic patients.

While they tend to be less agoraphobic and less socially phobic than younger adults, they are similar with regard to illness phobias. The elderly also have rates of secondary depression similar to those reported for young adults and endorse a greater degree of depression. This presents somewhat of a difficulty for the elderly, particularly since the diagnosis often is overlooked or the problem is misdiagnosed as irritable bowel syndrome, mitral valve prolapse, or Parkinson's disease.

The researchers estimate that the late onset of panic disorder is usually a result of an inherited vulnerability to the disorder based on family history or nervousness. It may also be attributable to alcoholism or to the fact that the patient had it for years before diagnosis.

Despite their age, panic-disordered elderly patients respond to standard drug treatments fairly well.

Children

"Do children panic?" That question has been posed from time to time in the professional literature.

Actually this has become somewhat of a controversial issue and will most likely spur the additional research that is clearly needed. It is currently one of the fastest growing areas of interest in clinical child psychology since there are so few reports on panic attacks in children and adolescents. The controversy has been fueled by several studies that concluded that young children may experience the physical sensations associated with panic disorder (e.g., hyperventilation and lightheadedness), but are unlikely to "catastrophize" their symptoms as adults do (Nelles & Barlow, 1988).

It was found that adolescents who possess greater cognitive sophistication may be more prone to experiencing a full-blown panic disorder since their catastrophizing capability is greater.

In spite of the paucity of clinical reports, there is a growing consensus that panic disorder does exist in youths with some regularity. Ollendick, Mattis, and King (1994) concluded from a study that although the phenomenon of panic is present in adolescents, it is less frequently seen in younger children. Children who report panic attacks describe cognitive symptoms, although less often than physiological symptoms.

In general, the consensus among clinical researchers today is that panic disorder does occur in adolescents, with an overall prevalence rate of about 1% (Lewinsohn, Hops, Roberts, et al., 1993). How many children actually suffer panic disorder remains controversial, but the overall prevalence of spontaneous panic attacks in youngsters in general is almost certainly higher than what was reported previously.

In examining 17 youths, Last and Strauss (1989) found that the most commonly reported symptoms were heart palpitations, trembling, flushes or chills, shortness of breath, dizziness, and sweating. Surprisingly, only one diagnosis of separation-anxiety disorder was identified in this sample, which contradicts earlier arguments that panic disorder in youths is related to the separation-anxiety syndrome.

With regard to treatment, treatments similar to those used with adults are essential. The child who experiences paniclike symptoms usually demonstrates concern for physiological responses associated with anxiety, however, less sophisticated cognitive processes also occur and, therefore, some of the more straightforward behavioral techniques may be effective as opposed to focusing on cognition.

For more information with regard to the treatment of panic disorder in children and adolescents, the reader is referred to Kendall and associates (Kendall, Chansky, Kane, et al., 1992).

2

Theories of Panic

It is generally accepted by health-care professionals that panic attacks are common among various types of anxiety disorders. In fact, almost anyone can have a panic attack, depending on the circumstances and one's condition. In many cases, individuals who experience panic are able to identify the cues that trigger the panic reaction; however, they are often unable to identify cues that would allow them to predict an oncoming attack, rendering the disorder debilitating. It is precisely this issue that has sparked interest among researchers and also has raised controversy. A number of theories have been proposed that attempt to explain the origin of spontaneous panic attacks and panic disorder and what constitutes their onset and duration.

Most major theories include the general tenet that uncued panic attacks involve intense fear reactions that stem from unjustified activations of a hypersensitive alarm system in the body. Thus, the panic reaction is triggered in the absence of objective evidence of danger and constitutes what may be considered a false alarm. However, different conceptualizations have been proposed to account for the origin of such episodes of panic. Various biochemical and/or psychological mechanisms have been considered and studied at length. Among the theories attempting to account for the advent of spontaneous panic attacks are the psychodynamic, the biological, and the cognitive-behavioral.

Psychodynamic Theory

Even though panic attacks existed before Freud's era, Freud was among the first to call the syndrome anxiety neurosis (Freud, 1894). His description included many of the characteristic traits exhibited by individuals who suffer panic disorder today. He also was among the first theorists to suggest that anxiety neurosis had a somatic, rather than psychological, etiology. He associated it with particular sexual practices (Milrod, Busch, Cooper, & Shapiro, 1997), postulating that anxiety neurosis altered the ego as a result of emerging forbidden wishes. Contending that anxiety acted as a signal,* triggering the ego to employ a variety of defense mechanisms that aided in avoiding perceived danger, Freud hypothesized that symptoms of anxiety would arise from a compromise between the wishful impulse and the defense mechanism elicited by the wish. Unfortunately, Freud's work at the time referred to a general variety of anxiety neuroses with no specific delineations of what is now referred to as panic attacks.

Approximately 32,480 books on psychodynamic theory have been published; most of these texts deal with some aspect of fear (Haley, 1996), but very few specifically address the concept of panic.

Modern psychodynamic theory posits that panic disorder develops as a result of life events preceding the onset of panic, premorbid personality traits, and the patients' perceptions of their parents. This theory is based on the concept that symptoms result from mental processes that may be outside of the client's conscious awareness and that by elucidating these processes, symptoms may be reduced (Milrod, Busch, Cooper, & Shapiro, 1997; Kohut, 1972). Triggers preceding the onset of panic may include a real or fantasized loss or rejection of security symbols that demands more independent behavior of the patient. Examples may include, but are not limited to, a change in jobs or a move to another location, graduation, marriage, and births. In addition, the role of unconscious configuration is extremely important, together with personality traits that predispose certain people to panic in the context of particular life stressors. Such personality characteristics as dependency, perfectionism, and obsessive-compulsive traits are often found among panic-disordered sufferers.

---

*This later became known as signal anxiety in classical psychoanalytic theory.

In a study conducted by Kleiner and Marshall (1987), agoraphobic patients who suffered panic attacks reported a history of dependency associated with unassertiveness. They also described themselves as highly anxious socially and as being fearful of negative evaluations by others. In addition, they described experiencing difficulties in coping with anger and criticism and a tendency to comply with others (pp. 318–319). Furthermore, Tucker (1956) described patients' reports of a lack of parental affection, overprotection, and criticism by parents as being major precursors to panic (p. 827).

The separation-anxiety hypothesis is another popular explanation for the onset of panic disorder (Weissman, Leckman, Merikangas, et al., 1984). This theory contends that panic-disordered individuals commonly report that life events preceding the onset of panic involve real or fantasized separation or loss from ambivalent objects. Thoughts associated with panic attacks may include a fear of being alone and unable to care for oneself. Weissman and colleagues (Weissman, Leckman, & Merikangas, 1984) found that panic disorder in parents conferred more than a threefold risk of separation-anxiety disorder on their children 6 to 17 years of age.

The psychodynamic treatment of panic disorder, therefore, places a great deal of emphasis on investigating the individual's intense fears of separation and the sense that he or she cannot function alone. While these symptoms have their roots in early childhood conflict, they are also connected in some way to ongoing interpersonal difficulties.

Another hypothesis contends that anger often plays a key role in panic disorder (Busch et al., 1991; Shear et al., 1994). The authors believe that fear of angry feelings, along with the conscious and unconscious vindictive fantasies accompanying these feelings, can trigger panic episodes. In a sense, panic symptoms may serve as a precursor to underlying anger, or even rage.

Biological Theories

Biological theories argue that panic is essentially the result of biochemical dysregulations associated with a genetic predisposition (Sheehan, 1982; Weiss & Uhde, 1990). These theories share a common theme that minimizes the role of psychological factors in the actual experience of panic attacks. The majority of these hypotheses suggest that panic disorder involves a specific abnormality in neurotransmission—either a defect in the metabolism or at a specific receptor site (e.g., Sheehan, Ballenger, & Jacobsen, 1980). Other abnormalities may involve anatomical dysfunction of specific brain areas (e.g., locus ceruleus, circuit of Papez). Panic attacks are usually associated with dysfunction of lower cortical areas, such as the brain stem (e.g., Charney & Heninger, 1986; Gorman, Liebowitz, Fyer, & Stein, 1989; Klein, 1993, 1994). These areas of the brain are more primitive and are connected to an ancient hardwired alarm system (Barlow, 1988; Barlow & Cerny, 1988). More highly developed areas of the brain are not directly involved in fear and panic reactions, but do play a role in the evaluation of danger and anticipatory anxiety where phobic avoidance is involved (e.g., Barlow, 1988; Barlow & Cerny, 1988).

According to the biological perspective, spontaneous panic attacks are truly unsolicited since they result from a disorder in the brain. Thus, the onset of panic attacks is not associated with predisposing factors or predictive signs (Rapee, 1996). Specific etiological hypotheses include dysregulation in the noradrenergic system, also referred to as the locus ceruleus theory (Svensson, 1987; Charney, Heninger, & Breier, 1984; Charney & Heninger, 1986b; Charney, Woods, Price, et al., 1990), and dysregulations in the serotonergic system (Charney & Heninger, 1986b; Charney, Woods, Goodman, & Heninger, 1987). Other theories include the septohippocampal hypothesis (Gray, 1982), the GABA/benzodiazepine hypothesis (Skolnick & Paul, 1983), and the cholecystokinin tetrapeptide (cck-4) hypothesis (Bradwejn, Koszycki, Payeur, et al., 1992). More recently, Klein's suffocation-false-alarm theory (1993, 1994) has been proposed as a more palatable theory.

The main evidence used to support the neurochemical dysregulation hypotheses include (1) results from twin, family, and linkage studies suggesting a genetic predisposition toward experiencing panic, and (2) the induction of panic experiences in a laboratory setting through artificial stimulation of neurotransmission. Direct (e.g., infusion of sodium lactate, inhalations of carbon dioxide) and indirect (e.g., yohimbine, flumazenil) agents have been used successfully to stimulate specific neurotransmitters and to induce panic in a laboratory setting (e.g., Charney, Heninger, & Breier, 1984; Boulenger, Uhde, Wolff, & Post, 1984; Appleby, Klein, Sachar, & Levitt, 1981; Nutt, Glue, Lawson, & Wilson,

1990). Results have suggested that panic-disordered individuals are hypersensitive to neurotransmitter stimulation caused by exposure to certain agents (McNally, 1995).

Research on the biological theory of panic has revealed some biochemical imbalances associated with the experience of panic. Nevertheless, there is little evidence to support the notion that a purely biological etiology for panic disorder exists in every case, or that any of the mentioned dysregulation hypotheses is specific to panic disorder. Several interesting studies currently under way are examining the tendency for panic disorder to run in families. These studies are investigating DNA structures of panic and agoraphobic individuals by comparing blood samples among those family members reporting a history of the disorder. At present, there is no sure method to test for a chemical imbalance in the brain. While the explosion of research using magnetic resonance imaging (MRI), positron emission tomography (PET) scans, and brain electrical area mapping (BEAM) has generated tremendous interest in psychobiological theories of panic disorder, the complexity of brain-related behavior continues to stall a comprehensive understanding of brain mechanisms involved in panic and anxiety disorders.

However, locating a neurobiochemical correlate of panic is not out of the question since every behavior and emotion has a somatic substratum. Unfortunately, a parameter has yet to be established for diagnosing the biology of panic disorder (Barlow & Cerny, 1988; APA, 1994). Moreover, it is not clear as to whether or not such chemical dysregulations are a cause or a consequence of panic. Even in the event that they play a causal role, a question remains as to whether they stand alone or coexist with the notion of the patient's interpretation of internal cues. Much remains to be determined in this area.

Cognitive-Behavioral Theory

The cognitive-behavioral theory (CBT) of panic constitutes a comprehensive and integrative approach that includes cognitive, neurobiochemical, affective, and behavioral aspects of panic (e.g., Clark, 1986; Barlow, 1988; Ehlers & Margraf, 1989; McNally, 1990). It also takes into account the role of predisposing or vulnerability factors (biological and psychosocial) as well as that of precipitating elements, whether internal (bodily sensations) or external (environmental) (e.g., Raskin, Peeke, Dickman, & Pinsker, 1982; Dattilio, 1986; Dattilio & Foa, 1988; Ottaviani & Beck, 1987; Rapee, 1996).

While acknowledging that neurochemical components of autonomic symptoms do play a vital role in panic, CBT places more emphasis on the causal influence of the perception of threat or danger. More specifically, catastrophic misattributions of a wide range of distressing bodily sensations originate from different sources in vulnerable individuals, serving as the combination necessary to produce a sensation of panic (e.g., Beck, Emery, & Greenberg, 1985; Clark, 1986; Clark & Ehlers, 1993; Rapee, 1996). According to this theory, the activation of the panic response is not the automatic result of perceiving any specific sensation, but stems from the threatening appraisal of a particular bodily change (e.g., palpitations, lightheadedness) (Clark, 1986; Rapee, 1996).

This conceptualization has three key components. The first is the perception of physical symptoms that act as interoceptive cues for triggering a threat appraisal, and, consequently, the panic response. These sensations can be triggered by a myriad of sources, which may include internal cues (e.g., palpitations induced by mitral valve prolapse, physical exercise, respiratory distress from a hyperventilatory hypocapnia) or external cues (e.g., exposure to a feared stimulus or cardiovascular reactions to barometric pressure changes, infusions of sodium lactate, carbon dioxide inhalations, and so on). Whereas physical symptoms can range from normal bodily sensations to abnormal physical reactions, there does not appear to be a specific neurobiological mechanism for all panic attacks. In order to play a relevant role in generating panic, however, these sensations not only must be present, but also must be perceived by the individual as threatening (Rapee, 1996). Specifically with individuals experiencing panic disorder, the catastrophic interpretation of internal cues (autonomic symptoms) is more pronounced than with external cues (enclosed places) (Dattilio & Foa, 1988).

The second factor is an erroneous self-explanation of such bodily changes, typically misattribution to perceived danger of cues (e.g., a heart attack, hypertensive crisis, fear of losing total control and of going insane (Clark, 1989). Attribution and information processing are important aspects of panic disorder, particularly since panic-disordered individuals often cannot verbalize what happens to them (Rapee, 1996).

The third aspect is the presence of a psychological vulnerability that predisposes the person not only to making the erroneous attributions, but, in some cases, to unintentionally inducing bodily sensations.

In the cognitive-behavioral perspective, laboratory-induced panic attacks constitute a biological challenge that successfully provokes bodily changes that are feared by vulnerable individuals (Clark, 1986; Van den Hout, 1988; Rapee, 1995, 1996). Several studies have demonstrated how beliefs and expectative manipulations mediate an individual's response to such biological challenges and procedures and, in some cases, can serve to eliminate panic (Margraf, Ehlers, & Roth, 1986b; Sanderson, Rapee, & Barlow, 1989; Shear, Fyer, Ball, et al., 1991).

In summary, to adopt a reductionistic perspective on panic disorder does not seem justified, or productive. Research evidence has demonstrated that alternative psychobiologically based theories of panic have received stronger support from empirical research (e.g., Beck, Emery, & Greenberg, 1985; Clark, 1986, 1988; McNally, 1990).

Alternative Hypotheses

Predisposing Factors to Panic Attacks

Research, as well as clinical practice, appears justified in considering separately the predisposing factors that render some individuals prone to experiencing uncued panic attacks, and the precipitating factors as those stimuli that actually trigger the initial surge of anxiety. Interactions between these two aspects of panic account for interpersonal and intrapersonal response variability when exposed to a stressor. Thus, precipitating stimuli affecting a vulnerable person generate a panic reaction, whereas they will not produce the same reaction in a nonvulnerable individual. Moreover, vulnerable individuals not exposed to precipitants do not present with panic attacks.

The basic objective of psychotherapy for panic disorder is to reduce the patient's vulnerability to panic attacks and to provide him or her with an alternative and a more objective view of the phenomenon, as well as with effective coping mechanisms.

At present, there is no consensus regarding the length of time prior to an actual experience of spontaneous panic that would define such an event as being predisposing or precipitating. This may explain why the literature shows the same factor as being considered as being both pre-disposing and precipitating by different investigators.

Understanding the nature of panic would be easier if we identified pre-cipitants to those factors (e.g., biological dysregulations, psychosocial ex-periences) that immediately precede the onset of panic (for example, within the preceding 24 hours). It would also illuminate our understand-ing if we could relate predisposing factors to events more distant from the panic experience (e.g., several days to years prior to the episode).

Biological Vulnerabilities

Genetic Predisposition Hypothesis

Data from family, twin, and adoption studies analyzing the genetic eti-ology of anxiety disorders suggest a hereditary transmission of factors that predispose individuals to manifesting symptoms of panic. However, it is not clear as to exactly which factors are inherited (Last, 1993). One hypothesis suggests that a specific trait is transmitted that consists of a high arousal level and a slow habituation to stimuli, thus causing a person to increase his or her propensity to experience panic symptoms (Johnson & Melamed, 1979). Another hypothesis suggests that the heredity of certain temperamental characteristics, such as the tendency to withdraw from unfamiliar stimuli or slow adaptability to change, with highly intense expressions of mood, possibly explain the predis-position (Goldsmith, 1983; Thomas, Chess, Birch, et al., 1963; Torger-sen, 1981, 1987, 1989).

Another possibility is that there is a specific genetic basis for in-heriting a predisposition to panic disorder as opposed to generalized anxiety disorder (e.g., Torgersen, 1983). Recent research on deoxy-ribonucleic acid (DNA) has analyzed the genetic structure of panic vic-tims and members of their families who also report a history of experiencing panic or related symptoms.

The issue of whether or not a genetic linkage is familial with individu-als diagnosed with panic disorder has been hypothesized for some time (Knowles & Weissman, 1995; Weissman, 1993; Weisman & Merikan-gas, 1986). This is particularly true of individuals who describe an early onset of panic (Goldstein, Wickramaratne, Horwath, & Weissman, 1997).

Recently, a series of studies were undertaken in order to test this hypothesis (Hamilton et al., 1999; Knowles et al., 1998).

In the more recent study, the investigators used a family-based design to test for genetic association and linkage between panic disorder and a functional polymorphism in the promoter of the gene 5-HTT. In this study, 340 individuals in 45 families, as well as 75 Haplotype Relative Risk "trios," were genotyped at the polymorphic locus, which consists of 44 base pair deletion/insertion. The results yielded no significant differences in Allele frequencies or occurrence of genotypes within the triads. Furthermore, no linkage between the 5-HTT polymorphism and panic disorder was observed in the multiplex families, using a variety of simulations for dominant and recessive models of inheritance. The results of this study suggest that the genetic basis of panic disorder may be distinct from anxiety-related traits assessed by personality inventories in normal populations (Hamilton et al., 1999).

On a different note, David Barlow's (1988) emotion theory of panic disorder suggests that there is a genetically inherited predisposition to having panic attacks. Hypothetically, this vulnerability operates under the same theory as those for other physical illnesses, such as hypertension and headaches (Antony & Barlow, 1989). Therefore, when in distress, biologically vulnerable individuals will experience panic attacks in the absence of any specific triggers. Barlow's theory is supported by several twin studies (e.g., Torgersen, 1985; Kendler, Heath, Martin, & Eaves, 1987; Martin, Jardine, Andrew, & Heath, 1988; Kendler, Walters, Neale, et al., 1995) and linkage studies (Crowe, Noyes, Wilson, et al., 1987), which suggest that panic attacks may have a specific genetic etiology. They also suggest that panic disorder and agoraphobia with panic attacks are genetically related anxiety disorders (Torgersen, 1983, 1990). Although fascinating, these results are far from conclusive. There are only a few twin studies, each involving a small number of pairs. Moreover, most monozygotic twin pairs are discordant in the sense of their not having the same anxiety disorder (Torgersen, 1983, 1990). The observed correlation between monozygotic twin pairs is of moderate magnitude. According to Torgersen (1993), twin and linkage studies tend to magnify the influence of genetic factors and may not provide an objective account of why such an influence occurs.

In conclusion, research data suggest that some individuals seem to be genetically predisposed to developing anxiety disorders. However, the genetic specificity hypothesis for panic is still controversial since genetic studies have not been able to isolate which element is specifically inherited. The authors, along with others who adhere to the information-processing view (e.g., Rapee, 1996), are more inclined to support the hypothesis of an inherited general vulnerability to anxiety than the hypothesis that there is a specific predisposition to panic. This may explain why psychological treatments of panic combined with the short-term use of medications have been able to produce more effective and longer-lasting outcomes (Craske, Maidenberg, & Bystritsky, 1995).

Differential Respiratory Response Under Stress

A number of researchers and clinicians have noticed that the bodily sensations that accompany panic attacks bear a striking similarity to the sensations produced by hyperventilation (e.g., Ley, 1985a; Barlow, Vermilyea, Blanchard, et al., 1985; Clark, 1986). As a result, it has been hypothesized by several theorists that hyperventilation may play an important role in predisposing a person to panic or initiating panic attacks.

Several researchers (e.g., Ley, 1985a, 1985b; Rapee, 1985, 1986; Clark, 1986; Salkovskis & Clark, 1989) have suggested that people demonstrate different respiratory reactions when under stress. Those who tend to overbreathe are especially prone to developing panic attacks.

The theory porports that hyperventilation contributes to excessive carbon dioxide to be expelled from the lungs, triggering an excessive loss of carbon dioxide (pCO_2) by the blood. Reduction that diminishes the stimulation of the respiratory reflex center increases the level of pH, producing blood alkalosis. Such changes in the blood's chemistry and the metabolic homeostasis manifest as uncomfortable body sensations (i.e., dyspnea, palpitations) to which the individual responds with apprehension. This increased apprehension subsequently causes further augmentation in the hyperventilation cycle, and the greater the reduction in carbon dioxide, the more intense are the physical sensations. These spiraling events quickly evolve into a full-blown panic attack (typically in 10 minutes or less) (Dattilio, 1990, 1994b).

Cognitive-behavioral theorists (e.g., Clark, Salkovskis, & Chalkley, 1985) contend that it is either the perception of a feared stimulus itself or the induction of fear already elicited by other stimuli that contributes to the catastrophic reaction during this event, precipitating the sequence of panic. Thus, hyperventilation in some cases is considered to play a causal role in the onset of panic, whereas in other cases, it is the result of experiencing panic. In either role, the sudden, unexpected, and apparently unexplainable bodily sensations accompanying the overbreathing associated with the emotional arousal of the initial fear is what triggers the panic (Ley, 1985b; Dattilio, 1994b).

The main hypothesis that accounts for this differential respiratory reaction during stress is the chronic hyperventilation theory (Ley, 1987a). According to this theory, hyperventilation is one of the autonomic nervous system responses to stress and anxiety. People who are chronically tense or anxious show a heightened baseline of physiological arousal, and a significant number of them maintain a chronic hyperventilation hypocapnia (Lum, 1976). When the level of overbreathing is low, its accompanying somatic effects are of low intensity (i.e., lightheadedness, nausea) and may go unnoticed or individuals simply adapt to them quickly (Lum, 1976; Ley, 1987a). In chronic hyperventilation, blood pH is somewhat high (i.e., 7.63) and the carbon-dioxide tension level is relatively low (i.e., 18.67 mmHg) (Okel & Hurst, 1961; Lum, 1976). These are usually conditions that lower the threshold of tolerance. Since the person is on the brink of hyperventilatory hypocapnia, sometimes even a mild autonomic arousal associated with an emotional change may produce increased overbreathing. This increases the blood pH level and decreases carbon dioxide to levels at which the somatic effects are difficult to tolerate (Ley, 1987a). It is proposed that, in individuals with normal breathing, the alterations of pH and pCO_2 for the same emotional arousal will not be excessive. Their resting level maintains the pH and pCO_2 within the normal range, resulting in a higher threshold of tolerance.

People exposed to stress or anxiety for prolonged periods have a greater chance of becoming chronic hyperventilators (Ley, 1987a). Also, those with physical abnormalities in their nasal passages (e.g., obstruction of the nasal orifices) or nasal diseases (e.g., tubanitis, sinusitis, allergies) may generate chronic overbreathing (Adams, Boies, & Paparella, 1978). This usually causes the expelling of higher levels of CO_2.

Studies partially support the hyperventilation hypothesis, suggesting that about half of panic-disordered subjects evinced chronic hyperventilation (e.g., Craske, 1991); about half of those with panic disorder display symptoms of hyperventilation when panicking (i.e., 40% in

Garssen, Van Veenendaal & Bloemink's 1983 study). On the basis of research data, Briggs, Strech, and Brandon (1993) proposed a distinction between panic suffocation and nonsuffocation, considering the presence or absence of respiratory distress. While this tends to obscure the aforementioned findings, further research has supported such a classification (Taylor & Rachman, 1994).

In summary, the vulnerability factor for a significant proportion of individuals with panic disorder would be a pattern of chronic hyperventilation that predisposes the individual promptly to exceed the normal range of specific biochemical parameters (pCO_2, blood pH).

Suffocation False Alarm

Klein's (1993, 1994) suffocation theory proposed that some spontaneous panic attacks occur when a hypersensitive suffocation monitor in the brain erroneously indicates a deficiency of useful air, triggering the suffocation-alarm system. This system activation generates respiratory distress, hyperventilation, and panic. Thus, individuals with a pathologically low threshold for activation are prone to unpredictable false-alarm activation. In this theory, psychosocial aspects, including stress and anxiety, do not seem to play a significant role in activating the false alarm.

As mentioned previously, panic-disordered individuals can be differentiated in two ways: those who suffer respiratory distress during the attacks and those with little or no respiratory distress. Nevertheless, this distinction neither supports nor disclaims the hypothesis that a pathologically lower biochemical threshold of the brain monitors the center for suffocation. Despite the fact that scores on the Suffocation Fear Scale predicted respiratory responses to a behavioral suffocation challenge (Taylor & Rachman, 1994), there is no clear support for Klein's etiological hypothesis since there are other competing hypotheses to account for such association (i.e., chronic hyperventilation plus misattribution).

In a recent study, Taylor and colleagues (Taylor, Woody, Koch, et al., 1996) tested part of Klein's theory (1993), which proposed that CBT is less effective for suffocation panickers than for nonsuffocation panickers since the etiology of the former is organic (the suffocation-alarm system). Results fail to support Klein's contention: both suffocation and nonsuffocation panickers significantly improved as a result of the CBT treatment program and there were no differences between them at post-test or during follow-up three months later. Research is required to test Klein's theory more extensively.

Psychosocial Vulnerabilities

Separation Anxiety

Fear of separation from caregivers during infancy is a normal developmental phenomenon that peaks between the ages of 9 and 13 months, starts to diminish progressively when infants reach the age of two and a half (Marks, 1987), and typically ends between the ages of three and five years, when children are more independent. This anxiety reaction, also observed in many animals, is assumed to be an ethological mechanism with the survival role of protecting children from being alone and vulnerable to harm (Marks, 1987).

Some children, nevertheless, do not overcome this developmental stage and remain anxious about being separated from those to whom they feel attached. For example, they often have dreams or fantasies of accidents, illnesses, or other events that could lead to separation from their caregivers. Also, if they are by themselves in a unfamiliar environment, as well as when they travel by themselves, they become extremely anxious and homesick (e.g., at school, at a friend's house, or at summer camp).

Thus, if before the age of 18, a person experiences unreasonable and intense fear of and worry about an actual or anticipated separation from his or her major attachment figures, he or she may be diagnosed as having a separation-anxiety disorder (APA, 1994).

Some investigators (e.g., Klein & Fink, 1962; Klein, 1964; Mendel & Klein, 1969; Weissman, Leckman, Merikangas, et al., 1984) have suggested that separation-anxiety disorder is a selective precursor of panic and agoraphobia in the future and, consequently, is etiologically related. Moreover, the DSM-III-R (APA, 1987, pp. 226, 231) adopted this hypothesis in a tentative fashion: "Separation-anxiety disorder in childhood and sudden object loss apparently predispose to the development of . . . agoraphobia and panic disorder." Also, the DSM-IV (APA, 1994, p. 111) endorsed a possible connection between seperation anxiety disorder and panic disorder with agoraphobia: "The (separation-anxiety) disorder may precede the development of panic disorder with agoraphobia."

Support for this hypothesis originated in anecdotal reports and prevalence studies that revealed that a significant proportion of agoraphobics reported a history of childhood separation anxiety. This is demonstrated in approximately 50% in Klein's (1964) and Mendel and Klein's (1969) studies. Thorpe and Burns' (1983) national survey in Great Britain yielded 38%, and between 20% and 30% of subjects in Coryell, Noyes, and Clancy's (1983), and Breier, Charney, and Heninger's (1984) studies respectively. However, a number of important critiques have been formulated and should be taken into account in interpreting such results.

Thyer (1993) critiqued the methodological shortcomings of such studies, particularly the retrospective nature of their data and the lack of validity of the instruments used for the assessment of childhood separation anxiety. Furthermore, the differences in the definition of separation used in each study render it difficult to determine how comparable these results are.

Since the hypothesis suggests that separation anxiety is a precursor of panic and agoraphobia, several studies have been conducted to contrast the prevalence of the history of separation-anxiety disorder during childhood in panic disorder with or without agoraphobia as compared with individuals with other anxiety disorders and with the general population. Overall, the results do not strongly support the hypothesis. For example, it has been found that the same prevalence of separation-anxiety disorder, loss of significant relationships during childhood, and separation were identified as precipitants of anxiety in a sample of individuals with panic disorder, as well as in a sample of generalized anxiety-disordered subjects (e.g., Raskin, Peeke, Dickman, & Pinsker, 1982). Studies comparing subjects with specific phobias have provided mixed results. Some studies have shown that separation anxiety appears to be more common in agoraphobics. For instance, 50% in the agoraphobic group reported more separation anxiety as compared with 27% in the specific-phobic sample in a study conducted by Klein, Zitring, Woerner, and Ross (1987). Although these differences appear to be true for females, they differ for male agoraphobics (Gittelman & Klein, 1984). Nevertheless, Thyer and associates (Thyer, Nesse, Cameron, & Curtis, 1985; Thyer, Nesse, Curtis, & Cameron, 1986; Thyer, Himle,

& Fischer, 1988; Thyer, Himle, & Miller-Gogoleski, 1989) found no differences between agoraphobics and panic-disordered individuals as compared with specific phobics in the prevalence of childhood separation (e.g., parental deaths) or separation anxiety. Roy-Byrne, Geraci, and Uhde (1986a) found no significant differences in the number of life events involving separation and loss between a sample of 44 panic-disordered patients and a matched sample of 44 nonclinical subjects.

Thyer (1993) also critiqued the studies exploring the relationship between school phobia and adult agoraphobia. He proposed that these studies erroneously equated school phobia with separation-anxiety disorder when, in reality, school refusal may be attributable to causes other than separation anxiety (e.g., oppositional behavior) (Last, Francis, Hersen, et al., 1987; Last & Strauss, 1990).

Cognitive Vulnerability

People vulnerable to panic disorder share certain common beliefs about the harmfulness of sudden bodily changes. As this cognitive frame causes them to fear their own fear and physical changes, it has been referred as the "fear of fear" hypothesis (Goldstein & Chambless, 1978) or anxiety sensitivity (Reiss & McNally, 1985). More recently, Williams, Chambless, and Ahrens (1997) suggested that this may also be a result of a fear of emotions.

Panic-vulnerable individuals seem to be particularly concerned with physical (e.g., death) or psychological threats (e.g., becoming insane or losing control) even before the first panic attack occurs. For example, in a retrospective study conducted by Fava, Grandi, and Canestrari (1988), it was found that, compared with nonclinical subjects, panic-disordered subjects reported significantly more hypochondriacal concerns and anxiety prior to the first panic attack. Also, consistent with research evidence revealing that anxiety disorder biases individuals toward selectively attending threatening information (e.g., Bradley, Mogg, Millar, & White, 1995; Bryant & Harvey, 1995), panic-disordered individuals focus their attention on their bodily changes since they are associated with impending doom.

This information-processing bias—which includes distorted interpretation and selective attention—found among panic-disordered subjects not only could be the outcome of experiencing one or more spontaneous panic attacks, but might stem from the individual's belief system and enduring cognitive style (e.g. Chambless, Caputo, Bright, & Gallagher, 1984; McNally & Lorenz, 1987; Clark, 1988; McNally, 1989; Van den Hout, Van der Molen, Griez, & Lousberg, 1987; Clark & Ehlers, 1993). Moreover, Cox, Endler, and Swinson (1995) found that catastrophic cognition generated during a panic attack in panic-disordered individuals is related more to the individual's cognitive style than it is to the severity of the physical symptoms.

According to investigators (Rapee, 1993; McNally, 1995; Mogg, Bradley, & Williams, 1995), this information-processing bias among those with anxiety disorders functions automatically in the sense of being involuntary and often preconscious, but it is not capacity-free. This last property makes it possible to control it and to change it. Several studies have shown that, with proper interventions, panic-disordered patients learn to change their bias. For example, in a recent study, Westling and Öst (1995) found that a sample of 45 panic-disordered patients, as compared with 45 matched normal controls, interpreted their internal sensations, but not external events, in a significantly more threatening manner. After a cognitive-behavioral intervention, panic-free individuals, as compared with still panicking patients, revealed a greater reduction in their threatening interpretation of bodily sensations at posttreatment and follow-up. This notion was also investigated in a study by Dattilio (1986), while comparing the cognitive response of panic-disordered subjects with that in other types of anxiety disorders. Panic subjects demonstrated the highest response to internal threat as compared with any other type of anxiety disorder.

Precipitants of Spontaneous Attacks

Panic-disordered individuals consistently report that their fear response does not seem to be associated with specific life events that precede by minutes, or even hours, the experience of panic. Again, from this phenomenology stems the notion that these symptoms are uncued and, consequently, unpredictable. In other words, for the panic-disordered individual, spontaneous panic attacks have no precipitating factors. Nevertheless, research has led us to consider several possible factors.

Disruption of Social Support

The DSM-III-R (APA, 1987, p. 237) and DSM-IV (APA, 1994, p. 398) propose that, in some cases, a sudden loss or disruption of a significant interpersonal relationship may precipitate or exacerbate panic disorder. It can be inferred that vulnerable individuals, that is, those with separation-anxiety disorder, are prone to experiencing panic attacks when facing an actual, or possible, loss of social support (e.g., through divorce, death, or moving away).

Studies examining the prevalence of disruption of social support just prior to the onset of panic disorder with or without agoraphobia have shown that between 10% and 35% of patients reported having been exposed to such stressors. For example, Doctor (1982) found that 31% of the 404 agoraphobics sampled reported separation and loss before the onset of their anxiety disorder. Roy-Byrne, Geraci, and Uhde (1986b) found the same proportion (33%) among 33 panic-disordered individuals. Other studies have reported lower prevalence rates for similar samples. For instance, in a study conducted by Öst & Hugdahl (1983), only 12% of a sample of 80 agoraphobics reported the same stressor, and 16% of 58 agoraphobics reported the stressor in a study conducted by Last, Barlow, and O'Brien (1984).

Most investigators (Doctor, 1982; Last, Barlow, & O'Brien, 1984; Roy-Byrne, Geraci, & Uhde, 1986b; Thyer, 1993) conclude that separation and the loss of significant others is one of the stressors that may precede the onset of panic disorder in some individuals, but there is a wide range of other types of life events that can also act as precipitants. For example, in Last, Barlow, and O'Brien's (1984) study, approximately half of the stressors that preceded the first panic attack in a sample of 58 agoraphobics were not of an interpersonal nature, but were health-related issues (e.g., drug reactions, major surgery, endocrine reactions). Moreover, in the same study, many of the patients reported having been exposed to more than one distressing life event prior to the initial attack.

It should also be mentioned that the time between the separation experience and the surge of fear is more than a few hours, and usually one to two months. Consequently, the disruption of social support does not seem to act as a true precipitant of panic, but more like a medium-range predisposing factor.

Bodily Changes

The onset of panic attacks is explained as a feedback/feedforward process among the physical sensations considered threat signals. A number of studies have revealed how a variety of sensations have triggered the panic reaction in natural, as well as laboratory, settings. Moreover, various benign cardiovascular, respiratory, and audiovestibular procedures have been designed as part of the treatment protocol of panic-disordered patients in an effort to induce the relevant bodily changes until the patients learn how to cope with them effectively and/or become desensitized to the changes (e.g., Orwin, 1973; Zarate, Rapee, Craske, & Barlow, 1988; Dattilio, 1990, 1994b).

Among the factors that may cause these bodily sensations in natural settings are the following.

Diseases

Several diseases (e.g., hypoglycemia, pheochromocytomas, hyperthyroidism) involve significant biochemical changes that elevate an individual's autonomic arousal, which also affects the person's information-processing style and habitual mood. Some, but not all, of these individuals experience panic attacks (e.g., Starkman, Zelnik, Nesse, & Cameron, 1985). Pheochromocytoma in particular tends to mimic a panic attack closely. This syndrome involves an adrenaline-producing tumor in the kidney or adrenal glands, which causes autonomic activity. (See "Medical Conditions" for more details.)

Physical Abnormalities

Several physical abnormalities have been known to produce symptoms very similar to panic attacks. One such abnormality, which has been studied in depth, is the mitral valve prolapse syndrome (MVPS). This benign heart abnormality typically produces palpitations, cardiac arrhythmias, shortness of breath, dyspnea, faintness, and chest pain without posing any real threat to the sufferer's health. Several studies consistently have found that the prevalence of MVPS is significantly higher among panic-disordered patients (e.g., 7% in Mavissakalian, Salerni, Thompson, & Michelson, 1983; 16% in Hartman, Kramer, Brown, et al., 1982; 44% in Kantor, Zitrin, & Zeldis, 1980; 50% in

Gorman, Fyer, Gliklich, King, & Klein, 1981) than in the normal population (e.g., 0.4% in Liberthson, Sheehan, King, & Weyman, 1986; 5% in Shear, Devereaux, Kramer-Fox, et al., 1984; 9% in Kantor, Zitrin, & Zeldis, 1980). Despite the variability in the prevalence rates found in different studies, the higher incidence of MVPS among panic-disordered individuals than in normal populations is widely accepted. Nevertheless, the syndrome does not appear to play a direct role in the onset of panic. Psychosocially vulnerable individuals with MVPS are more likely than are nonvulnerable individuals to misinterpret symptoms of MVPS.

Another physical abnormality found to be associated with spontaneous panic attacks is vestibular misfunctioning. For example, Jacob and colleagues (Jacob, Moller, Turner, & Wall, 1985) found that panic-disordered patients whose main complaint during attacks was dizziness, presented a high proportion of abnormal vestibular and audiological functioning. These researchers suggested two possible mechanisms to support this finding: Anxiety may result from a threatening interpretation of vestibular symptoms, or vice versa, that is, vestibular symptoms stem from heightened levels of anxiety.

Relaxation

The phenomenon of relaxation-induced anxiety and panic has been reported. The experience of feeling relaxed is clearly associated with significant bodily changes, that is, the level of respiration is lowered, which parasympathetically reduces blood pressure, increases skin temperature, and so on. Consequently, this initial change in the body's homeostasis may result in initial anxiety (Lazarus & Mayne, 1990). As a result, individuals sometimes interpret such sensations in a catastrophic manner. Some believe that something dangerous to their health is taking place. Ley (1988) suggested that hyperventilation may account for this phenomenon. Accordingly, when an individual's breathing rhythm does not keep pace with the reduction in metabolism and carbon-dioxide production associated with relaxation, the person will experience hyperventilatory hypocapnia. Nevertheless, most individuals with relaxation-induced anxiety and panic seem to be more troubled by their fear of losing control of themselves, than by fear of their bodily changes in terms of becoming ill (Lazarus & Mayne, 1990).

Spontaneous Cognitive Activity

A person's interpretation of an event (actual or future) as a threat triggers the person's alarm reaction, which is accompanied by bodily changes. The greater the perceived threat, the more intense are the symptoms. The automatic quality of many of these negative thoughts gives the individual the false impression that he or she is not doing anything to provoke his or her anxiety and initial accompanying symptoms. Vulnerable individuals tend to react with fear to their own bodily changes, initiating the feedback/feedforward process involved in the development of panic attacks.

Exercising: Palpitation and Hyperventilation

Engaging in almost any sport leads to cardiovascular and respiratory changes (e.g., Ley, 1985b, 1987a). Those prone to cognitive vulnerabilities tend to be surprised by these bodily changes, interpreting them in a catastrophic manner that may initiate the panic cycle.

A previous study conducted by Margraf and Ehlers (1989) investigated the reactions of panic-disordered individuals to hyperventilation and compared them with a normal population. The influence of subjects' expectancies was tested by manipulating instructions that were presented during an exercise. Two groups (panic and normals) were informed that they were participating in a "biological panic attack test" whereas the others (panic and normals exposed to a second condition) were told that they were involved in a "fast-paced breathing task." Apparently, the increase in panic subjects' anxiety and arousal was contingent on what they were told by the experimenter. The expectation that they were taking a panic test produced physiological reactions and self-reported elevations in levels of both anxiety and arousal. Conversely, the manipulation of the instructions and expectations had no effect on normal subjects' responses.

Sexual Activity

As with exercise, sexual activity also involves the increase of autonomic activity by virtue of the behavioral stimulation involved (e.g., foreplay, coitus). Consequently, in some cases, this level of excitation has produced sensations similar to those experienced during episodes of panic (Dattilio, 1988, 1989, 1992a; Kaplan, 1988).

Surprisingly, however, in many cases, the opposite occurs due to the cognitive correction that individuals make to allow them to enjoy the sexual experience (Dattilio, 1992). This exception tends to underscore the influential role that cognition plays in overriding physiological sensations.

Biological Challenges

A series of biological challenges in the laboratory produce marked bodily changes and panic attacks in panic-disordered individuals more often than in people with other anxiety disorders or in normal controls. Agents used to conduct the biological challenges include sodium-lactate infusions, carbon-dioxide inhalations, caffeine administration, and voluntary hyperventilation.

Sodium-Lactate Infusions

One of the first methods employed to induce panic in a laboratory setting was the intravenous infusion of sodium lactate (Pitts & McClure, 1967). Research data indicated that such infusions induced panic attacks only in subjects who had a history of spontaneous panic, and did not provoke panic in normal subjects who had no history of panic. Repeated studies yielded similar results (e.g., Appleby, Klein, Sachar, & Levitt, 1981; Sheehan, Carr, Fishman, et al., 1985; Dager, Cowley, & Dunner, 1987; Goetz, Klein, & Gorman, 1994).

Recent studies have demonstrated that not all panic-disordered individuals panic when infused with sodium lactate (e.g., 33% in Cowley & Arana, 1990). Individuals with other disorders also panic in response to lactate; for example, 11% of patients with generalized anxiety disorder (Cowley, Dager, McClellan, et al., 1988), 14% of patients with obsessive-compulsive disorder (Gorman, Liebowitz, Fyer, et al., 1985), as well as some nonpsychiatric controls (e.g., 13% in Cowley & Arana, 1990). It has been also found that about two-thirds of remitted patients treated for panic disorder who no longer are receiving treatment do not panic with sodium-lactate infusions: 77% of a sample treated with tricyclic antidepressants (Fyer, Liebowitz, Gorman, Davies & Klein, 1985) and approximately 70% of patients treated with CBT (Guttmacher & Nelles, 1984; Shear, Fyer, Ball, et al., 1991). There does not seem to be a familial transmission of sodium-lactate sensitivity (e.g., Reschke, Mannuzza, Chapman, et al., 1995).

Recent findings have led researchers to rule out different hypotheses concerning the potential biochemical mechanisms responsible for sodium lactate's induction of panic (Ballenger, 1986; Sandberg & Liebowitz, 1990; Gorman, Davies, Steinman, et al., 1987; Gorman, Goetz, Dillon, et al., 1990; Coplan, Sharma, Rosenblum, et al., 1992). Several additional critiques have been formulated concerning the sodium-lactate specificity hypothesis. For example, Margraf, Ehlers, and Roth (1986a) pointed out that differences between panic groups and normal controls in terms of their subjective anxiety reports (subjective units of discomfort, or SUDs) and physiological variables mainly reflect initial differences in the baseline arousal level for both groups, since the actual increments in such variables in the two groups are similar.

Ley (1986) also questioned the sodium-lactate hypothesis. In his reexamination of the original data of the 1967 study by Pitts and McClure, he discovered that it was actually an increase in sensitivity to uncomfortable symptoms that panic subjects experienced. Clark (1986) called attention to the possible effects of experimental expectancy manipulations of sodium-lactate studies. Panic groups are informed that they might have a panic attack during the infusion, whereas normal control subjects are warned to expect an anxiety surge similar to the one experienced when speaking in public. These findings give rise to a need to determine whether it was an actual chemical chain reaction that occurred or catastrophic misinterpretation that caused the individuals in this study to panic.

An overview of the findings cast doubt on the intrinsic panicogenic property of a lactate infusion and its hypothesized biochemical mechanism of action (Nutt & Lawson, 1992). An alternative CBT explanation seems more plausible: a lactate infusion typically triggers a severe involuntary hyperventilation (Liebowitz, Gorman, Fyer, et al., 1985), whose accompanying sensations are interpreted in a threatening manner, reinforcing the symptoms in a vicious spiral (e.g., Clark, 1986, 1988; Ley, 1986, 1996).

Carbon-Dioxide Inhalations

Another method frequently used in biological challenges to induce panic is the inhalation of a mixture of 35% CO_2/65% O_2. It has been found that 35% carbon-dioxide inhalations provoke the sudden onset of paniclike physical symptoms in both panic-disordered patients and normal controls (Van den Hout, 1988). The symptoms are more severe in individuals with panic disorder (Griez, Lousberg, Van den Hout, & Van der Molen, 1987), who also tend to panic far more often than do those with other anxiety disorders and than normal controls. For example, 72% of panic patients panicked in response to carbon-dioxide inhalations versus 30% of social phobics and 4% of normal controls (Papp, Klein, Martinez, et al., 1993). The mechanism whereby carbon-dioxide inhalations are associated with panic seems to be the provocation of bodily changes accompanying a hypocapnic alkalosis characteristic of hyperventilation (Van den Hout & Griez, 1985; Gorman, Fyer, Goetz, et al., 1988).

Some researchers have suggested that panic-disordered individuals have hypersensitive carbon-dioxide receptors in the brain stem (Gorman & Papp, 1990; Papp, Klein, & Gorman, 1993). Klein (1993) suggested another biological hypothesis: panic-disorder patients possess an abnormally low threshold for triggering their suffocation-alarm system. Thus, any agent that causes a loss of oxygen and the risk of suffocation, including, but not limited to, elevations in CO_2, fires the alarm system and consequently causes fear. An alternative CBT perspective suggests that carbon-dioxide inhalations produce intense physical symptoms that, when interpreted catastrophically, intensify the initial sensations and provoke panic. Several empirical findings support this conceptualization: The stimulation of involuntary hyperventilation through exposure to other agents, such as doxapram, which does not affect carbon-dioxide or oxygen levels, has also provoked panic attacks in the majority of panic patients (i.e., 80% in Lee, Curtis, Weg, et al., 1993). Research shows that carbon-dioxide infusions produce similar biochemical and physiological reactions in both panic-disordered patients and normal controls (Woods, Charney, Goodman, et al., 1987). Differences in interpretation of such effects account for the fact that only patients tend to panic. Moreover, it has been found that when panic-disordered patients believe that they can control and reduce the bodily sensations resulting from CO_2 inhalations, the frequency of panic episodes diminishes (Sanderson, Rapee, & Barlow, 1989).

Also, nonclinical individuals who rate high on the Anxiety Sensitivity Index panic in response to carbon-dioxide inhalations in the same proportion that panic-disordered patients do (Telch & Harrington, 1992).

Cognitive-behavioral hypotheses do not exclude the possibility that some panic patients may have hypersensitive carbon-dioxide receptors. Evidence suggests that these individuals' hypersensitivity levels provoke more intense cardiorespiratory responses to increments in carbon-dioxide concentration than do reactions to similar increments in other populations (Griez, Lousberg, Van den Hout, & Van der Molen, 1987).

Caffeine and Drug Ingestion

Several studies (e.g., Boulenger, Uhde, Wolff, & Post, 1984; Charney, Heninger, & Jatlow, 1985) have demonstrated that panic-disordered patients are hypersensitive to the effects of caffeine. The rate of caffeine-induced panic attacks is higher in panic-disordered patients than in healthy controls. Results indicated this in 37.5% of patients versus 0% of controls in Uhde's (1990) study, and 71% versus 0%, respectively, in the Charney, Heninger, and Jatlow 1985 study. Patients who panic as a result of caffeine induction report symptoms that are similar to those experienced during naturally occurring panic attacks (Charney, Heninger, & Jatlow, 1985).

Commensurate with Pitts and McClure's (1967) sodium-lactate hypothesis, Charney and colleagues (Charney, Heninger, & Jatlow, 1985) hypothesized the presence of neurochemical abnormalities in panic-disordered patients to explain caffeine's induction of panic. Caffeine seems to be connected to panic in various ways, for example: (1) by blocking adenosine receptors, which affects the norepinephrine regulation and stimulates the locus ceruleous (Charney, Heninger, & Jatlow, 1985), and (2) by increasing ventilation and carbon-dioxide sensitivity (Papp, Klein, & Gorman, 1993).

Other studies have found that many individuals with panic disorder reported aversive experiences as a result of drug use (e.g., marijuana, alcohol, anesthesia, cocaine), which triggered the first unexpected panic attack (Last, Barlow, & O'Brien, 1984b; Aronson & Craig, 1986).

Overall, research outcome suggests that the panic episodes experienced by some panic-disordered patients as a result of sodium-lactate infusions, carbon-dioxide inhalations, drug administration, and so on, seem to be better explained by their propensity to experience threat-related cognitions in response to the bodily changes triggered by these chemical agents.

High Stress Level

A number of research studies, as well as clinical reports, have revealed that a variety of negative and significant life events may have closely preceded the first panic attack in panic-disordered patients (e.g., Snaith, 1968; Solymon, Beck, Solymon, & Hugel, 1974; Sheehan, Sheehan, & Minichiello, 1981; Mathews, Gelder, & Johnston, 1981; Doctor, 1982; Last, Barlow, & O'Brien, 1984b; Margraf, Ehlers, & Roth, 1986b). The average prevalence among panic disorder samples of such distressing events is approximately 80% (Barlow & Cerny, 1988), and in some studies it has been as high as 91% (Sheehan, Sheehan, & Minichiello, 1981) and 96% (Roth, 1959).

Faravelli and Pallanti (1989) found that panic-disordered patients report significantly more severe distressing events during the year preceding the onset of panic disorder as compared with demographically matched normal controls (64% versus 35% respectively); most of the stressors occurred during the month previous to the first panic attack. It has also been found that the incidence of stressful life events in agoraphobic samples is significantly greater than that for control patients with other types of neurosis, as well as subjects without any psychiatric history (Roth, 1959; Roy-Byrne, Geraci, & Uhde, 1986a).

With the consistency of the findings from different studies, the relationship between stress and the panic experience has become widely accepted. Nevertheless, the nature of such a relationship has not been clearly established. Several mechanisms have been proposed in an attempt to explain the relationship of stress to panic. Barlow and Cerny (1988, p. 34) adopt the "weak organ" model, according to which the stress precipitates any physical or emotional disorder to which the individual may be predisposed. They assume that when people are under stress, their vulnerability to "break down" in a particular way (e.g., a panic attack, diabetes, tuberculosis, headache, ulcers) depends on their constitution or genetic load. Under acute stress, no antecedents are required for biologically vulnerable individuals to experience a panic attack (Barlow & Cerny, 1988, p. 35). In the emotional theory of panic, psychological factors can predispose people to false-alarm activations, but they seem only to moderate the stress response to significant life stressors.

The authors agree that acute stress may be physically manifested in specific physical and neurochemical abnormalities, according to the person's biological vulnerabilities, but the corresponding somatic sensations will only precipitate a panic attack if they are interpreted catastrophically. In our view, psychosocial factors play a moderating role for the stress response (e.g., social support, self-efficacy, optimism, self-complexity, a copying style) and other psychological factors play a mediating role (e.g., catastrophic misattributions, distorted beliefs, anxiety sensitivity) between the physical consequences of stress and the fear experienced in panic. This perspective is the basic assumption of a CBT or information-processing view of panic (e.g., Clark, 1986, 1996; Ehlers & Margraf, 1989; McNally, 1990; Van den Hout, 1988; Rapee, 1996).

As with depression, there is also the possibility that some cases of spontaneous panic are better accounted for by Barlow and Cerny's (1988) "weak organ" model. In other cases, the mediational–information-processing model provides a better explanation of the first and subsequent panic attacks. Results from outcome studies using CBT for panic disorder lead us to believe that the mediational–information-processing model fits most cases of panic disorder.

More studies need to be conducted to improve our understanding of the role of stress in the spontaneous onset of panic. Previous studies have been criticized for being retrospective (Barlow & Cerny, 1988), which may pose some question as to their validity. They can also be criticized with regard to the definition used to explain stress. In these studies, stress was defined as exposure to distressing life events (stressors), but the researchers did not measure the actual stress response developed after exposure to such events. To determine better the role played by stress in the onset of panic attacks, it would be necessary to consider both aspects combined (stress as stimulus and as a response), as well as stress response moderators. More longitudinal studies need to be conducted to explore antecedents of the onset of panic attacks and the development of panic disorder.

Onset of a Spontaneous Panic Attack

Within a broad CBT view of panic, two main approaches hypothesize different mechanisms for the first panic attack. In Barlow's emotion theory of panic (Barlow, 1988; Barlow & Cerny, 1988), the first panic experience is neither connected to predisposing factors other than a biological vulnerability nor associated with precipitants, except for stress. Thus, the first panic attack is an uncued false-alarm reaction that occurs against a background of intense stress. The role of psychological factors is to moderate the stress experience. From an information-processing perspective (e.g., Clark, 1986; Rapee, 1996), the first spontaneous panic is due to a combination of vulnerability and precipitant factors. Thus, a cognitively vulnerable individual will experience the first panic attack at the point of interpreting unexpected bodily changes in a catastrophic manner. Subsequently, this perception will trigger more changes, reinforcing the initial threatening perception and generating a vicious circle of symptoms and responses (Dattilio, 1994b, 1996).

The cognitive-behavioral conceptualization of panic has also attempted to account for nocturnal panic attacks (Craske & Barlow, 1989, 1990). This type of panic may be interpreted as proof of the "spontaneous" nature of the disorder since the individual is asleep and it is rarely induced by frightening dreams. Nevertheless, according to Craske and Barlow (1989, 1990), nocturnal panic attacks are not really different from daytime panic attacks, except that they are triggered by physiological changes that take place while one is asleep. Physiological observations conducted on panic-disordered individuals while asleep have shown how some bodily changes (e.g., palpitations, body movements, muscle twitches) occur just minutes or seconds prior to the person's awakening with a panic attack (Hauri, Friedman, Ravaris, & Fisher, 1985; Hauri, Friedman, & Ravaris, 1989; Mellman & Uhde, 1989; Roy-Byrne, Mellman, & Uhde, 1988). These sensations constitute interoceptive threatening cues for the individual with high anxiety sensitivity (McNally & Lorenz, 1987). Thus, once one is awake, one's awareness of the bodily changes precipitates a fearful misappraisal. The feedback/feedforward initiated then may end in a panic attack.

Physiological changes generated while panic-disordered patients are sleeping have been attributed to the same possible mechanisms of the sensations that originate during the day (e.g., Ley, 1987). No electroencephalographical abnormalities have been associated with nocturnal panic experiences (Cameron & Thyer, 1985; Hauri, Friedman, Ravaris, & Fisher, 1985; Lesser, Poland, Holcomb, & Rose, 1985; Hauri, Friedman, & Ravaris, 1989; Mellman & Uhde, 1989).

From the First Panic Symptom to Panic Disorder

Anyone may experience a spontaneous panic attack, if he or she un-expectedly undergoes what he or she considers abnormal and signifi-cantly threatening bodily changes. In nonvulnerable individuals, this panic experience is not followed by anticipatory anxiety and subsequent panic episodes. These nonclinical panickers typically frequent hospital emergency rooms in the belief that they are suffering a serious event, such as a heart attack, stroke, or hypertensive crisis; however, once informed that the symptoms were caused by stress, they realize that they misattributed the sensations and view the event as situation specific without anticipating more panic episodes. Consequently, they may con-clude that it was a false alarm. Vulnerable individuals, on the other hand, react differently. If they go to the emergency room and are told that they are physically healthy, they typically do not believe it and continue thinking that there is something seriously wrong. They tend to believe that it was not a false alarm, and develop anticipatory anx-iety.

Typically, after the first attack, vulnerable individuals develop a "fear of fear." Their attention tends to be focused on their bodily sensations. Because of the intense and unexpected nature of such sensations, the vulnerable person believes that something very dangerous, either phys-ical or psychological, is impending. The physical symptoms become the threat, a perception that, in turn, increases the fear intensity until it culminates in a panic attack. This vicious circle, where the physical sensations act simultaneously as the cause and effect of the threat ap-praisal, contributes greatly to the perception of the apparently sponta-neous nature of these anxiety surges.

There are several interrelated mechanisms whereby the first panic at-tack in biopsychosocially vulnerable individuals develops into panic dis-order.

1. *Anticipatory anxiety.* The first panic episode or symptom generates anticipatory anxiety for more attacks, heightening these individuals' sense of vulnerability, chronic stress, and hyperventilation.
2. *Hypervigilance and selective attention.* The anticipation of more un-predictable and uncontrollable panic attacks causes them to become hypervigilant about bodily changes. Their attention is focused on

scanning for bodily cues that may warn of the possibility of another panic attack. Thus, psychologically vulnerable individuals selectively attend and react to subtle physical changes that would be unnoticed by most people (Rapee, 1996).

3. *Misattribution and distorted beliefs.* Such individuals tend to misattribute such bodily changes to false catastrophic origins. Such threatening interpretations of physical sensations increase the number and type of sensations as the person becomes more aroused. These feedback/feedforward processes constitute a vicious circle that ends with very intense physical changes and the sensation of imminent danger. In other words, psychosocially vulnerable subjects involuntarily provoke their panic attacks.

4. *Interoceptive conditioning.* In addition to the catastrophic misattribution, aversive interoceptive conditioning is a second learning process involved in the development of panic disorder. After the first panic attack(s), psychosocially vulnerable individuals might learn a fear-conditioned response to internal physiological stimuli. That is why some authors have referred to spontaneous panic attacks as "interoceptive phobias." Thus, the uncued nature of spontaneous panic is apparent only because the cues are internal rather than external as in other phobias. There is mounting evidence that panic-disordered individuals are extremely sensitive to and fearful of interoceptive cues (e.g., Rapee, 1986; Van den Hout, Van der Molen, Griez, & Lousberg, 1987). Barlow and his colleagues have shown how this is also true of bodily changes that occur during sleep (Barlow, 1988; Barlow & Craske, 1988).

Control Schemata

The notion of losing control has been addressed as a fear during the onset of panic, but we believe that there is much more to the concept that pertains to the thinking style of those predisposed to panic.

This notion of schemata plays an integral role for many individuals who experience panic. One of the most frequent schemata reported by panic sufferers is the fear of "losing control" or of "doing something uncontrolled." Although this is only one of the eight criteria required for the formal diagnosis of panic, it is probably one of the most frequently anticipated by panic sufferers. Several researchers have shown that this fear of loss of control is among those symptoms most commonly experienced (Breggin, 1964; Liebowitz, Gorman, Fyer, et al., 1985). This is particularly true in cases where the individual does not know what symptoms to expect (Rapee, Mattick, & Murrell (1986).

What is intriguing about this concept is the role that perception plays in the anticipated loss of control and its relationship to the recurrence of symptomatology (Dattilio, 1989).

In an interesting pilot study conducted by the first author at the University of Pennsylvania School of Medicine (Dattilio, 1988, 1992a), three men and seven women diagnosed with panic disorder (without agoraphobia) were presented with a modified version of the Body Sensations Questionnaire (BSQ) developed by Chambless, Caputo, Bright, and Gallagher (1984). The participants were asked to place checkmarks next to the sensations they experienced during panic, rather than to rate the items in the traditional fashion. Approximately one week later, during the intake process, the subjects were given the same modified BSQ, but this time were instructed to place checkmarks next to the sensations they experienced during sexual arousal, including orgasm (if applicable). Subjects were not informed of the premise of this study until after both questionnaires had been administered. A follow-up interview was also conducted to obtain additional information and to explain the nature of the study.

In this small pilot sample, the results indicated a significant overlap in both men and women regarding sensations experienced during sexual arousal and during unrelated panic episodes. In a larger study conducted about a year later using 30 subjects, the same modified BSQ, as well as the Beck Anxiety Inventory (BAI) (Beck, 1987), was administered in the same fashion as in the pilot study (Dattilio, 1988; 1989). In this sample, all subjects were diagnosed as having panic disorder according to the Structured Clinical Interview schedule (SCID-R), and the presence of any other Axis I or II disorder was ruled out before admission to the study group (Spitzer, Williams, & Gibbon, 1985). The Beck Depression Inventory (BDI) was also administered to each participant, and subjects with a score of 21 or higher were excluded from the study. Individuals who reported a history of physical and/or sexual abuse or who were currently on psychotropic medication were also excluded from the sample.

Subjects consisted of 22 women (age = 34.3, SD = 6.2) and eight men (age = 36.1, SD = 8.6), all of whom carried a DSM-III-R diagnosis of panic disorder. The results were analyzed using the Pearson correlation coefficient to calculate the overlap of sensations that occurred during sexual arousal and panic.

The sensations that overlapped significantly ($p = .01$) were (1) heart palpitations, (2) shortness of breath, (3) butterflies in the stomach, (4) dry mouth, (5) sweating, (6) disorientation, and (7) nausea.

Subjects were later questioned during the debriefing period about the perceived differences in sensations during panic and sex, which had been characterized as occurring at the same level of intensity. The majority responded by stating that in the first situation, they perceived the symptoms as dangerous (panic), whereas in the second, they perceived them as pleasurable (sex). Most subjects strongly agreed that the physical sensations experienced during both panic and sex were virtually the same. When questioned further about what made these sensations during panic "frightening" or "dangerous," subjects reported that it was the perceived loss of control, which was not experienced during sexual relations. Oddly enough, however, one of the overlapping symptoms reported in the study was disorientation, which might be perceived by some as a prelude to losing control.

The results of this study may lend some support to the theory that the interpretation assigned to certain bodily sensations contributes to the feeling of a loss of control and the escalation of panic. What is particularly interesting is that many of the sensations experienced during heightened autonomic arousal in panic as well as sexual arousal physiologically emanate from the same centers in the brain (septum and hypothalamic structures, particularly the circuit of Papez). Similar activity is evidenced neurochemically with the release of excitatory neurotransmitters and adrenaline (Weiss & Uhde, 1990).

This study raises some question about the perception of control and the role of cognition in the mediation of physiological arousal.

People may function for years without any thoughts or worries about losing control until someone or something draws their attention to the issue. Once one's focus shifts to the perceived or potential loss of control, one's sense of vulnerability comes more into awareness and may escalate physiological arousal. A perfect example of this is the case of Lorimar, who had served as an international flight attendant for more than 30 years. She enjoyed her work and had often stated to her family and friends that she would consider working as long as she could, despite the attractive retirement package that the airline had offered her—until the day that she abruptly came face to face with the potential danger her job posed.

Lorimar had been scheduled to work on a flight to Europe—a route that had become familiar to her over the past three years. But when she received an invitation to a social gathering that would include several family members whom she had not seen in many years, she decided to ask a coworker to switch flight schedules with her so that she could attend the function. Her friend agreed willingly.

Five days later, the jetliner that was to have carried Lorimar to Europe exploded in midair 18 minutes after takeoff, killing all aboard: 386 passengers and 28 crew members, including Lorimar's friend and an extra flight crew on special assignment. The tragedy was devastating to Lorimar as she grieved the loss of her friends and coworkers. She had also restricted herself to such a ferocious regime of introspection that some two months later, she began to have limited symptom attacks, and experienced anticipatory anxiety prior to her overseas flights. Lorimar began calling in sick and eventually decided to take a short leave-of-absence from her flight duties because her anxiety symptoms had escalated. She was referred to a clinical psychologist through her company's employee assistance program and given a three-month leave.

Lorimar was treated with traditional CBT, which included progressive relaxation, cognitive restructuring for misinterpretation of bodily cues, and visual imagery. An additional component of treatment involved focusing on Lorimar's issues of control. She maintained that she had always felt in control while flying and had never experienced any heightened state of anxiety in her 30 years as a flight attendant. The tragic accident reminded her of her vulnerability and of her good fortune over the years not to have encountered any threat of danger while in flight. She also expressed a great deal of guilt for having asked her friend to switch flight itineraries with her. Lorimar repeatedly told herself and her family, "I was supposed to die on that flight, that was my intended fate." This idea raised the existential question: "Why was my friend killed and not me?" This question was further dealt with in treatment, an integral part of which was a focus on Lorimar's need to relinquish control and to accept fate on fate's terms. We consider it extremely important to address this issue in treating individuals suffering from panic, regardless of the modality employed. The concept of control is often at the base of panic disorders and may play a key role in relapse.

Conclusion

The broad range of hypotheses regarding the nature of panic offers a fertile field for study and speculation. There remain, however, many questions that will only be answered through continued empirical research. Overall, research data suggest that biological abnormalities predispose a person to developing panic disorder, although their nature and role have not been clearly established. Moreover, no biological factors have demonstrated a specific causal role in this disorder. In contrast, the causal role of cognitions in panic has been established more precisely and may be more reliable in explaining the onset of panic. Distorted beliefs and catastrophic appraisal of bodily changes are crucial to the experience of panic. Without such cognitions, even intense bodily changes would not produce panic if they were not interpreted catastrophically. Also, other psychosocial factors appear to play a role in inducing a person to panic. Consequently, CBT interventions appear to be a necessary component of a treatment protocol for panic that seeks to produce effective and permanent results.

3

The Diagnosis of Panic Disorder

The taxonomy of the earlier psychiatric classification systems (DSM-I and DSM-II: APA, 1952, 1968) was based on hypothetical etiological constructs. But such an approach proved to be ineffective, and an alternative approach was implemented. Subsequent classification systems (DSM-III, DSM-III-R, DSM-IV: APA, 1980, 1987, 1994, respectively) have attempted to be atheoretical and are based on empirical research focusing on patterns of observable behaviors and reportable experiences. Among the techniques used to improve the classification system of psychiatric disorders, cluster analysis has become the preferred method of constructing the new diagnostic categories (Millon, 1991). As opposed to the classical taxonomical approach, which conceives disorders as discrete entities with qualitatively different defining features, the current taxonomical approach is prototypical. According to the classical approach, all features that define a disorder must be present for it to be considered a member of a particular diagnostic category (Cantor & Mischel, 1979). Alternatively, the prototypical perspective refers to the most common features of a diagnostic category. Such profiles of features constitute a prototype that represents a standard against which people can be assessed and compared. Therefore, individuals do not have to present all features to become part of a diagnostic group (Cantor & Mischel, 1979). Furthermore, different individuals with the same diagnosis may present with somewhat distinct profiles (Horowitz, Post, French, et al., 1981). That is, we should not expect every panic-disordered person to present with the same symptoms and the same level of severity. Experiences in clinical practice have proved how varied panic patients can be.

In this chapter, the degree of comorbidity that exists between panic disorder and other anxiety and nonanxiety disorders is discussed in detail. The differential diagnosis of panic disorder and other psychiatric disorders with somewhat similar symptoms is also considered.

Issues of Reliability

The importance of having a reliable taxonomy cannot be over-emphasized. Without a reliable taxonomy of psychiatric/psychological disorders, research would be of little use, knowledge would not advance, and clinical applications would be limited. Empirical evidence suggests that the panic-disorder diagnosis is a robust diagnostic category, as it seems to maintain its composition even in the presence of other disorders.

Stability and Homogeneity of Panic Symptoms

Panic attacks involve two main groups of symptoms: autonomic activity and catastrophic cognitions. Several studies have demonstrated how the symptomatology of panic attacks is highly reliable. Usually, the phenomenology of different and consecutive panic episodes for the same individual involves similar symptoms (including catastrophic cognitions) and symptom sequences (Zoellner, Craske, & Rapee, 1996; Katerndahl, 1990; 1996).

Reliability of the Panic Disorder Diagnosis

That a diagnostic category is considered reliable means that two or more researchers or clinicians conducting independent assessments on the same person reach the same conclusion as to what the primary disorder is.

Barlow and his associates (DiNardo, Moras, Barlow, et al., 1993) conducted a study using the Anxiety Disorders Interview Schedule—Revised (ADIS-R) (DiNardo & Barlow, 1988) as a measure of diagnostic criteria for panic disorder. Individuals were interviewed independently by two experimenters so that interrater reliability could be determined. They found moderate to high reliability for two panic-disorder categories. Specifically, for a sample of individuals ($n = 38$) with panic disorder without agoraphobia the kappa value was .43. Panic disorder with agoraphobia (PDA) was divided into three subgroups, according to the intensity of the disorder: mild ($n = 89$), moderate ($n = 50$), and severe ($n = 7$); the kappa coefficients were .60, .71, and .44 respectively. The kappa values for the three PDA groups combined ($n = 131$) was .72, and for the panic-disorder and PDA groups combined ($n = 152$) was .79.

Differential Diagnosis

Paniclike symptoms often accompany a variety of psychiatric disorders other than panic disorder itself, as well as certain medical conditions. In addition, panic-disordered individuals may also experience other disorders, which can be confusing when making a differential diagnosis. To improve our understanding of panic disorder as a separate diagnostic category, and to design more efficacious treatment plans, it is important to differentiate it from other psychiatric disorders and medical illnesses. This section discusses various differential diagnostic criteria between panic disorder and other potentially confusing psychiatric disorders or medical conditions. The object is to improve knowledge in formulating an accurate and comprehensive differential diagnosis.

Differential Diagnosis with Relevant Medical Conditions

One of the clinician's initial steps in the process of making a differential diagnosis of panic disorder is to rule out the presence of medical conditions that might be producing paniclike symptoms.

Medical Conditions Presenting with Panic and Anxiety Symptoms

A number of medical conditions commonly involve symptoms or signs that overlap symptoms of anxiety, especially in panic disorder. Mental health professionals who treat panic should be familiar with the types of medical conditions that can simulate panic disorder and ensure that the patient submitting for treatment has received a thorough medical examination prior to the assessment phase.

Following are various medical disorders that may be commonly found among panic-disordered individuals; there are listed in Table 2 (p. 60) with their related symptoms and the medical procedure for diagnosing them. Symptoms of panic are likely to develop as a result of the presence of these disorders.

Cardiovascular-Related Disorders

Angina Pectoris

Angina pectoris refers to heart pain that is perceived by the victim as pain in either the chest, shoulder, neck, upper back, or as any combination of these. This condition typically involves the release of excessive catecholamines in the system, which produces autonomic activity similar to that found with panic attacks.

Hyperdynamic Beta-Adrenergic Circulatory State

The excessive release of catecholamines in the body may cause autonomic activity resembling the symptoms of panic attacks.

Mitral-Valve Prolapse (Systolic Click-Murmur Syndrome)

This disorder involves the mitral valve, a barrier in the heart that blocks retrograde blood flow from the left ventricle into the left atrium. This barrier is designed to prevent the back flow of blood (regurgitation). Mitral-valve prolapse is often a hereditary disorder that causes the barrier to malfunction, thus allowing excess blood to flow backward into the left atrium. Even though a benign disorder, it may cause the heart to experience single extra beats or sustained arrhythmias, which may also arouse autonomic activity and create symptoms very similar to those of panic. Many who present with panic disorder also carry a

Table 2. Medical Conditions Producing Paniclike Symptoms

Main Symptoms	Condition Suspected	Test/Initial Evaluation*
Palpitations, tachycardia	Anemia	Blood count
	Paroxysmal atrial tachycardia	ECG monitoring
	Cardiac arrhythmias induced by electrolyte (especially potassium) deficiency	ECG monitoring Serum electrolyte tests
	Hyperthyroidism	Thyroid function tests
	Pheochromocytoma	24-hour urine catecholamine-level analysis
	Temporal lobe epilepsy Stimulant drug overdose	EEG with nasopharyngeal leads ECG–drug screen
Chest pain	Myocardial infarction	ECG monitoring, cardiac enzymes
	Angina pectoris	ECG monitoring
	Costochondritis	Physical exam
	Pheochromocytoma	24-hour urine catecholamine-level analysis
Dizziness	Orthostatic hypotension	Blood pressure and pulse standing v. sitting/lying down.
	Vertigo	Otoneurological examination Barany maneuver
	Cardiac arrhythmias	ECG monitoring
Faintness	Cardiac arrhythmias	ECG
	Pheochromocytoma	24-hour urine-catecholamine-level analysis, blood pressure analysis
	Hypoglycemia Anemia	Blood glucose analysis Blood count
Dyspnea, shortness of breath	Chronic obstructive pulmonary disease	Pulmonary function test (respirometry)
	Asthma	Pulmonary function test (respirometry)
	Congestive heart failure	ECG monitoring, chest X-rays
	Hyperthyroidism	Thyroid function tests
	Pulmonary embolism	

Main Symptoms	Condition Suspected	Test/Initial Evaluation*
Tremor	Hyperthyroidism	Thyroid function tests
	Hypoglycemia	Blood glucose analysis
	Insulin-secreting tumors (episodic hypoglycemia)	Blood-glucose and blood-insulin levels
Hot and cold flashes, sweating	Menopause	Hormone-level tests
	Carcinoid syndrome	5-HIAA in 24-hour urine
	Hyperthyroidism	Thyroid function tests
	Pheochromocytoma	24-hour urine catecholamine level analysis
Numbness, tingling, spasms of face, hands, and feet	Bell's palsy	Physical exam—nerve conductive studies
	Hypoparathyroidism	Serum calcium level and serum parathyroid hormone tests
	Spinal cord and/or peripheral nerve disorder, such as multiple sclerosis, brain tumor	Neurobiological evaluation—nerve conductive studies/CT or MRI brain scan
Feelings of derealization, hallucinations	Hypoglycemia	Blood glucose analysis
	Temporal lobe epilepsy	EEG with nasopharyngeal leads/CT or MRI brain scan

*Abbreviations: ECG = electrocardiogram; EEG = electroencephalogram; MRI = magnetic resonance imaging; CT = computed tomography.

diagnosis of mitral-valve prolapse (Gorman, Fyer, Gliklich, et al., 1981: Kantor, Zitrin, & Zeldis, 1980).

Although at one time it was thought that mitral-valve prolapse was a precursor to panic disorder, recent studies discredit this theory (Barlow, 1988).

Panic and Cardiovascular Activities

One of the more common and potentially more threatening symptoms during panic disorder is the occurrence of certain cardiac arrhythmias. This is an excessive rate or irregular rhythm of the heart and circulatory pulse, which may inspire the panic-inflicted individual to become vigilant about his or her heart's performance. Of all of the symptoms that are misinterpreted, cardiovascular symptoms are the most common among panic sufferers (Barlow, 1988). Because of their potentially lethal effects, it is important to educate individuals about the mechanics of the heart and its activities in order to help them identify which criteria constitute benign cardiovascular activity and which may differentiate the more serious irregularities. This, of course, can be very difficult to accomplish and should always be referred to a physician or cardiologist.

The following information may be helpful when educating panic-disordered individuals about cardiovascular mechanisms.

Heart rhythms are governed by a complex system of natural pace-makers and complex electrical impulses. Quite healthy individuals may experience a "glitch" (unusual activity) from time to time. Most of the time, these disturbances in heart rhythm are simply ordinary variations in the functioning of a healthy heart, just as with any type of automated mechanism that may emit a strange sound occasionally. Such variations may occur for a number of reasons, and are often benign.

Heart rhythms may also be disturbed by one's emotional state, physical condition, or what one eats or drinks. Even the use of certain medications may disturb one's heart rhythms, and thus it is important for panic sufferers to be sensitive to their daily routines.

Following are 10 common causes of arrhythmias:

1. *Fatigue or exhaustion* can disrupt a number of bodily functions that regulate the heart's rhythm, particularly if the fatigue is prolonged or accompanied by extreme stress.
2. *Emotional stress, anxiety, fear, or even anger* can trigger the release of excessive catecholamines, which produce catecholamine surges and stimulate the heart. Depending on the intensity, these stimuli can cause excessive cardiovascular activity.
3. *Flu or other viral infections*, especially with a high fever, may trigger various arrythmias, which can range from being merely annoying to causing alarm and real concern.
4. *Stimulants*, such as caffeine and nicotine, can cause the heart to pound or add beats because they mimic the effects of adrenaline, which results in autonomic activity. Stimulant drugs such as common decongestants, diet pills, certain asthma medications, and even cocaine, can have similar effects. A protein mix known as "Ultimate Orange," which is used by body builders, has been known to produce symptoms of autonomic arousal.
5. Premenstrual variations in the blood levels of female *hormones* can

result in the retention of water and sodium. This can disrupt the body's electrolyte balance, which in turn can disturb the heart rate.

6. The excessive use of *alcohol* can tax the cardiovascular system, and may cause a variety of symptoms.

7. Aggressive *dieting*, prolonged use of liquid diets, severe vomiting or diarrhea, and the use of diuretics may cause an abrupt decrease in potassium levels and magnesium in the blood, thus affecting the electric current that inspires each heartbeat.

8. *Gastric esophagitis* may also be a result of excess gas or spasms in the esophagus, stomach, or muscles of the chest wall.

9. *Sleep deprivation* alone can cause excessive autonomic activity, particularly when associated with the use of stimulant medication.

10. Other *medications* that a person may be taking for an indication unrelated to the panic disorder may cause similar symptoms.

Differentiating a Panic Attack from a Heart Attack

There is no doubt that making a distinction between a panic attack and a heart attack or myocardial infarction can be tricky—not only for the layperson, but also for trained professionals. Nevertheless, it is important to be aware of some criteria that one can consider before reaching the conclusion that what one is experiencing is an actual heart attack and rush off to the emergency room unnecessarily.

What exactly is a heart attack?

A heart attack or myocardial infarction results when the coronary artery becomes occluded. A small blood clot can suddenly become lodged in a fat-clogged artery and completely cut off blood and oxygen to a portion of the heart. An irregular heartbeat may be one signal of a heart attack. Sometimes a heart attack is so mild that one isn't aware of it. Consequently, a heart attack may not always be as well defined as one might expect.

There are a number of major warning signs of a heart attack that are somewhat different from those experienced during a panic attack.

1. The initial symptom often involves uncomfortable pressure, squeezing, or a pain in the center of the chest that is usually much deeper than the intercostal chest-wall tension experienced during panic. The

pain with a heart attack is generally beneath the breastbone and may last more than just a few minutes.

2. The pain may spread to (or be experienced only in) the shoulders, arms, back, elbows, or jaw. It may also be felt in the high abdominal area.

3. The pain may grow increasingly severe and be associated with dizziness, fainting, sweating, shortness of breath, nausea, vomiting, or severe anxiety, or even death.

It is important that both the treating clinician and patient consider any type of autonomic activity, particularly cardiovascular activity, seriously and not let it persist without taking further action. However, learning the different criteria for the two events can avoid false alarms and oversensitivity to activity that is actually benign.

Drug-Related Panic

Caffeinism (or Caffeine Intoxication)

High levels of caffeine are typically found in many beverages, particularly tea, coffee, cola, and even cocoa. This overabundance of caffeine causes the release of catecholamines, resulting in autonomic excitation that can initiate or exacerbate symptoms of panic disorder.

Caffeine is an xanthine derivative that is widely used in psychotropic agents in the United States. In doses above 600 mg per day, it can easily induce a syndrome of caffeinism, which is typically characterized by nervousness, anxiety, sleep disturbance, and psychophysiological symptoms, including rapid heartbeat, tightness in the chest, and dyspnea. These symptoms can be indistinguishable from those of panic disorder. Also, overuse of stimulants, such as decongestants, asthma medications, and thyroid supplements, may produce similar effects.

Withdrawal from Central Nervous System Depressants, Alcohol, and Tobacco

Withdrawing from any of these can produce autonomic effects, as can withdrawal from tobacco, which is now classified as a stimulant since it contains nicotine. Many of the general autonomic sensations found with the anxiety disorders, particularly panic, can occur.

Endocrinological Disorders

Hyperadrenalism (Cushing's Disease)

The condition is marked by an increase in adrenal corticosteroids as a result of tumors or hyperplasia of the adrenal cortex or the pituitary. With the increase of these hormones, heightened autonomic activity can produce autonomic symptoms or, most commonly, depression, but when anxiety does occur, it usually presents in the form of hyperactivity.

Hyperthyroidism

One of the most commonly observed endocrinological disorders that is responsible for anxiety symptoms, including panic, it is typically eight times more prevalent in women than in men (MacLeod, 1981), estimated as affecting 20 out of every 1,000 women (Hoffenberg, 1981). Symptoms usually consist of irritability or emotional lability, overactivity, distractibility, and a general uneasiness. Autonomic symptoms may also include exacerbated heart rate, sweating, and dyspnea. The most common sign is weight loss.

Hyperthyroidism can usually be ruled out by performing a blood test that specifically measures thyroid levels or levels of thyroid-stimulating hormones.

Hypoglycemia

A syndrome induced by low blood sugar, it triggers excessive adrenaline secretion, and consequently autonomic activity that may produce sweating, headaches, tremor, and palpitations. It usually results from fasting or an overdose of insulin. It may also be a side effect of various medications, or even follow certain surgical procedures. The disorder can be ruled out by measuring blood sugar levels during or around the time of a hypoglycemic attack.

Neoplastic Disorders

Pheochromocytoma

An adrenaline-secreting tumor of the adrenal gland that produces autonomic symptoms, this disorder in particular has been noted to involve episodes that mimic panic attacks owing to paroxysms of the excess secretion of catecholamines in the system. They typically include chest pain, palpitations, sweatiness, increased blood pressure, and occasionally syncope. Urine screens are used to determine whether or not there is an increased level of catecholamines or their metabolites (McCue & McCue, 1984) before the diagnosis can be confirmed.

Respiratory States

Hypoxia of Various Origins, Most Often Chronic Obstructive Pulmonary Disease

Low oxygen levels in the blood and brain cause the pulse, blood pressure, and respiratory rate to increase, together with the stimulation of adrenaline, which once again may produce autonomic activity, including panic symptoms.

In pulmonary embolism, which also may cause shortness of breath and rapid heart rate that mimic panic disorder, the pulmonary artery or one of its branches is closed by an embolus (a clot or a plug), resulting in swelling (edema) or a hemorrhagic infarction.

Seizure Disorder

Temporal-Lobe Epilepsy

Characterized by recurrent and transient disturbances of mental function or movements of the body as a result of the excessive discharge of groups of brain cells, the disorder causes cerebral neurons to become excessively excited—which can affect the autonomic nervous system and produce many of the symptoms that are commonly observed during panic.

Inner-Ear Disorder

This disorder refers to a primary disease of the inner ear (viral, degenerative, etc.) or the buildup of fluid in the middle ear, which results in contiguous pressure on the inner ear, causing dizziness and nausea. This can contribute to the escalation of autonomic activity similar to that experienced during panic attacks.

Lyme Disease

Caused by a microorganism that is transmitted through deer ticks, symptoms include skin lesions, flulike symptoms, cardiac abnormalities, and neurological problems that mimic the symptoms of panic.

In order to rule out the potentially undiagnosed conditions cited above, prior to the diagnosis and treatment of panic disorder, patients should submit to a thorough medical evaluation, with an extensive blood profile, including a CBC (complete blood count), platelet studies, SMA 12, or a CHEM 20, which should include a thyroid profile. Both electrocardiograms and electroencephalograms may be administered in the routine evaluation. Individuals who present with any unusual cardiac activity, such as atrial fibrillation, may be referred for an echocardiogram or a thallium stress test. Likewise, an electroencephalogram and brain imaging may be ordered if abnormal brain activity is suspected.

Differential Diagnosis with Other Psychiatric Disorders

Social Phobia

Sometimes it is difficult to differentiate panic-disordered individuals from social phobics, since both may experience anticipatory anxiety and so avoid public places (e.g., churches, shopping malls, theaters, restaurants). Social phobics fear and avoid situations in which they anticipate being subjected to public scrutiny, humiliation, or embarrassment. Similarly, panic-disordered individuals often report anticipatory anxiety about having a panic attack in public. Their main concern is that they will embarrass themselves during a panic attack. Liebowitz, Gorman, Fyer, and Klein (1985) refer to a secondary social phobia for panic-disordered individuals who, after developing panic disorder, anticipate having a panic attack in public and start to avoid social situations. On the other hand, primary social phobia refers to the existence of a social phobia prior to the onset of the panic disorder. Hence, despite the similarities, there are some important differences between the two disorders.

Research has consistently found that the onset of social phobia is earlier than for panic disorder, and that more women than men consult for panic disorder, whereas the two numbers are similar for social phobia (e.g., Amies, Gelder, & Shaw, 1983; Liebowitz, Gorman, Fyer, & Klein, 1985; Page, 1994).

Focus of Concern

According to the fourth edition of the *Diagnostic and Statistical Manual of Mental Disorders* (DSM-IV); (APA, 1994), an important criterion that distinguishes panic-disordered individuals from those who are socially phobic is the focus of their fears. It has been found that panic-disordered individuals are mainly concerned about having panic attacks (e.g., "I will die"; "I will pass out and nobody will be there to help me"; "I will lose control and act crazy"). Consequently, they undergo anticipatory anxiety about being exposed to any (public or nonpublic) situation in which they might panic. Social phobics, on the other hand, are mainly worried about acting in a socially inappropriate manner while in public. Among these concerns are the their apparent nervousness during social interactions and the fact that they might be evaluated negatively by others (e.g., "I will shake and blush, and that will be very embarrassing"). That is, for social phobics, the fear of becoming anxious is limited to public situations in which they feel they will attract attention. Hence, even though acting in an embarrassing fashion can also be upsetting for panic-disordered individuals, it is not their main concern (Zoellner, Craske, & Rapee, 1996). A study conducted by Ball and colleagues (Ball, Otto, Pollack, et al., 1995) compared patients suffering panic disorder alone with patients diagnosed as social phobics alone based on their fear of negative evaluation and assertiveness. The panic-disorder group revealed significantly less fear of negative evaluation and a higher assertiveness than did the social-phobic group.

Such differences in the focus of concern explain why social phobics can be relaxed in public places whenever they are not required to perform in front of others, whereas agoraphobic individuals cannot. For example, going to the movies or a shopping mall can be an enjoyable excursion for a social phobic, but a very difficult one for a panic-disordered person with social fears. The latter tends to anticipate panic, thus calling other people's attention to his or her inappropriate behavior.

Phobic Stimuli

Both panic-disordered people and social phobics fear autonomic activity and ongoing anxiety, although for different reasons. For panic-disordered individuals, autonomic changes are interpreted as heralding an imminent physical threat (e.g., a stroke) or a psychological threat (e.g., losing control). Again, for a subgroup of panic individuals, the danger also involves social threat (e.g., embarrassment). For social phobics, on the other hand, a noticeable autonomic activation (e.g., sweating, blushing, stuttering) is the main precipitant of anxiety. It has been suggested that panic-disordered individuals are more highly sensitive to anxiety than are those with a social phobia (e.g., Page, 1994). However, the majority of the studies have failed to support the anxiety-sensitivity specificity hypothesis for panic disorder (e.g., Ball, Otto, Pollack, et al., 1995; Harvey, Richards, Dziadosz, & Swindell, 1993).

With regard to exteroceptive phobic stimuli, panic-disordered individuals typically avoid agoraphobic-type situations (e.g., unfamiliar places, being alone, or places from which they cannot escape easily, such as airplanes, churches, and theaters). Social phobics usually have no problem with being in those places; their difficulty is with social situations, where they feel they are the center of attention (Amies, Gelder, & Shaw, 1983).

Types of Panic

A related differential criterion is the fact that social phobics usually experience anticipatory anxiety or panic attacks in social situations, whereas panic-disordered individuals may also have panic attacks in nonsocial contexts. Consequently, social phobics tend to predict more precisely than do panic-disordered individuals where and when they will have a panic attack. This is why the "spontaneous" nature of panic episodes in panic-disordered individuals is an important differential marker for the disorder (Mannuzza, Fyer, Liebowitz, & Klein, 1990). Although social phobics may also experience "spontaneous" panic attacks, these are significantly less frequent than in panic-disordered persons (Barlow, Vermilyea, Blanchard, et al., 1985). It is far more common for social phobics to panic in the context of social exposure, actual or anticipated. For example, social phobics may become gradually and increasingly anxious in a nonsocial context when they anticipate that they are going to have to perform in public in the near future (e.g., at a wedding ceremony or making a speech).

Symptomatology/Phenomenology

There are studies suggesting that the autonomic symptoms of anxiety/panic experienced by panic-disordered and socially phobic individuals are somewhat different. Persons with panic disorder tend to evince more symptoms of fainting, difficulty with breathing, chest pain, palpitations, dizziness, and fear of impending doom and dying than do social phobics (e.g. Amies, Gelder, & Shaw, 1983; Dattilio, 1986; Reich, Noyes, & Yates, 1988; Page, 1994). As mentioned above, social phobics, on the other hand, tend to endorse visible symptoms, such as blushing, sweating, muscle twitching, or shaking.

Using the "Symptom Checklist 90," Munjack, Brown, and McDowell (1987) compared a sample of 20 panic-disordered persons with secondary social phobia with a sample of 20 primary social phobics with no history of spontaneous panic attacks. It was found that those with panic disorder scored significantly higher on the somatization factor than did social phobics. It was also found that social phobics scored higher than did panic-disordered persons on interpersonal sensitivity.

Personality

Other differences between the disorders seem to be related to the personalities of those with the disorder. A study conducted by Noyes and associates (Noyes, Woodman, Holt, et al., 1995) compared those with panic disorder alone (without social-phobia comorbidity) with those with social phobia alone regarding their personality traits. It was found that social phobics differed from the panic-disordered individuals with respect to personality in that the former had much higher avoidant, schizoid, schizotypical, and paranoid personality traits than did the latter.

Other Comparisons.

Norton and colleagues (Norton, McLeod, Guerin, et al. 1996) compared a sample of 28 social phobics with 30 panic-disordered persons regarding the frequency of lifetime major affective disorder episodes and suicide attempts; they found no differences between the two groups on the two measures. When compared as to alcohol consumption, it was found that a much higher proportion of social phobics abused alcohol as compared with those with panic disorder. Noyes and colleagues (Noyes, Woodman, Holt, et al., 1995) found the two groups to be comparable on measures of social impairment and lifetime comorbidity.

Generalized Anxiety Disorder

Both panic-disordered and generalized-anxiety-disordered (GAD) individuals have in common a high level of persistent anxiety. However, there are some empirical differences between panic disorder and GAD.

Focus of Concern
Panic-disordered individuals experience heightened arousal mainly in anticipation of panic attacks. Consequently, their concern revolves around the topic of panic. GAD individuals, on the other hand, may experience anxiety regarding a wide variety of topics. Basically, their focus of concern can be anything important that they do not want to happen (e.g., with regard to family, financial matters, religion, health). Furthermore, usually the theme of concern changes periodically, and every new topic is as frightening as the previous one.

Aversive/Phobic Stimuli
For GAD individuals, aversive stimuli are chains of threatening automatic thoughts. For panic-disordered individuals, the phobic stimuli are both cognitive and interoceptive (bodily changes perceived as indicators of an oncoming panic attack); however, misattributions lead panic-disordered individuals to avoid the situations in which they have experienced panic or anticipate doing so.

Symptomatology/Phenomenology
The main difference between GAD and panic disorder is the absence of recurrent panic attacks in the former. They also can be distinguished with regard to the intensity and nature of anxiety symptoms. When panic-disordered and GAD individuals were compared regarding the intensity of the anxiety symptoms as measured by the Beck Anxiety Scale (BAI) and the revised Hamilton Anxiety Rating Scale (HARS-R), the former scored higher on both measures (Steer & Beck, 1996): for panic disorder, the mean scores were 27.11 (SD = 13.73) and 18.69 (SD = 8.11) for BAI and HARS-R, respectively, whereas for GAD, the

respective BAI and HARS-R means were 20.02 (SD = 9.95) and 15.91 (SD = 6.72).

In addition, several studies (Anderson, Noyes, & Crowe, 1984; Rapee, 1985, 1986; Dattilio, 1986) have found that panic-disordered individuals report more cardiovascular (e.g., palpitations, dizziness) and respiratory symptoms (e.g., breathlessness) than do those with GAD. Furthermore, panic-disordered persons with and without agoraphobia have higher mean respiratory rates (Munjack, Brown, & McDowell, 1993) and lower mean pCO_2 values than those with GAD (Rapee, 1986; Munjack, Brown, & McDowell, 1993). However, evidence exists to the effect that not every panic patient chronically hyperventilates (e.g., Holt & Andrews, 1989). Consequently, these differential criteria with GAD are valid for many panic-disordered individuals, but not in every case (Gorman, 1988). For example, in the 1993 study by Munjack and associates, 86% of the panic-disordered sample were outside the normal limits with regard to respiration rate (more than 16 beats per minute) and 30% in venous pCO_2 values (less than 24 mmHg) compared with 44% and 8% of GAD individuals on the same variables. Also, 29% and 4% of a normal control sample had values outside the normal limits for respiration rate and venous pCO_2 respectively.

Hypothesized Neurochemical Differences
It has been hypothesized that GAD and panic disorder involve different neurochemical mechanisms. Generalized anxiety disorder has been associated with the benzodiazepine/GABA receptor complex (Cowley & Roy-Byrne, 1991) and is said to respond to benzodiazepines but not to tricyclics (Klein, 1967). Panic disorder, on the other hand, has been mainly associated with disregulations in the noradrenergic or serotonergic systems (Charney & Heninger, 1986b; Evans, 1989). Also, Klein (1967) suggested that panic is alleviated by tricyclics, but not by benzodiazepines. However, a number of studies have failed to support this hypothesis (e.g., Noyes, Anderson, Clancy, et al., 1984; Ballenger, Burrows, DuPont, et al., 1988; Charney & Woods, 1989).

Hypothesized Differences in the Underlying Emotional States
In addition to the empirical differences, Barlow (Barlow, 1988; Antony & Barlow, 1989) has suggested that GAD and panic disorder involve two different emotional states: anxiety and fear respectively. Panic dis-

order is associated with fear, that is, with a primitive alarm response to the perception of present danger. Hence, panic consists of intense negative affect, high arousal, and a little cognitive mediation. Generalized anxiety disorder, on the other hand, is basically the emotional result of catastrophic cognitions about a future danger. Thus, anxiety involves a cognitive-affective unit whereas fear (panic) is purely emotional, that is, it does not involve cognitive components. Findings by Noyes and colleagues (Noyes, Woodman, Garvey, et al., 1992) partially supported Barlow's theory, indicating that GAD individuals endorsed more symptoms indicative of central-nervous-system hyperarousal, whereas panic-disordered individuals reported mostly symptoms of autonomic hyperactivity. However, Barlow's emotion theory has been questioned by proponents of the information-processing view of panic, who argue that panic only results from misinterpretation of autonomic arousal (e.g., Rapee, 1996). Further empirical testing of these conceptualizations is needed.

Specific Phobias

For clinicians, defining the differential diagnosis between panic disorder and a specific phobia usually is not a difficult task. Specific phobias are predictable, irrational fear reactions to exteroceptive and well-defined phobic stimuli, whereas panic disorder involves relatively unpredictable fears in response to interoceptive cues and much more pervasive apprehension than do specific phobics. However, there is one type of simple phobia that can be easily confounded with panic disorder: claustrophobia.

A study conducted by Craske, Zarate, Burton, and Barlow (1993) compared two samples (clinical and nonclinical) reporting specific fears (of driving, of flying, of being in enclosed places, of heights, of blood/injury, and of animals) with a sample of patients diagnosed as panic disordered with agoraphobia. Participants were compared as to their focus of apprehension, symptom profile, and predictability of the phobic fear. Claustrophobics showed stronger fear/outcome expectancies, endorsed many more symptoms, and perceived the fear more unpredictably than did participants with other fears. Moreover, on all three dimensions, there were no significant differences from panic-disordered participants. Compared with the panic-disordered patients' symptomatology, patients with specific fears had significantly fewer anxiety symptoms. According to Craske and associates, these findings suggest some overlap between claustrophobia and panic disorder.

Focus of Concern

Simple phobics are typically very limited in their focus of concern since it involves a specific and well-defined stimulus. Consequently, they frequently report limited consequences in their everyday activities and normal anxiety levels, except when exposed to the phobic stimulus. In this respect, they are very different from panic-disordered individuals, who suffer high levels of chronic anxiety and significant impairment.

Aversive/Phobic Stimuli

Any external stimulus can become phobic, depending on the learning experiences. Panic-disordered individuals not only develop phobias to external stimuli, but also to internal bodily and emotional changes. However, panic-disordered individuals without agoraphobia only present phobia in response to internal changes. Also, the type of external stimuli that can become phobic for panic-disordered individuals with agoraphobia tend to be places where they feel physically or socially trapped, open or closed spaces, or overstimulating places where they feel as though they are losing control.

Hypochondriasis

Panic disorder and hypochondriasis share some common features that can make their differentiation as separate diagnoses difficult. Specifically, both panic-disordered and hypochondriacal individuals tend to be hypervigilant concerning their bodily changes, to misinterpret such changes as indications of harm, and to feel anxious (e.g., Clark, 1986; Warwick & Salkovskis, 1990; Salkovskis & Clark, 1993). Furthermore, many with panic disorder initially believe that they are suffering an undiagnosed medical illness (e.g., heart disease) rather than a psychosocial or psychiatric disorder. As a result, both hypochondriacs and many persons with panic disorder not only seek medical reassurance, but persist in worrying about becoming ill in spite of that reassurance.

Despite the similarities, investigators (e.g., Warwick & Salkovskis,

1990; Salkovskis & Clark, 1993; Taylor, 1994, 1995) point out several differences between the two diagnoses:

Focus of Concern

Hypochondriacs fear acquiring or developing a wide variety of potential diseases (e.g., diabetes, cancer, arthritis, ulcer, lupus, multiple sclerosis). Panic patients' range of feared consequences is more limited. They are mainly afraid of losing control of themselves and acting insane or of developing a sudden life-threatening condition (e.g., having a heart attack or a stroke, or suffocating).

Phobic Stimuli

Hypochondriacs fear a wide range of physical symptoms, most of which are normal bodily changes (e.g., pain, muscular twitches, dizziness, lumps). Sometimes, their focus of concern can be sensations involved in anxiety experiences (e.g., tachycardia). They interpret such sensations as possibly indicating a disease. Panic-disordered individuals, on the other hand, are mainly, although not exclusively, concerned with arousal symptoms (e.g., shortness of breath, tachycardia, hot/cold flashes, dizziness), that is, bodily changes typical of acute anxiety (McNally, 1990; Taylor, Koch, & McNally, 1992). Compared with anxious nonpanic individuals and nonanxious controls, panic patients tend to misinterpret arousal symptoms more catastrophically than do the other two groups. Moreover, no significant differences were observed among the three groups regarding the bodily changes that are the main concern of hypochondriacs (Clark, Salkovskis, Gelder, et al., 1988). Given the nature of the physical symptoms of panic attacks, those with panic disorder mostly seek medical advice from cardiologists, neurologists, and gastroenterologists (Clancy & Noyes, 1976; Katon, Hall, Russo, et al., 1988).

Symptomatology/Phenomenology

For hypochondriacs, the anticipated harm is much less imminent than for panic-disordered individuals (Salkovskis & Clark, 1993). Even if they believe they have a disease, the fear of a catastrophic outcome is not vivid. Consequently, for hypochondriacs, the typical fear associated with worries of becoming ill is usually less intense than that experienced by panic individuals. As soon as the latter perceive the relevant bodily changes, they tend to believe that they are about to face a catastrophe (e.g., they are having a heart attack). These differences between the two groups are reduced in cases of panic disorder with limited symptoms attacks.

Posttraumatic Stress Disorder

Posttraumatic stress disorder (PTSD) originates in an exposure to a real, unpredictable, sudden, out-of-the-ordinary, and life-threatening situation (APA, 1994). For most people, such exposure is traumatic, of course, but for some, the impact is so severe that it results in the development of PTSD. For the diagnosis of panic disorder, however, no traumatic event is required (APA, 1994), although McNally and Lukach (1992) have suggested that panic attacks can be traumatic stressors since "spontaneous" panic attacks have similar potentially traumatic features; they are unpredictable, sudden, out of the ordinary, and perceived as life-threatening. In their study, McNally and Lukach found that for 7% of those with panic disorder, panic attacks generated symptoms that met the diagnostic criteria for a concurrent diagnosis of PTSD, according to the DSM-III-R (APA, 1987). It was also found that the PTSD symptoms produced by the panic attacks were less severe than those produced by such traumas as being the victim of a rape, serving in combat, or being involved in an automobile accident. For example, a higher proportion of persons with PTSD (not caused by panic) than those with panic disorder (and panic-induced PTSD) reported nightmares, flashbacks, psychogenic amnesia, concentration problems, loss of interest, and physiological reactivity to reminders of the trauma. McNally and Lukach concluded that, despite some similarities in the potentially traumatic events triggering panic disorder and PTSD, the prototypical events inducing PTSD seem to be far more traumatic. They speculate that the differential impact may be attributable to the relatively ambiguous threatening nature of panic attacks versus the definite nature of objective traumatic events.

Obsessive-Compulsive Disorder

It is not uncommon for symptoms of panic disorder and obsessive-compulsive disorder (OCD) to coexist. The comorbidity (coexistence of two or more disorders in the same person) is higher than expected whether one examines the question from the vantage point of panic disorder or of OCD. A study by Rasmussen and Tsuang (1986) found that 13% of the patients with OCD studied also had a history of panic disorder. Conversely, Mellman and Uhde (1987) reported that 27% of a group of patients with panic disorder whom they studied had symptoms of OCD as well.

When assessing whether an individual truly has both panic disorder and OCD, it is important to differentiate between panic attacks and panic disorder. Panic attacks are not unique to panic disorder, but can occur in the context of other conditions, including OCD. When someone with OCD reports that he or she has had a panic attack, the clinician should find out what precipitated the attack. If, for example, an individual with an obsession about germs states that he or she had a panic attack after being contaminated, this attack would be viewed as secondary to the OCD and would not warrant a second diagnosis of panic disorder. In contrast, however, if the panic attack occurred without warning and the individual feared that he or she was having a heart attack, then these symptoms would be consistent with a separate diagnosis for panic disorder.

The study by Mellman and Uhde (1987) cited earlier suggests that panic-disordered patients with OCD symptoms might have a different form of illness. Compared with patients with OCD symptoms alone, patients diagnosed with panic and OCD symptoms had an earlier age of onset of dual symptoms. The latter were more likely than those with panic disorder to have a personal and family history of major depression. Individuals experiencing panic disorder with OCD certainly would require different types of treatment, in the cognitive-behavioral realm as well as the choice of medication, for whom one of the selective serotonin reuptake inhibitors (SSRIs) would be beneficial for both conditions.

Comorbidity with Other Psychiatric Disorders

Comorbidity refers to the presence of two or more psychiatric disorders at the same time (concurrent comorbidity) or at distinct moments during one's life (lifetime comorbidity). The focus here is exclusively on concurrent comorbidity.

Studies have consistently demonstrated that panic disorder frequently occurs with other disorders (e.g., De Ruiter, Rijken, Garssen, et al., 1989; Sanderson, DiNardo, Rapee, & Barlow, 1990; Moras, DiNardo, Brown, & Barlow, 1994). Panic-disorder comorbidity may include other anxiety disorders and/or other (nonanxiety) disorders (e.g., mood disorder, substance abuse disorder) that may belong in either the Axis I or Axis II diagnostic category.

The severity of the panic disorder seems to be associated with the co-occurrence of other disorders. For example, Moras and his colleagues (1994) found that patients with mild panic disorder had 51% comorbidity, those with a moderate disorder had 48%, and patients with severe symptomatology had a 72% comorbidity rate.

It has been suggested that the high comorbidity with other anxiety disorders can be partially explained by the fact that all anxiety disorders seem to share a common disposition of vulnerability (e.g. Eysenck, 1967; Gray, 1982; Tellegen, 1985). Moreover, recent studies (e.g., Clark & Watson, 1991; Zinbarg & Barlow, 1996) have suggested not only an underlying neurobiological factor for a predisposition to anxiety disorders, but to depression as well.

The comorbidity relationship between panic disorder and other disorders can be heterogeneous since they may vary on temporal and causal dimensions. Specifically, some disorders may precede the onset of panic disorder, but they can have a causal or an independent (noncausal) relationship with the panic. Alternatively, other psychiatric disorders may develop after the panic onset, which does not necessarily mean that they are caused or predisposed by the panic disorder. Finally, there are disorders that begin simultaneously with the onset of panic. When the panic disorder is thought to predispose the onset of the other disorder, the former is viewed as the primary diagnosis and the latter as secondary to panic. Barlow and his colleagues (Sanderson, DiNardo, Rapee, & Barlow, 1990) suggested that when two or more comorbid disorders are judged to be independent, the distinction between primary and secondary disorders must be based on the severity of symptoms and the degree of interference with daily functioning. Hence, in specific cases, clinicians are expected to distinguish between primary and secondary disorders, since such distinction will determine the course of treatment. In view of the heterogeneity of panic-disorder cases, one will see individuals with just one primary disorder, others with one primary and one secondary disorder, a third with two primary disorders, some of whom may also have a secondary disorder, and so on.

A review of the literature on comorbidity, however, can be very confusing as researchers have used different criteria by which to label a disorder as primary or secondary. In some cases, the criterion has been the temporal relationship, with primary used when one disorder precedes another (e.g., Katerndahl & Realini, 1997). In other studies, the criterion was causal relationship; hence, primary refers to the disorder that is supposed to make one vulnerable to the other (e.g., Breier, Charney, & Heninger, 1984). For example, the depression resulting from agoraphobic impairment is secondary to panic (the primary disorder). In other studies, primary or secondary reflects the degree of severity and impairment (e.g., Sanderson, DiNardo, Rapee, & Barlow, 1990). To confuse common understanding even more, the actual definitions of what constitutes different types of temporal associations may vary. For example, "simultaneous" may involve the notion that panic and comorbid disorder(s) started within the same year, six months apart, within one month, and so on. Clinicians should keep this in mind when trying to compare and make sense of results from different studies.

Prevalence of Additional Axis I Diagnoses: Other Anxiety Disorders

A significant number of individuals with panic disorder also experience another type of anxiety disorder. Specifically, comorbidity with other anxiety disorders seems to occur in approximately 40% of cases (e.g., Moras, DiNardo, Brown, & Barlow, 1994; Brown, Antony, & Barlow, 1995).

Panic disorder has been found to coexist with all types of anxiety disorders (e.g., Ball, Otto, Pollack, et al., 1995). However, the most common comorbid diagnoses are with GAD (0.5%–26%: Renneberg, Chambless, & Gracely, 1992; Hoffart & Hedley, 1997); social phobia (11%–55%: Liebowitz, Gorman, Fyer, & Klein, 1985; Argyle & Roth,

1989; Barlow, DiNardo, Vermelyea, et al., 1986; Renneberg, 1992; Hoffart & Hedley, 1997); simple phobia (10%: Renneberg, Chambless, & Gracely, 1992 study). Brown, Antony, and Barlow (1995) reported an interesting finding concerning the association between panic disorder and other anxiety disorders. Their study found that 40% of patients with panic disorder had comorbidity (at least one additional anxiety diagnosis) at pretreatment, but that prevalence was reduced to 17% at posttreatment for panic. After 24 months, the gains regarding the panic disorder had been maintained, but 30% had developed an additional diagnosis. The researchers interpreted this finding as evidence of the relative independence among anxiety-disorder diagnoses.

Comorbidity with Depression

Depression is common among individuals with panic disorder. In some cases, the depression can be relatively independent of the panic disorder, as with persons who are already depressed when they develop their panic disorder. Also, there are cases in which, during the course of the panic disorder, an activating event occurs (such as a divorce or the death of a family member) that triggers the depression. For example, in a sample of 60 panic-disordered individuals (with and without agoraphobia), Breier, Charney, and Heninger (1984) found that in 8.33% of the cases of comorbidity, the depression had preceded the onset of the panic disorder. In these cases, recovery from depression is not usually accompanied by relief of the panic symptomatology.

In other panic patients, the depression develops as a result of their panic disorder. In such cases, the typical triggers of depression are (1) the restrictions on their mobility (limiting their family, social, and work life); (2) the sense of being different from "normal" people; and (3) a sense of helplessness in trying to overcome the panic attacks. For example, in Breier and colleagues' 1984 study, 25% of the panic patients because depressed following the appearance of the panic disorder. It has been found that where the depression results from the panic disorder, the depression improves when the panic symptomatology is alleviated as a result of treatment (e.g., Laberge, Gauthier, Cote, et al., 1992).

Comorbidity Prevalence

A number of studies have consistently shown that an important proportion of panic patients also meet the criteria for major depression. Some studies have reported a major depression comorbidity rating as high as 91% (e.g., Raskin, Peeke, Dickman, & Pinsker, 1982). The majority, however, have reported a comorbidity prevalence of between 48% and 75% (e.g., Dealy, Ishiki, Avery, et al., 1981; Breier, Charney, & Heninger, 1984; Uhde, Boulenger, Roy-Byrne, et al., 1981; Breier, Charney, & Heninger, 1984; Uhde, Boulenger, Roy-Byrne, et al., 1985; Barlow, DiNardo, Vermilyea, et al., 1986). A few studies have reported a lower prevalence (e.g., 15% in Renneberg, Chambless, & Gracely, 1992).

The variability in the prevalence of depression comorbidity reported in various studies may be attributable to the fact that different studies used the same names (e.g., primary major depression, secondary major depression) to refer to different constructs (e.g., Clancy, Noyes, Hoenk, & Slymen, 1978; Raskin, Peeke, Dickman, & Pinsker, 1982; Breier, Charney, & Heninger, 1984). Furthermore, other studies did not differentiate between primary and secondary depression. In addition, other sources of variance might be related to the use of different assessment methods to collect data (e.g., Raskin, Peeke, Dickman & Pinsker, 1982).

A common finding is that panic-disordered individuals with agoraphobia have significantly higher levels of depression than do panic individuals without agoraphobia (e.g., Lesser, Rubin, Pecknold, et al., 1988; Katerndhal & Realini, 1997). Such an association may be attributable to an impairment accompanying the agoraphobia, which impoverishes the individual's social, occupational, and recreational life.

Panic Disorder Course—Implications

Panic-disordered patients suffering major depression seem to have more severe panic symptoms and more frequent attacks (Clum & Pendry, 1987; Breier, Charney, & Heninger, 1984; Chambless, 1985; Rief, Trenkamp, Auer, & Fichter, 1997). Moreover, they also seem to be more socially anxious, to be more impaired in social-role areas (Breier, Charney, & Heninger, 1984; Chambless, 1985; Witchen, 1988), and to experience fewer anxiety-free periods, as well as poorer social adjustment (Clancy, Noyes, Hoenk, & Slymen, 1978; Rief, Trenkamp, Auer, & Fichter, 1997).

Treatment and Outcome Implications

It has been suggested that concurrent depression can interfere with panic-disordered patients' responsiveness to treatment aimed at alleviating the panic symptoms (e.g., Marks, 1987; Telch, 1988; Mills & Salkovskis, 1988; Grunhaus, Pande, Brown, & Greden, 1994; Rief, Trenkamp, Auer, & Fichter, 1997). It has been hypothesized that depression can interfere with treatment for panic via the following nonexcluding mechanisms: (1) interfering with the physiological habituation to the feared stimuli during exposure (Mills & Salkovskis, 1988); and (2) promoting low compliance with homework exposure assignments, either because the patients are not motivated to comply with them (Marks, 1987), or because they evaluate their progress negatively, which discourages them from persevering with their self-exposure program (Telch, 1988) and so they terminate the treatment prematurely.

Laberge and associates (Laberge, Guthier, Cote, et al., 1992) elaborated on this issue, suggesting that panic patients suffering secondary depression do respond well to panic treatment, although those with concurrent primary depression may not respond as well. A number of studies provide partial support for this contention. It has been found that CBT interventions are effective for patients with diagnoses of both panic disorder and secondary depression (e.g., Clark, Salkovskis, & Chalkley, 1985; Salkovskis, Jones, & Clark, 1986; Klosko, Barlow, Tassinarie, & Cerny, 1988). A 1997 study conducted by Rief and colleagues compared panic patients with and without concurrent major depression. The two groups were compared at the end of treatment and at follow-up one year later. Both responded equally well to treatment concerning avoidance of places, the fear of body sensations, and disability. However, a significantly lower proportion of patients in the comorbid group were panic-free during the last week before follow-up: 43% and 74% for the panic-with-depression and panic-alone groups respectively. Also, the comorbid groups had significantly more catastrophic cognitions at follow-up than did the panic-alone group. Unfortunately, the study did not explore whether the depression anteceded or preceded the panic disorder.

In order to determine conclusively that depression plays a role in the treatment outcome of panic-disordered patients, the interactions of relevant variables need to be studied more carefully, including the severity of the depression, of the panic attacks, and of the agoraphobic avoidance; whether the depression resulted from the panic disorder or it was an independent entity; and the nature of the interactions among such variables. Different levels and combinations of these variables may have different effects on treatment outcome.

The preliminary research in this area suggests that it may be useful to adapt the intervention strategy to the individual's circumstances: (1) in panic-disorder cases evincing concurrent moderate depression resulting from the panic disorder, the treatment must focus on the panic; (2) in similar cases, but the depression is severe, the depression must be targeted first or simultaneously (e.g., combining CBT with antidepressant medication); (3) in cases with moderate depression that started before the panic, the treatment first must focus on the panic disorder, and later on the depression.

A recommendation based on such assumptions was that depression should be treated before initiating the panic intervention (Marks, 1987; Telch, 1988; Mills & Salkovskis, 1988). This seems to be particularly important when the depression is severe, whether or not it results from panic.

Panic Disorder and Suicidal Ideation

Even though the more severe psychiatric disorders, such as schizophrenia and major mood disorders, are associated with suicide and suicidal attempts, there has been controversy over the likelihood that individuals experiencing panic disorder also experience suicidal ideation. Weissman, Klerman, Markowitz, and Oullette (1989) reported that persons who meet the criteria for either panic disorder or panic attacks may be at a greater risk for suicidal behavior. These researchers studied 18,011 individuals who participated in the National Institute of Mental Health Epidemiological Catchment Area Study and found that 254 adults who were diagnosed according to the diagnostic criteria had panic disorder. Those with histories of panic disorder and panic attacks reported more suicidal attempts and ideation than did those with other psychiatric disorders. The suicide-attempt rates were 20% and 12%, respectively, for persons with panic disorder and with panic attacks, and 6% for persons with other psychiatric disorders. Furthermore, the higher suicide-attempt rates and level of suicidal ideation among persons with panic disorder or panic attacks were not related to the coexistence of other psychiatric disorders, such as major depression, alcoholism, and drug abuse. Beck and colleagues (Beck, Staer, Sanderson, & Madland-Skeie, 1991) studied 900 consecutive outpatients who were given diagnoses of DSM-III or DSM-III-R disorders, and found that none of the 73 patients with primary panic disorder without agoraphobia reported even having attempted suicide. One (1.3%) of the 78 patients who had panic disorder with agoraphobia, 34 (7.0%) of the 485 patients who had mood disorders, and four (1.5%) of the 264 patients who had other psychiatric disorders reported suicide attempts. This study concluded that the rates of suicidal ideation and behavior for psychiatric outpatients who had panic disorders did not agree with those reported by earlier groups of investigators for a random community sample of persons who reported ever having had panic attacks or who met the criteria for panic disorder. Furthermore, in a retrospective study of 100 consecutive suicides by Barraclough, Bunch, Nelson, and Sainsbury (1974) that focused on data obtained from medical records and/or family interviews shortly after the suicides had occurred, the researchers found that only seven of the 100 had reported having had panic attacks at some time before their suicides. Moreover, panic attacks ranked 35th in frequency among patients who subsequently committed suicide. Depression, on the other hand, was a major determinant of suicide.

The report by Beck and colleagues suggests that, taken together with previous studies of suicidal behavior, there is insufficient support for the conclusion that panic in and of itself constitutes a risk factor for suicide. Analyses of the diagnoses of patients who committed suicide do not indicate that panic disorder preceded the suicide. Furthermore, analyses of the diagnoses of patients who made nonfatal suicide attempts also failed to show such an association.

Therefore, it is likely that whereas individuals who suffer from panic disorder or panic attacks may occasionally have thoughts of wanting to be dead or to be freed from their suffering, it is questionable as to whether or not they, as a whole, may be considered suicidal, unless, of course, a coexisting major depressive disorder or other psychiatric disorder is present.

Comorbidity with Hypochondriasis

Panic-disordered individuals tend to be hypervigilant about their bodily changes, and also catastrophize the perception of such changes. A number of studies have found that between 50% and 70% of panic-disordered patients report hypochondriacal concerns, such as worry over physical illness, preoccupation with the body, and fear of death (e.g., Buglass, Clarke, Henderson, et al., 1977; Sheehan, Ballenger, & Jacobsen, 1980). Noyes, Reich, Clancy, and O'Gorman (1986) derived similar hypochondriacal scores as measured by a questionnaire completed by panic-disordered patients and hypochondrics.

A number of studies have explored the actual co-occurrence of the two diagnoses. For example, Friedman and Chernen (1994) found in a sample of panic-disordered individuals that 7% had concurrent hypochondriasis. In another study, by Barsky, Barnett, and Cleary (1994), it was found that about 25% of the panic-disordered individuals had concurrent hypochondriasis, whereas 13.3% of those with a primary diagnosis of hypochondriasis had panic disorder. This group (hypochondriasis plus panic) somatized more and visited hospital emergency rooms more frequently than did individuals with panic disorder alone.

It has also been found that hypochondriacal symptoms significantly decreased as a result of treatment for panic (e.g., Noyes, Reich, Clancy, & O'Gorman, 1986; Fava, Kellner, Zielezny, & Grandi, 1988).

Comorbidity with Substance-Related Disorders

Some panic-disordered individuals also have a coexistent substance-dependence or substance-abuse–related disorder (alcohol and/or drugs). The prevalence of substance abuse has been found to be approximately 30% (e.g., Cassano, Perugi, Musetti, & Akiskal, 1989; Katerndahl & Realini, 1997).

Substance-dependence or substance-abuse disorder may precede the onset of the panic disorder (e.g., use of cigarettes or alcohol). In such cases, the panic disorder may result from either the abuse or the withdrawal reactions. For example, nicotine- or alcohol-dependent individuals tend to develop severe adverse physiological and emotional reactions to withdrawal after an abrupt interruption in drug consumption. Depending on the nature of the substance, the symptoms of intoxication or withdrawal tend to involve paniclike symptoms, particularly increments in sympathetic arousal, such as tachycardia, sweatiness, exaggerated startle response, agitation, and anxiety (e.g., George, Zerby, Noble, & Nutt, 1988; APA, 1994). In such cases, the panic disorder is secondary to the substance-related disorder since the panic symptoms are caused by the chemical effects of the substance (APA, 1994).

It has also been found that panic-disordered individuals often tend to self-medicate with sedative-hypnotic agents in order to control their anxiety and panic symptoms (e.g., Quitkin, Rifkin, Kaplan, & Klein, 1972). In such cases, the substance-related disorder is secondary to the panic disorder. Alcohol and benzodiazepines are the self-prescribed drugs most commonly used to deal with anxiety and panic.

A careful historical and functional analysis of the substance-related disorder and the panic disorder must be conducted to determine which is the primary diagnosis and how the two are interrelated. The goal is to plan treatment according to the idiosyncratic features of each case so as to be more effective. Detecting the presence of a substance-related disorder with panic disorder has important implications for assessment and treatment. For example, Norton, Block, and Malan (1991) found that alcoholics who have panic attacks presented with greater psycho-pathology than did alcoholics without panic attacks. Such differences were observed regardless of whether the alcohol abuse preceded or followed the panic experiences.

Prevalence of Additional Axis II Diagnoses

Studies have consistently found that panic disorder can coexist with personality disorders. More specifically, between 25% and 50% of panic-disordered patients also have one or more personality disorders (e.g., Friedman, Shear, & Frances, 1987; Reich, Noyes, & Troughton, 1987; Mavissakalian & Hamann, 1988; Green & Curtis, 1988; Renneberg, Chambless, & Gracely, 1992).

Types of Comorbid Personality Disorders
Studies have revealed that panic disorder can coexist with all types of personality disorders (Renneberg, Chambless, & Gracely, 1992). However, comorbidity seems to be more common with DSM-IV Cluster C

personality disorders, which include the anxious types—avoidant, dependent, obsessive-compulsive, and passive-aggressive personalities (Renneberg, Chambless, & Gracely, 1992; Diaferia, Sciuto, Perna, et al., 1993; Hoffart & Hedley, 1997). The next most frequent type of personality disorder is Cluster B or dramatic—histrionic, narcissistic, borderline, and antisocial personalities (Renneberg, Chambless, & Gracely, 1992; Diaferia, Sciuto, Perna, et al., 1993).

A number of studies have reported that the most frequent single personality disorder coexisting with the panic disorder is the avoidant, dependent, or histrionic personality (e.g., Reich, Noyes, & Troughton, 1987; Mavissakalian & Hamann, 1988; Green & Curtis, 1988; Renneberg, Chambless, & Gracely, 1992; Hoffart & Hedley, 1997).

Comorbidity and Types of Panic Disorder

Panic-disordered patients with agoraphobia tend to display a higher prevalence of personality-disorder diagnoses than do patients without agoraphobia (e.g., Reich, Noyes, & Troughton, 1987; Friedman, Shear, & Frances 1987; Green & Curtis, 1988). However, the duration and severity of the agoraphobia have not been found to be related to the presence of a concurrent personality disorder in panic patients. This is suggestive of their independence as diagnostic categories (Mavissakalian & Hamann, 1988; Renneberg, 1992).

Complications

A coexisting personality disorder seems to complicate the treatment of panic disorder. In general, findings suggest that panic patients with at least one personality-disorder diagnosis seem to have more other Axis I disorders than do panic patients without personality-disorder diagnoses (Renneberg, Chambless, & Gracely, 1992). The most frequent Axis I diagnoses seen in panic patients were dysthymia and social phobia. Friedman and Chernen (1994) compared a sample of panic-disordered individuals (with or without an Axis II disorder, except for borderline personality disorder (BPD) with a second panic-disorder sample who also met the criteria for BPD. When the influence of depression was statistically controlled, the following variables differentiated the two groups: panic disorder plus BPD individuals had higher affective instability; longer panic attacks; more fearful thoughts during panic attacks; more anger, suicidal ideation, and other self-destructive behaviors; more severe family conflicts and other chronic life stressors (e.g., poverty, joblessness); as well as more visits to hospital emergency rooms. Also, the panic-disorder plus BPD sample revealed a greater history of alcohol/drug abuse and a traumatic early environment.

Treatment and Outcome Implications

It has been found that the presence of concurrent personality disorder is a significant predictor of a negative outcome of cognitive therapy for panic (Renneberg, Chambless, & Gracely 1992; Black, Wesner, Gabel, et al., 1994; Hoffart & Hedley, 1997). For example, Hoffart and Hedley found that pretreatment dependent-personality scores in panic-disordered patients predicted the results of symptom-focused treatment. Friedman and Chernen (1994) found that panic patients with a coexistent diagnosis of borderline personality disorder had poorer treatment response than did panic disorders with other Axis II diagnoses.

These results suggest that it is important to identify the presence of a concurrent personality-disorder diagnosis in panic-disordered individuals since the specificity of the typical treatment protocols for panic may overlook the complications accompanying an additional Axis II diagnosis (Friedman & Chernen, 1994). Effective interventions for such cases may require longer-term and more comprehensive psychological/pharmacological treatment than for other types of panic-disordered individuals.

Methodological differences among studies may account for different conclusions regarding the prevalence of Axis II disorders in persons meeting the criteria for panic disorder. Also, differences in diagnostic procedures (Dubro, Wetzler, & Kahn, 1988), the presence or not of agoraphobia in panic patients (Renneberg, Chambless, & Gracely, 1992), and changes in the Axis II diagnostic criteria for personality disorders and panic disorder from DSM-III to DSM-IV may account for the variable study results.

Comorbidity with Psychotic Features

Although panic attacks usually do not involve psychotic symptomatology, a few reports suggest that such complications may occur. For example, Galynker, Ieronimo, Perez-Acquino, and Lee (1996) reported three panic-disordered women (ages 40, 44, and 48) who had multiple panic attacks a day. Hallucinations or delusions originated during severe panic attacks, but they disappeared when the attacks subsided.

Conclusions

The diagnosis of panic disorder as a cluster of symptoms describing a specific group of anxiety responses has proved reliable and valid for identifying panic-disorder cases.

Paniclike symptoms, "spontaneous" panic attacks, avoidance, and social fears can be found in various psychiatric disorders and medical conditions. Consequently, differential diagnosis is a crucial task for clinicians. The first step is to rule out the possibility of a general medical condition that might account for the paniclike symptoms. If none is found, the next task is to consider potentially confounding disorders, and to use the differential diagnostic criteria to determine whether or not the disorder is panic disorder, and whether there are symptoms that might fit into any other diagnostic category.

Panic disorder can co-occur with any other anxiety disorder, but most commonly with social phobia. Other nonanxiety Axes I and II disorders can also be present with panic disorder. Major depression, on Axis I, and avoidant personality disorder, on Axis II, are the most common comorbid disorders. As depression is more likely to coexist with panic disorder than with any other anxiety disorder, clinicians treating panic disorder often find themselves using multiple diagnoses, which include additional Axes I and II diagnoses. In some cases, such diagnoses are considered secondary to panic disorder; in other cases, the opposite may be true, or the diagnoses can be independent.

Comorbidity, particularly with major depression, substance and alcohol abuse, and Axes II disorders, affects the course of the disorder and may interfere with treatment. Such disorders usually compromise the patient's motivation to improve and the capacity to remain focused and to comply with the panic-disorder treatment plan. Hence, clinicians assessing panic cases must evaluate not only potential concurrent comorbidity, but also the severity of any other psychiatric disorder and the relationship between the latter and the panic disorder with regard to their origin and maintenance. The two main factors to take into account thus are the severity of the other disorder and whether or not there is a functional relationship. Such variables are very important in designing an effective treatment plan, and in understanding patients' difficulties in responding to treatment, as well as their propensity to relapse. As a general guideline, when the comorbid disorder is of mild to moderate severity and has a functional relationship with the panic disorder, the clinician can safely predict that it will disappear once the panic has been successfully treated. But if the comorbid disorder is severe (e.g., PTSD, major depression, personality disorder) it probably will require specific treatment, along with the intervention targeting panic.

4

The Assessment of Panic Disorder

The main objective when assessing panic-disordered individuals is to obtain the information on which to base an accurate diagnosis and effective treatment plan. But an assessment consists of far more than simply assigning the right label to the problem; it also includes constructing a model of the nature and development of the condition and the person's level of impairment. To fulfill this goal, clinicians not only must assess and integrate a wide range of data, but must tap into various areas of knowledge in order to produce a valid case conceptualization. This conceptualization is essential in orienting oneself to the patient and in determining the treatment interventions to which he or she is most likely to respond. Hence, a comprehensive assessment will explore a broad spectrum of circumstances in the patient's life, rather than being limited to those factors that are common among panic-disordered patients. Finally, the assessment must be a continuous process during treatment and follow-up, thus allowing the clinician to evaluate the efficacy of the various interventions throughout the course of treatment.

What Needs To Be Measured?

According to the biopsychosocial perspective of panic disorder, a multidimensional evaluation of each case is necessary. Hence, the assessment for panic disorder should include the assessment of biological, cognitive, affective, behavioral, and social factors. The following is a general guide to the specific areas and measures to be considered when assessing cases of panic disorder.

Diagnostic Information and Treatment-Outcome Measures

Panic Symptomatology

Some of the instruments used by researchers and clinicians specifically measure the anxiety symptomatology in order to determine whether or not the individual meets the diagnostic criteria for panic disorder. This area includes not only the frequency of panic attacks within a given time, but also the type of attack and the nature and severity of the symptoms. The most popular assessment measures include:

- Anxiety Disorders Structured Interview—IV (ADIS-IV) (DiNardo, Brown, & Barlow, 1995).
- International Diagnostic Checklists (IDCL) (Hiller, Zaudig, & Mombour, 1993).
- Panic Attack Symptoms Questionnaire (PASQ) (Clum, Broyles, Borden, & Watkins, 1990).
- Panic Attack Questionnaire (PAQ); (Norton, Dorward, & Cox, 1986).
- Panic and Agoraphobia Scale (P&A) (Bandelow, 1995).
- National Institute of Mental Health Panic Questionnaire (NIMH PQ) (Scupi, Maser, & Uhde, 1992).

Phobic Avoidance

In order to understand better the nature of a patient's condition, it is necessary to ascertain the existence of and to measure the extent of any agoraphobic behavior (avoidance of certain situations). It is also important to determine the extent to which individuals avoid engaging in various activities, such as exercise, sex, and relaxation. In this way, the clinician will come to understand the schemata involved with the patient's anxiety disorder. Consequently, a number of instruments have been designed to assess this aspect of the disorder.

- Anxiety Disorders Structured Interview—IV (ADIS-IV) (DiNardo, Brown, & Barlow, 1995).
- Mobility Inventory (MI) (Chambless, Caputo, Bright, & Gallagher, 1984).
- Panic Attack Questionnaire (PAQ) (Norton, Dorwards, & Cox, 1986).
- Behavioral Avoidance Tests (BAT); Agras, Leitenberg, & Barlow, 1968; Mathews, Gelder, & Johnston, 1981).
- Panic and Agoraphobia Scale (P&A) (Bandelow, 1995; Bandelow, Hajak, Holzrichter, et al., 1995).
- Fear Questionnaire (FQ) (Marks & Mathews, 1979).

Disability/Competence in Everyday Functioning
Another important factor to consider in the assessment of panic disorder is the extent to which the disorder has affected the individual's lifestyle, especially where the limitations have hampered the individual's daily activities. Hence, one of the goals is to restore lost competencies and facilitate the acquisition of new skills to deal effectively with everyday situations. The avoidance instruments mentioned in the previous sections can be used as measures of the degree of limitations and disability. Such instruments used in studies with panic-disordered individuals include:

- Self-monitoring (e.g., behavioral diaries).
- Short-Form Health Survey (SF-36) (Ware & Sherbourne, 1992).
- Anxiety Disorders Structured Interview—IV (ADIS-IV) (DiNardo, Brown, & Barlow, 1995).

Psychiatric and Panic History and Familial Information

Panic History
An accurate history of an individual's panic symptoms is vital to the success of treatment. This includes any experience of anxiety involving

separation from parents or familiar surroundings, school phobia, or even simple phobias. Much can be gained from studying the pattern of anxiety reactions in a panic-prone person, including a detailed family history of anxiety and health problems related to anxiety, as well as a history of other psychiatric disorders. For that purpose, clinicians and researchers may use an interview schedule or a self-report questionnaire:

- Panic History Form (PHF) (Schmidt & Telch, 1997; Telch, Silverman, & Schmidt, 1996).
- Panic Attack Questionnaire (PAQ) (Norton, Dorwards, & Cox, 1986).
- National Institute of Mental Health Panic Questionnaire (NIMH PQ) (Scupi, Maser, & Uhde, 1992).
- Anxiety Disorders Structured Interview—IV (ADIS-IV) (DiNardo, Brown, & Barlow, 1995).

Significant Life Events

When exploring the person's history it is also important to evaluate significant events marking the person's life, particularly in recent years. Several studies have found that panic-disordered individuals report having experienced more frequent distressing life events than did normal controls, especially just before seeking treatment (e.g., Goldstein & Chambless, 1978; Faravelli, 1985; Faravelli, Webb, Ambonetti, et al., 1985; Roy-Byrne, Geraci, & Uhde, 1986a,b; De Loof, Zadbergen, Lousberg, et al., 1989). However, these findings do not imply that this excessive number of distressing events is unique to panic-disordered individuals (e.g., Holmes & Rahe, 1967; Paykel & Hollyman, 1984). More research is needed in this area to establish the nature, frequency, and proximity of relevant life events in cases of panic disorder. For example, Williams, Chambless, and Ahrens (1997) suggested that the typical stress preceding the onset of panic disorder involves interpersonal problems in which the person feels trapped or out of control. Also, more studies comparing panic-disordered and other anxiety-disordered individuals regarding such events would be useful in determining the role of these factors in the vulnerability to panic disorder. Two popular instruments for assessing life events are:

- Social Readjustment Rating Scale (SRRS) (Holmes & Rahe, 1967).
- Clinical interview.

Maintenance Factors or Process Measures

Other instruments must be used in order to obtain key information for the case's conceptualization, treatment design, and measurement of progress attributable to that treatment. Specifically, these instruments assess current biopsychosocial processes involved in the maintenance of the panic disorder. It has been demonstrated by extensive research that it is important to assess all of the following areas.

Fear of Fear (Interoceptive Phobic Reactions)

Goldstein and Chambless (1978) suggest that panic-disordered individuals learn to fear their anxiety symptoms. Through a classical conditioning process, the bodily changes accompanying anxiety become interoceptive phobic stimuli. That is, "fear of fear" develops as a consequence of one's experiencing spontaneous panic attacks and continues to perpetuate the cycle of panic. Goldstein and Chambless (1978), as well as Weekes (1976), have suggested that fear of fear is particularly characteristic of individuals with panic disorder with and without agoraphobia as compared with those with other anxiety disorders.

Several instruments have been developed to measure individuals' fear of arousal sensations accompanying anxiety, including:

- Body Sensations Questionnaire (BSQ) (Chambless, Caputo, Bright, & Gallagher, 1984).
- Agoraphobic Cognitions Questionnaire (ACQ) (Chambless, Caputo, Bright, & Gallagher, 1984).
- Agoraphobic Cognitions Scale (ACS) (Hoffart, Friis, & Martinsen, 1992).

Panic Attributions and Outcome Expectancies

In addition to the possible conditioning process, automatic negative cognitions occurring before, during, and after panic attacks have proved to play a crucial role in the origin and maintenance of panic attacks and agoraphobic behavior (e.g., Beck, Emery, & Greenberg, 1985; Clark,

1986; Salkovskis, 1988; Marks, Basoglu, Alkubaisy, et al., 1991). Cat-astrophic misinterpretations of arousal symptoms accompanying the autonomic nervous system activation initiate the vicious circle that re-sults in a panic attack. Panic-prone individuals are particularly attentive to such physical, emotional, and cognitive changes. Furthermore, they tend to attribute them to dangerous causes, such as dying, going insane, and losing control. Furthermore, the inference that a previous panic experience was caused by a particular situation—and the anticipation of an attack in a certain situation—leads panic-disordered individuals to avoid such situations, thus developing a pattern of agoraphobic be-havior.

Current instruments aimed at assessing cognitive processing occurring before, during, and after panic attacks concentrate mainly on negative and catastrophic cognitions (e.g., "I'm going to die"). However, treat-ment for panic does not focus only on reducing or eliminating patients' catastrophic cognitions, but also on generating a more realistic and pro-ductive perspective. It can be assumed that reducing negative cognition will result in an increase in positive cognition; however, such an as-sumption could be erroneous. Hence, an assessment limited to cata-strophic cognitions seems to be an incomplete evaluation (Cox, 1996).

Catastrophic cognitions were initially conceptualized from two dis-tinct approaches. Chambless and her colleagues (Chambless, Caputo, Bright, Gallagher, 1984) viewed catastrophic cognitions as part of the "fear of fear" aversive-conditioning phenomenon. This conceptualiza-tion is different from the cognitive approach to panic attacks and panic disorder (Beck, Emery, & Greenberg, 1985). According to Clark (1988), persons cognitively vulnerable to panic may misinterpret arousal symp-toms associated not only with fear, but also with other emotions (e.g., anger) and physical states (e.g., sexual arousal, physical exercise, caf-feine arousal). Hence, it is not fear, but the perception of danger asso-ciated with the arousal that triggers the panic response. Recently, Chambless and her colleagues (Williams, Chambless, & Ahrens, 1997) extended their conceptualization of the "fear of fear" construct to in-clude the fear of any strong emotional arousal, even including positive emotions. The new construct, referred to as "fear of emotions," suggests that vulnerable individuals who fear their emotions are particularly afraid of losing control of their emotions and their reactions to them. Hence, the approaches are very similar.

The most frequently used measures of the beliefs regarding the dangers, causes, and consequences of arousal changes are:

- Panic Attack Cognitions Questionnaire (PACQ) (Clum, Broyles, Borden, & Watkins, 1990).
- Catastrophic Cognitions Questionnaire (CCQ) (Khawaja & Oei, 1992).
- Panic Appraisal Inventory (PAI); (Telch, 1987; Telch, Brouillard, Telch, et al., 1989).
- Self-monitoring.

In addition to the objective measures listed, a new method of eliciting an individual's automatic thoughts during a panic attack has been created by Dattilio (1990, 1994b). The SAEB System (symptoms–automatic thoughts–emotions–behaviors) is a self-monitoring instrument that is particularly useful in helping panic patients to see the sequential interaction between their catastrophic thoughts, bodily and emotional changes, and avoidant behavior. Hence, it facilitates panic patients' awareness of how, through their distorted interpretations of bodily changes, they create and exacerbate the vicious circle that may escalate into a panic attack. An application of the SAEB System is detailed in Chapters 5 and 7. Figure 1 provides a blank form that can be reproduced and used during panic assessments.

Panic Coping and Self-Efficacy
The lack of self-sufficiency of panic-disordered individuals in controlling their arousal symptoms plays a crucial role in the maintenance of their panic disorder. This inability to control panic exacerbates their fear of panic and avoidance. Consequently, psychological interventions for panic target patients' way of coping with arousal experiences with the aim of facilitating the development of effective coping techniques. There are several scales that assess this dimension:

- Panic Appraisal Inventory (PAI) (Telch, 1987; Telch, Brouillard, Telch, et al., 1989).
- Self-Efficacy to Control a Panic Attack Scale (SE-CPAS) Ivers, Bouchard, Gauthier, et al., 1994).

NAME

DATE

SAEB: Panic Sequence.

Symptom   Automatic   Emotion/
                           Thought   Behavior

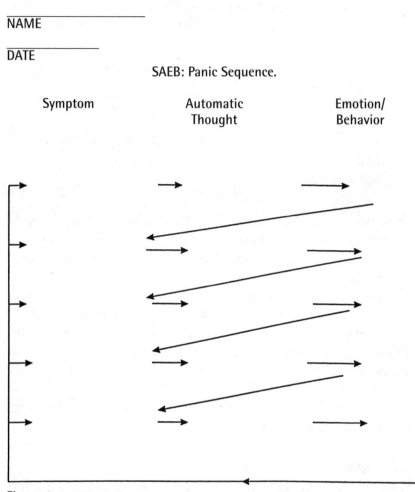

Figure 1. SAEB: panic sequence.

Safety Behaviors and Safety Signals

Avoidance is not an all-or-nothing phenomenon (e.g., the patient either avoids a certain situation or doesn't). It is a very complex set of behaviors and beliefs that can take on heterogeneous forms. Panic-disordered individuals engage in a variety of "safety behaviors," which are subtle and defensive coping mechanisms, and are intended to prevent the person from having a panic attack. In reality, safety behaviors protect patients from the distorted nature of their negative beliefs, and include holding one's breath when exposed to a particular situation, requesting not to be talked to when anxious, and carrying a cellular phone along when traveling more than 10 miles from home. Safety behaviors are superstitious and ineffective behaviors that are conditioned through negative reinforcement, and those who engage in them often are unaware of doing so. The clinician's role is to help patients to confront their fears directly so that they can overcome their catastrophic anticipation of consequences resulting from their anxiety and arousal symptoms (Clark, Salkovskis, Hackmann, et al., 1994; Salkovskis, 1995a). Hence, it is very important to identify panic patients' safety behaviors in order to conceptualize the case and design treatment.

Another important concept is that of safety signals (Rachman, 1984; Barlow & Cerny, 1988), which refer to stimuli perceived by panic individuals as a source of protection, and include other people (e.g., spouse, mother, even infants), places (e.g., home, hometown), animals or inanimate objects (e.g., empty or filled bottle of anxiolytic pills, water, a cellular telephone) (Rachman, 1984). The presence or absence of such signals can be a key factor, not only in the way the individual feels in a particular situation, but also in his or her perceived capability to expose himself or herself to the situation at all. Safety behaviors and safety signals can be assessed through various instruments, such as:

- Safety Seeking Behaviour Scale (SSBS) (Salkovski, 1995a).
- Self-monitoring.
- Clinical interview.
- Clinician's observation during exposure.

Assessment of Predisposing Factors

Clinicians should also assess variables that may act as predisposing factors for developing and maintaining spontaneous panic attacks and panic disorder. Conceptualized as traits or enduring personal characteristics that pose a risk factor for panic, anxiety sensitivity and state and trait anxiety are variables that have been found to play a role.

Anxiety Sensitivity
Reiss and his colleagues' (e.g., Reiss, 1987; Reiss, Peterson, Gursky, & McNally, 1986) conceptualization of anxiety sensitivity is somewhat different from Goldstein and Chambless' (1978) concept of "fear of

fear." The latter is viewed as result of a conditioning process occurring after experiencing the first panic attack, whereas anxiety sensitivity is considered a risk factor—a personality trait—that precedes panic experiences. According to Reiss (1987), as with any other personality trait, individuals in the general population differ as to their sensitivity to anxiety, that is, as to their level of distress over becoming anxious.

It could be argued that not only does a very intense experience such as panic produce a conditioning response, but less intense anxiety experiences may also originate a conditioned fear response to autonomic arousal. There are two main scales that measure the anxiety sensitivity construct:

- Anxiety Sensitivity Index (ASI) (Reiss, Peterson, Gursky, & McNally, 1986).
- Brief Panic Disorder Screen (BPDS) (Apfeldorf, Shear, Leon, & Portera, 1994).

High Level of Stress and Anxiety

It is widely accepted that in vulnerable individuals chronic high stress may result in panic attacks. Three scales commonly used to measure these constructs are:

- State-Trait Anxiety Inventory (STAI) (Spielberger, Gorsuch, & Lushene, 1970; Spielberger, 1983).
- Depression Anxiety Stress Scales (DASS) (Lovibond & Lovibond, 1993).
- Beck Anxiety Inventory (BAI) (Beck, Epstein, Brown, & Steer, 1988; Beck & Steer, 1990).

Another way to measure chronic stress and high anxiety is to conduct a psychophysiological assessment. Biofeedback apparatus allows clinicians to assess precisely most panic patients' common somatic complaints: tachycardia, palpitations, shortness of breath, hot/cold flashes, shakiness, and hyperarousal.

A frequent and justified criticism of the use of physiological recording to measure clinical change has been its lack of stability or reliability over time (e.g., Barlow, 1988). However, in our clinic, we have found that psychophysiological changes during a session are very informative about the individual's reaction to the intervention used in that session. Furthermore, consistent with previous findings (e.g., Barlow, Cohen, Waddell, et al., 1984), we have also observed significant bodily changes (e.g., skin conductance, skin temperature, heart rate) across sessions in response to imagined or simulated repetitive exposure to the same phobic stimuli.

Of the many bodily changes that take place during panic, over-breathing has been of particular interest to clinicians and patients since, in many cases, it is an important causal and maintenance factor (e.g., Clark, Salkovskis, & Chalkey, 1985; Munjack, Brown, & McDowell, 1993). We have noticed that individuals' breathing patterns tend to be stable over time unless they have been trained in respiratory control. We have obtained the most effective changes in breathing patterns after a few (two to four) sessions of breathing-feedback–assisted relaxation.

The most useful biofeedback modalities for assessing panic and bodily changes are:

- Thermal feedback for skin temperature variations (e.g., hot/cold flashes) and shakiness.
- Heart-rate feedback for tachycardia and palpitations.
- Skin conductance for arousal before phobic stimuli.
- Breathing feedback for hyperventilation syndrome.
- Electromyographical feedback for shakiness, chest pain, and chest discomfort.

Since most psychotherapists do not have biofeedback instrumentation available, the direct measurement of such variables has not been a common clinical practice. However, with the advent of new and less expensive units, the use of biofeedback instrumentation is increasing.

Other Vulnerability Factors
Other variables that may constitute vulnerability factors for developing panic disorder are an ineffective coping style (mainly the avoidance of meeting everyday demands), a perceived lack of social support, separation anxiety, and a lack of assertiveness. However, either too few empirical studies of these factors have been carried out, or the results of existing studies have been inconsistent. Hence, whether or not they constitute important vulnerability factors has not been clearly determined.

Comorbidity and Other Relevant Areas

As pointed out in the previous chapter, given the complexity of the numerous factors contributing to the idiosyncrasies of each case of panic disorder, adjunctive measures can also provide useful information. These areas and instruments may not discriminate in most cases of panic, but they can be very helpful in developing an effective case conceptualization and treatment design.

Comorbidity

Considering the high comorbidity of panic disorder with other Axis I and II disorders (e.g., depression, other phobias, alcohol dependence), the assessment of specific panic cases must include an evaluation of possible coexisting disorders. The presence of a coexisting disorder must be considered in assessing the impact of the treatment design, in order to maximize compliance and treatment success.

Medical Conditions Associated with Panic Symptoms

In some individuals presenting with paniclike symptoms, the symptoms are generated by a medical condition. In these cases, panic attacks are mainly the result of the direct biochemical and physiological effects of the disease rather than psychosocial factors (Mackenzie & Popkin, 1983; Taylor, 1987; Barlow, 1988). Consequently, clinicians must become familiar with the relevant medical conditions and their differential diagnoses with panic disorder.

To determine whether or not panic symptoms are masking a potential medical problem, the evaluation of panic cases should include both psychological and medical factors. Hence, before starting to treat a panic patient, clinicians must first rule out the possible presence of such conditions by requesting a medical evaluation. In many instances, however, panic patients are referred to clinicians after receiving medical clearance by their primary-care physician or by a specialist (e.g., internist, cardiologist, endocrinologist).

Since panic-disordered individuals tend to believe that they have a serious medical problem, the clinician's interest in their health history and medical condition promotes their trust and compliance with treatment.

The most common medical conditions associated with anxiety, and whose symptoms may mimic panic-attack symptoms, are mitral-valve prolapse, paroxysmal atrial tachycardia, cardiac arrhythmias, myocardial infarction, angina pectoris, costal chondritis, pheochromocytoma, hypoglycemia, hyperthyroidism, orthostatic hypotension, hypothyroidism, chronic obstructive pulmonary disease, temporal lobe epilepsy, asthma, congestive heart failure, audiovestibular disorders, pernicious anemia, insulin-secreting tumors, menopause, and carcinoid syndrome. See Chapter 3 for a list of paniclike symptoms that are associated with each of these medical conditions (Table 2), as well as for a more detailed description of these conditions.

Paniclike symptoms also may be attributable to the abuse of or withdrawal of medications or substances. A common trigger of anxiety is caffeine abuse, as is the use of illicit drugs, such as cocaine and its derivatives. Withdrawal from smoking, caffeine, alcohol, prescription medications (e.g., psychotropic medications, bronchodilators), and some over-the-counter medications (e.g., antihistamines; decongestants), can precipitate panic, as can withdrawal from illicit drugs (e.g., cocaine, heroine, marijuana). In such cases, the diagnosis would be substance-induced anxiety disorder with panic attacks, rather than panic disorder (APA, 1994, p. 400).

When a medical condition associated with anxiety and paniclike symptoms is diagnosed, the DSM-IV suggests the diagnosis "anxiety due to a general medical condition with panic attacks," rather than panic disorder (Diagnosis Code 293.89; APA, 1994, p. 400). In order to make a 293.89 diagnosis, laboratory findings and a medical examination must indicate the presence of an organic disorder, and that the disorder is responsible for the panic attacks (APA, 1994). However, Barlow (1988) and Goldberg (1988) suggest that the identification of either of the two disorders—anxiety due to a general medical condition with panic attacks or substance-induced anxiety disorder with panic attacks—does not necessarily preclude the diagnosis of panic disorder since they may coexist. Furthermore, the panic disorder may precede the medical condition, which exacerbates the existing panic. And many panic patients may have a coexisting illness (e.g., peptic ulcer, arthritis) that is not related to the panic attacks.

Measurement Instruments

Early studies on panic/agoraphobia used more indirect measures, such as self-report inventories of generalized anxiety. During the past 12 years, however, researchers have developed more direct measures of panic that provide accurate information regarding diagnosis and the assessment of progress as a result of treatment.

The instruments assessing the relevant dimensions in panic disorder can be divided into: (1) self-report questionnaires, (2) structured interviews, (3) self-monitoring forms, (4) behavioral tests, (5) physiological measurement, and (6) medical screening for panic disorder. In this section, we discuss instruments in the first four categories. A detailed description of the physiological measures and medical screening is beyond the scope of this text.

Structured Interviews

Barlow and his colleagues (Nelson & Barlow, 1981; Barlow, 1988) recommended the use of a "graduated tunnel" approach for structured interviews. In this approach, the interview begins with global questioning (e.g., nature of the complaints, history of complaints and other problems, functioning in general areas of life, such as marriage, job/school); the clinician then elaborates on the patient's responses in order to obtain a precise and idiosyncratic image of the symptoms and how they affect the patient's life.

Anxiety Disorders Interview Schedule—IV

The Anxiety Disorders Interview Schedule—IV (ADIS-IV) (DiNardo, Brown, & Barlow, 1995) is a structured interview process designed to assess comprehensively the DSM-IV (APA, 1994) anxiety and mood disorders. It also evaluates for the presence of coexisting disorders and aids the clinician in rendering a differential diagnosis between panic disorder and other anxiety disorders. In addition, it evaluates symptom severity, degree of impairment, and clinical history. The ADIS-R is widely used by clinicians and in research facilities treating panic.

International Diagnostic Checklists (IDCL)

The International Diagnostic Checklists (IDCL) (Hiller, Zaudig, & Mombour, 1996) are recommended by the World Health Organization (WHO) as a way to validate the diagnosis of panic disorder. They consist of a number of items that allow clinicians to differentiate panic from other symptoms of anxiety.

Self-Report Questionnaires

The purpose of this section is to offer clinicians a list of instruments with published psychometric data that can be used in cases of panic disorder with and without agoraphobia. The validity of the assessment instruments is relative to how well they tap into each of the specific areas, offering a useful image of the key features of the disorder.

Panic Attack Symptoms Questionnaire (PASQ)

Description
The Panic Attack Symptoms Questionnaire (PASQ (Clum, Broyles, Borden, & Watkins, 1990) assesses the presence and duration of 36 different physical, emotional, and cognitive sensations during a panic attack. It also contains an open item for other possible symptoms. The item pool was taken from the DSM-III panic symptom list, as well as from symptoms reported in the literature on panic research and from interviews with panic-disordered individuals. Patients rate each item on a six-point Lickert scale, indicating the duration of each symptom. The PASQ score is the sum of ratings of all items.

Psychometric Properties
Clum and colleagues indicated an internal consistency for the PASQ (alpha) of .88. No test/retest reliability has been reported. The PASQ has been found to discriminate between individuals who have had panic attacks and those who have not (Clum, Broyles, Borden, & Watkins, 1990).

Reference Values

Clum and his colleagues failed to provide a direct comparison of panic-disordered individuals with controls or with nonpanic individuals with other disorders. Instead, they compared 60 anxiety-disordered individuals who had had at least one panic attack (87% had panic disorder with agoraphobia) with 33 anxiety-disordered subjects who had never had panic attacks. They found that the PASQ was able to discriminate between the two groups on 18 of the 36 items; panickers had significantly higher scores than did nonpanickers.

Clum, Broyles, Borden, and Watkins (1990) did not provide normative data for panic-disordered individuals only, nor did they provide comparisons of panic patients with nonclinical/normals or other anxiety-disordered individuals.

Panic Attack Questionnaire (PAQ)

Description

The Panic Attack Questionnaire (PAQ) (Norton, Dorwards, & Cox, 1986) is a comprehensive questionnaire aiming to assess different aspects of panic phenomenology. In order to create a common understanding of the term "panic attack" among those taking the PAQ, it starts by defining a panic attack (according to the DSM-III). On the basis of that information, individuals construct their self-assessment.

The first assessment area of the PAQ is frequency of panic attacks. Specifically, it assesses the number of panic attacks experienced during the past year and during the past three weeks, whether the attacks were more frequent in the past, and the presence of agoraphobic behavior as a result of panic attacks. The second section assesses the context in which the panic attacks occurred. For those individuals who reported having experienced panic attacks during the last year, the PAQ requests them to indicate from a list of 23 situations where they experienced the attacks. A third area is the intensity of panic symptoms. The PAQ asks individuals to indicate on a five-point Lickert scale (0–4) the severity of each of the 12 symptom criteria for panic (APA, 1980) during their panic attacks. A forth section of the PAQ asks individuals to use a five-point Lickert scale to indicate how long it took for the panic attack to peak, the percentage of panic attacks with an onset of less than 10 minutes, and the average duration of the attacks. The final section asks

Table 3. PAQ Scores at Different Levels of Panic-Disorder Severity (Cox, Endler, & Swinson, 1995)

PD Alone			PDA Mild			PDA Moderate			PDA Severe		
n	Mean	SD	*n*	Mean	SD	*n*	Mean	SD	*n*	Mean	SD
22	2.12	.81	68	2.16	.61	63	2.36	.69	36	2.61	.81*

Abbreviations: PD—panic disorder; PDA—panic disorder with agoraphobia.
*The PDA severe group had significantly higher symptom severity as compared with the other three groups ($F(3,185)=4.10$, $p < .01$).

several open-ended questions: (1) whether the respondent had ever taken medication as treatment for panic; (2) the context (location, activities) of the first panic attack, as well as its symptomatology; (3) whether the individual was under unusual stress when the first attack occurred; and (4) whether the person had been treated for any of several illnesses and mental disorders.

Psychometric Properties
PAQ factor analysis identifies a three-factor panic symptom structure (Cox, Swinson, Endler, & Norton, 1994; Cox, Cohen, Direnfeld, & Swinson, 1996): dizziness-related symptoms, cardiorespiratory distress, and cognitive symptoms (catastrophic thoughts). The PAQ has very good convergent validity with the Beck Anxiety Inventory (Cox, Cohen, Direnfeld, & Swinson, 1996).

Reference Values
Table 3 (above) presents PAQ scores found in a study conducted by Cox, Endler, and Swinson (1995) with 195 panic-disordered individuals with agoraphobia (PDA) and without agoraphobia.

Panic and Agoraphobia Scale (P&A)

Description
The Panic and Agoraphobia Scale (P&A) (Bandelow, 1995: Bandelow, Hajak, Holzuchter, et al., 1995) evaluates patients' symptoms of panic disorder and agoraphobia. The scale has two versions, with the same 13 items: a clinician-rating version and a patient (self)-rating version. The P&A has five subscales on which symptoms are assessed in a 0–4

Lickert scale: panic attacks (frequency, severity, and duration), phobic avoidance, anticipatory anxiety, worries about health matters, and disability (occupational, social, family). The total score is the sum of all item scores.

Psychometric Properties

The P&A has good internal consistency (Cronbach's alpha = .88), and the range of total correlations is between .37 and .70. A principal-component analysis yielded a three-factor structure (agoraphobia/disability, panic, anticipatory anxiety/worries about health) explaining 65.6% of the variance. Convergent validity was explored by correlating the P&A with the Mobility Inventory (r = .50, $p < .001$, n = 73), with the state anxiety subscale from the State-Trait Anxiety Inventory (r = .50, $p < .001$, n = 78), and with patients' self-rating of impairment (r = .82, $p < .001$, n = 235).

Reference Values

No information was available regarding total and subscale scores for nonclinical as compared with panic-disordered samples, nor was information provided related to the P&A's sensitivity to detect treatment effects. The total scores for a sample of panic-disordered patients with and without agoraphobia (n = 235) was 24.7 (SD = 9.8) for the self-rated version, and 27.7 (SD = 10.8) for the clinician version. Scores obtained in both versions were highly correlated (r = .78, $p < .001$).

Mobility Inventory

Description

The Mobility Inventory (MI) (Chambless, Caputo, Jasin, et al., 1985) is a 26-item scale that assesses the extent to which the subject avoids a particular situation when accompanied (MI-AAC score) and when alone (MI-AAL score). The MI has an additional open item that allows the subject to indicate other feared situations not listed. Each item is rated twice on a five-point scale from 0 (never avoid) to 4 (always avoid), when the subject is alone and when accompanied. The final item defines a panic attack and asks the subject to indicate how many panic attacks he or she experienced during the past week.

Table 4. Comparison of Panic-Disordered Patients with Nonclinical Samples on the Mobility Inventory

	Panic Disorder			Nonclinical Sample		
	n	Mean	SD	n	Mean	SD
Brown & Cash, 1990	50	11.91	8.45	107	6.71	5.66†

*$p < .05$
†$p < .01$
‡$p < .001$

Psychometric Properties

The MI has internal consistency ranging from .91 to .97 and one-month test/retest reliability ranging between .89 and .90 when alone and between .75 and .86 when accompanied. Arrindel and associates (Arrindel, Cox, Van Der Ende, & Kwee, 1995) found that the MI has a structure based on three underlying factors: (1) public places, (2) enclosed spaces, and (3) open spaces. The MI has good concurrent validity with the agoraphobic factor of the Fear Questionnaire (e.g., r = .63, $p < .001$ for MI-AAC and $r = .84$, $p < .001$ for MI-AAL (Arrindel, Cox, Van Der Ende, & Kwee, 1995), and with the Anxiety Sensitivity Index ($r = .42$, $p < .001$ for MI-AAC and $r = .39$, $p < .001$ for MI-AAL (Arrindel, Cox, Van Der Ende, & Kwee 1995).

Reference Values

The MI has been found to discriminate between clinical and nonclinical samples (see Table 4, above, for normative data), and also to discriminate subjects from social phobics and to be sensitive to treatment effects.

Fear Questionnaire

Description

The Fear Questionnaire (FQ) (Marks & Mathews, 1979) has two parts. The first part consists of 15 items assessing the degree of fear and avoidance experienced in 15 situations. Each situation is rated from 0 (would not avoid) to 8 (always avoid). The FQ total score for the first part is calculated by summing the subject's ratings of each item, and can range

Table 5. Comparison of Panickers (Clinical and Nonclinical) with Nonpanickers (Clinical and Nonclinical) on the Fear Questionnaire

		Clinical Sample Panickers			Nonclinical Sample Nonpanickers			
		n	Mean	SD	n	Mean	SD	p
Norton, Dorwards, & Cox, 1986	Ag	22	8.7	7.5	50	6.6	7.5	ns
	Bl	22	11.2	7.1	50	11.7	7.7	ns
	So	22	14.5	6.7	50	11.7	7.0	ns
		Nonclinical Sample Panickers			Nonclinical Sample Nonpanickers			
		n	Mean	SD	n	Mean	SD	p
Brown & Deagle, 1992	FQ-T	50	32.78	16.98	121	30.85	16.43	ns

Note: FQ-T: Fear Questionnaire total score; Ag = agoraphobia subscale, Bl = blood and injury fears subscale, So = Social fears subscale.
*p < .05
†p < .01
‡p < .001, ns: nonsignificant.

from 0 to 120. The FQ provides three subscores: agoraphobia, blood-injury phobia, and social phobia. The second part of the scale (ADS: or anxiety and depression symptoms) consists of a global rating of distress according to anxiety, anger, and depression. This part has five items in which individuals indicate the degree of distress on a nine-point scale: 0 (hardly at all) to 8 (very troublesome). The ADS total score is obtained by adding up the five ratings.

Reference Values

Based on his data, Mavissakalian (1986a) suggested that a score of 30 or more on the FQ agoraphobia (Ag) subscale is indicative of severe agoraphobia. In another study, Mavissakalian (1986b) found that a posttreatment score of 10 or lower on agoraphobia identifies a significant clinical change since it is within the normal range. Results of other studies have been consistent with Mavissakalian's findings. Table 5 (above) compares FQ total scores and subscores of panickers and nonpanickers.

Table 6 (p.111) compares FQ total and subscale scores among panic-disordered individuals with different levels of symptom severity (Cox, Endler, & Swinson, 1995a).

Table 6. Comparison of FQ Scores on Different Levels of Panic-Disorder Severity

	PD Alone (a)			PDA Mild (b)			PDA Moderate (c)			PDA Severe (d)		
	n	Mean	SD	n	Mean	SD	n	Mean	SD	n	Mean	SD
Ag	22	3.55	4.00	68	8.57	5.77	63	19.41	9.07	36	27.67	8.75
Bl	22	5.50	3.64	68	9.29	6.89	63	10.92	7.07	36	14.25	9.59
So	22	8.82	6.79	68	11.38	7.99	63	13.22	9.07	36	17.31	9.06
To	22	17.86	10.83	68	29.25	15.90	63	43.56	19.51	36	59.22	23.78

Note: ANOVAS were all significant and post hoc analyses revealed that on the agoraphobic (Ag) fears: group d > a,b,c and c > a,b and b > a; on social (So) fears: d > a,b; on the blood injury (Bl) fears d > a,b,c and c .> a; on the FQ total: d > a,b,c and c > a,b.

Panic History Form

Description

The Panic History Form (PHF) (Schmidt & Telch, 1994; Telch, Silverman, & Schmidt, 1996) is a four-item instrument that assesses the history of spontaneous panic attacks, the possibility of having experienced four or more panic attacks in a one-month period, the presence of anticipatory anxiety about experiencing panic, and a history of psychiatric or psychological treatment.

Psychometric Properties

These researchers (Schmidt & Tech, 1994; Telch, Silverman, & Schmidt, 1996) found a moderate agreement between the endorsement of panic attacks and diagnosis via structured interview in a clinical sample ($k = .64$) and a nonclinical sample ($k = .58$).

Reference Values

No comparative data were available.

National Institute of Mental Health Panic Questionnaire (NIMH-PQ)

Description

The National Institute of Mental Health Panic Questionnaire (NIMH–PQ) (Scupi, Maser, & Uhde, 1992) contains 230 items designed to provide a comprehensive assessment of individuals with a confirmed or suspected diagnosis of panic disorder, with or without agoraphobia.

Hence, the NIMH–PQ was not intended as a diagnostic tool, but as a source of longitudinal and detailed data for enhancing diagnosis and treatment design and research. The authors' purpose was to provide researchers with the opportunity to quantify selective dimensions of panic psychopathology in different individuals.

The NIHM–PQ covers 13 areas, with an average of 21 questions or probes per area. The main areas are demographics; past and present medical history associated with panic; typical and atypical symptoms of panic; past responses to different types of medical and psychological treatments for panic; exogenous factors (e.g., major life events) that may be associated with the course of the disorder; nature and extent of current avoidance behaviors; presence/absence, intensity, and type of anxiety and depressive symptoms; precipitating events; longitudinal course of the panic disorder; and temporal relationships among the severity of symptoms and impairment. The authors assumed that such information can be very useful since different panic-disorder profiles (e.g., comorbidity versus no comorbidity) might result in preferential responses to a particular medication.

Psychometric Properties

The psychometric properties of the NIMH–PQ are limited; the authors only presented data on positive correlations between the NIMH–PQ and the answers to the interview Schedule for Affective Disorders and Schizophrenia (SACS) (Endicott & Spitzer, 1978). Only 16 of the NIMH–PQ items were tested by comparing subjects' responses with similar items in both scales; the items covered panic-attack symptomatology, nature of fears, avoidance, type of panic attacks, and anticipatory anxiety. A significant difference was found in only one of the 16 items (a higher proportion of patients on the NIMH–PQ as compared with the SACS perceived the panic as spontaneous). Scupi, Maser, and Uhde (1992) did not provide normative data on the NIMH–PQ.

Agoraphobic Cognitions Questionnaire (ACQ)

Description

The Agoraphobic Cognitions Questionnaire (ACQ) (Chambless, Caputo, Bright, & Gallagher, 1984) is a 14-item scale assessing the frequency with which certain anticipatory and catastrophic thoughts cross the subjects' mind when they are anxious. The ACQ has two seven-item parts: one concerns thoughts of catastrophic physical consequences of experiencing anxiety symptoms (e.g., "I am going to have a stroke"); the other assesses thoughts of catastrophic social or behavioral consequences resulting from losing control when anxious (e.g., "I am going to go crazy"). The ACQ also offers an additional and optional 15th item so that subjects can express thoughts not covered in the previous 14 items. Subjects estimate the frequency of each thought when anxious using a five-point Lickert scale ranging from 1 ("thought never occurs when I'm anxious") to 5 ("thought always occurs when I'm anxious"). The total score is the average of the 14 items. The factor scores are the averages of the respective seven items.

Psychometric Properties

The ACQ has a one-month test/retest reliability of .86 and an internal consistency of (alpha coefficient) .80. Cronbach's alphas were .65 for the physical-concern factor and .76 for the loss-of-control factor. The ACQ has been shown to have good concurrent validity with the State-Trait Anxiety Inventory, the neuroticism score of the Eysenck Personality Questionnaire, and the Mobility Inventory. It has also been found to discriminate agoraphobics from normal controls (r biserial = .79; Chambless, Caputo, Bright, & Gallagher, 1984) and subjects with other anxiety disorders. The AQC has been found to be sensitive to treatment effects.

Reference Values

ACQ total scores for panic-disordered individuals, with and without agoraphobia, as compared with a nonclinical sample are presented in Table 7 (p. 114).

Table 8 (p. 114) compares ACQ scores of panickers and nonpanickers in a nonclinical (undergraduate students) population.

Craske, Rachman, and Tallman (1986) did not find significant differences on the ACQ between a sample of agoraphobics and a sample of social phobics. However, Craske and colleagues used the total score, which seems to be less sensitive in discriminating agoraphobics from social phobics than are the separate factors, especially the physical-concern factor.

Table 9 (p. 115) compares changes in pre- and posttest measures on

Table 7. Comparisons of Panic-Disordered Patients with Nonclinical Samples on ACQ

	PD + Agoraphobics			Nonclinical Sample		
	n	Mean	SD	n	Mean	SD
Chambless, 1985	231	2.42	.63			
Feske & De Beurs, 1997	40	2.37	.69			
Brown & Cash, 1990	50	1.96	.49	107	1.63	.43†
Bibb, 1988	139	1.60	.47			

*$p < .05$
†$p < .01$
‡$p < .001$

Table 8. Comparison of ACQ Scores in Panickers and Nonpanickers Among Nonclinical Individuals

	Panickers			Nonpanickers		
	n	Mean	SD	n	Mean	SD
Brown & Deagle, 1992	50	1.78	.49	121	1.58	40†

*$p < .05$
†$p < .01$
‡$p < .001$

the ACQ (Brown, Beck, Newman, et al., 1997) for two samples of panic-disordered individuals with agoraphobia.

Agoraphobic Cognitions Scale (ACS)

Description
The Agoraphobic Cognitions Scale (ACS) (Hoffart, Friis, & Matinsen, 1992) is a 10-item instrument intended to assess the concept of fear of fear in agoraphobics. However, it primarily assessed the most common fears found in a sample of 963 agoraphobics, and only one of the items was designed to assess fear of fear. Subjects use a four-point Lickert scale to indicate the degree of fear.

Psychometric Properties
The ACS assesses three factors: (1) fear of bodily incapacitation, (2) fear of losing control, and (3) fear of embarrassing action. The "fear of

Table 9. Pre- to Posttreatment Changes on ACQ Subscale Scores

	Panic-Disordered Individuals with Agoraphobia					
	Pretreatment			Posttreatment		
	n	Mean	SD	*n*	Mean	SD
FCT	21	2.37	.72	21	2.00	.59
SCT	19	2.41	.57	19	1.86	.53

Note: For both groups, differences between pretest and posttest were significant [$F(1,32) = 32.56$, $p < .001$], but there were no significant differences between treatments. FCT: Focused Cognitive Therapy. SCT: Standard Cognitive Therapy.

fear" item has been found to load on both the fear of losing control and the fear of embarrassment.

The ACS has good internal consistency; Cronbach's alphas for the three factors are .81 (fear of bodily incapacitation), .63 (fear of losing control), and .74 (fear of being embarrassed). No test/retest reliability has been reported (Hoffart, Friis, & Matinsen, 1992). The correlations between the ACS fear of losing control and the ACQ (Chambless, Caputo, Bright, & Gallagher 1984) fear of losing control was .70, and between the ACS fear of bodily incapacitation and the ACQ fear of experiencing anxiety arousal was .57.

Reference Values

Chambless and associates (Chambers, Caputo, Bright, & Gallagher, 1984) reported higher ACS scores for panic disorder with agoraphobic individuals (mean = 2.32, SD = 0.07) than the scores obtained by nonanxious controls (mean = 1.38, SD = 0.34). In the study by Hoffart, Friis, and Matinsen (1992) with a sample (*n* = 67) of panic-disordered individuals with agoraphobia, the mean values were 1.78 for "fear of bodily incapacitation," 1.38 for "fear of losing control," and .95 for "fear of acting embarrassingly." Hoffart and Martinsen (1990) found the ACS to be sensitive to treatment.

Panic Attack Cognitions Questionnaire (PACQ)

Description

The Panic Attack Cognitions Questionnaire (PACQ) (Clum, Broyles, Borden, & Watkins, 1990) is a 25-item scale assessing the extent to which catastrophic cognitions dominated subjects' thoughts before, during, and after panic attacks. Subjects are asked to rate each item (e.g., "I am going to scream") from 1 (not at all) to 4 ("it totally dominated my thoughts"). The higher the score, the more frequent were negative thoughts. The PACQ items were derived from the Agoraphobic Cognitions Questionnaire, the DSM-III, and interviews with panic-disordered individuals. The range of possible scores is from 23 to 92, with the higher score indicating more catastrophic thoughts.

Psychometric Properties

The PACQ has an internal consistency (alpha) of .88. No test/retest reliability has been reported. The PACQ has been found to discriminate between individuals who have had panic attacks and those who have not (Clum, Broyles, Borden, & Watkins, 1990).

Reference Values

Clum and his colleagues did not provide a direct comparison of panic-disordered individuals with those with other anxiety disorders or of panic-disordered individuals with nonclinical subjects. Instead, they compared 60 individuals with different types of anxiety disorders (87% had panic disorder with and without agoraphobia) who have had at least one panic attack with 33 anxiety-disordered subjects who have never had panic attacks. They found that the PACQ discriminated between the two groups on the total score: panickers (mean = 87.53) scored significantly higher than nonpanickers (mean = 70. 10; $t2,71$ = 4.19, $p < .001$).

Separate analyses comparing both groups were conducted on each PACQ item. On eight of the 25 items, "panickers" scored significantly higher on seven items than did "nonpanickers"; and for one item ("I am going to scream"), the relationship was inverse (Clum, Broyles, Borden, & Watkins, 1990).

Panic Appraisal Inventory (PAI)

Description

The Panic Appraisal Inventory (PAI) (Telch, 1987; Telch, Brouillard, Telch, et al., 1989; Feske & De Beurs, 1997) is a composite of three scales that were factor analytically derived. The first subscale is Anticipated Panic, which measures patients' estimation of the likelihood (in percent) of experiencing panic in 10 situations when alone and without taking medications or alcohol. The second subscale, Panic Consequences, assesses the patients' concerns about possible catastrophic consequences of panic. This subscale comprises 15 items describing thoughts of catastrophic consequences that panic patients tend to generate when anxious. It provides a total score and three subscores, depending on the type of consequence: physical, social, and losing control. Patients are asked to rate the extent to which they are distressed by each thought on a 11-point scale (0–10). The final subscale, called Panic Coping, measures perceived self-confidence in coping effectively with future panic attacks. It includes a description of 15 strategies that patients may use to cope with panic.

Psychometric Properties

The 35-item version of the PAI had good test/retest reliability over a three-week period for the three subscales ($rs = .81 - .89$). It also had high internal consistency for the three subscales; Cronbach's alphas ranged between .85 and .94 (Telch, Brouillard, & Telch, 1989).

A revision of the PAI included the addition of five items to the Anticipated Panic subscale; consequently, there are now 45 items, with each scale consisting of 15 items. The current version of the PAI has excellent internal consistency; Cronbach's alphas were .88, .86, and .90 for anticipated panic, panic consequences, and panic coping, respectively; also, internal consistency for the three panic-consequences subscores was very good. The average range of interitem correlations was between .30 and .55.

Consistent with previous findings (e.g., Telch, Brouillard, & Telch, 1989; Cox, Endler, & Swinson, 1995b), Feske and De Beurs (1997) found that the PAI Anticipated Panic subscale had a strong positive correlation with the Mobility Inventory, especially with regard to severity of avoidance when alone (MI-AAL; $r = .74$, $p < .001$). The Panic Coping subscale had a strong negative association with MI-AAL ($r = -.46$, $p < .01$) and MI-AAC ($r = -.41$, $p < .01$); these correlations indicate that the lower the self-efficacy to deal with panic, the greater is the avoidance. Of all subscales, the Physical Consequences subscale had the strongest correlation with the physical-concern factor of the Agoraphobia Cognition Questionnaire (ACQ). And the Loss of Control

Table 10. Comparison of Panic-Disordered Individuals with and Without Agoraphobia on the Three PAI Subscales

	Panic Disorder with Agoraphobia			Panic Disorder Without Agoraphobia		
	n	Mean	SD	n	Mean	SD
Anticipated panic	39	66.99	18.8	37	14.46	12.56
Panic consequences	39	82.67	32.65	37	52.17	31.92
Panic coping	39	24.5	18.99	37	37.46	19.37

and Social Consequences subscales had the strongest association with the ACQ's Social Concern (rs = .78 and .54 respectively).

Reference Values
Table 10 (above) presents mean values for each of the scales in panic-disordered individuals with and without agoraphobia (Telch, Brouillard, & Telch, 1989).

The PAI has been demonstrated to be sensitive to treatment effects (e.g., Feske & De Beurs, 1997). Table 11 (p. 119) presents a comparison of pretreatment and posttreatment values in each of the PAI subscales.

Self-Efficacy to Control Panic Attacks Questionnaire (SE-CPAQ)

Description
The Self-efficacy to Control a Panic Attack Scale (SE-CPAQ) (Gauthier, Bouchard, Cole, et al., 1993; Ivers, Bouchard, Gauthier, et al., 1994) is a 25-item questionnaire assessing perceived self-efficacy to control panic attacks. Patients rate their level of confidence in the ability to control panic on a 0–100 scale. The SE-CPAQ has three scales: The first, Self-efficacy—Cognitions, assesses self-efficacy to control panic attacks when having six specific negative thoughts. These cognitions are part of the ACQ (Chambless, Caputo, Bright, & Gallagher, 1984). The second scale, Self-efficacy—Symptoms, measures self-efficacy to control panic attacks when experiencing nine physical symptoms. These sensations are part of the 16 physical symptoms described in the BSQ (Chambless, Caputo, Bright, & Gallagher, 1984). The third scale, Self-efficacy—Mobility, assesses patients' self-efficacy to control a panic attack in 10 specific agoraphobic situations. These locations are part of

Table 11. Pretreatment to Posttreatment Changes on PAI Subscale Scores

Feske & De Beurs, 1997	Panic-Disordered Individuals with Agoraphobia				
	Pretreatment		$(n = 40)$	Posttreatment	
	Mean	SD		Mean	SD
Anticipated panic	47.9	20.8		35.1	21.2*
Panic consequences					
Total	45.5	18.8		30.2	21.9*
Physical	40.8	28.8		25.0	23.2*
Social	53.1	26.9		36.7	30.1*
Loss of control	42.8	27.5		28.9	27.6*
Panic coping	31.2	17.3		50.0	23.7*

*$p < .003$ two-tailed.

Table 12. Pretreatment to Posttreatment and Follow-up SE-CPAQ Scores

Panic Disorder with Agoraphobia (Tx: Exposure)					
Pretreatment		Posttreatment		Follow-up	
Mean	SD	Mean	SD	Mean	SD
41.88	17.36	68.94	22.05	76.05	20.33

Panic Disorder with Agoraphobia (Tx: Cognitive Restructuring)					
Pretreatment		Posttreatment		Follow-up	
Mean	SD	Mean	SD	Mean	SD
42.08	23.16	60.20	25.75	56.83	19.66

the MI items (Chambless, Caputo, Jasin, et al., 1985). The total SE-CPAQ score is the average of the answers to the 25 items.

Psychometric Properties
The SE-CPAQ has good internal consistency (Cronbach's alpha of .91) and a six-week test/retest reliability of .72 (Bouchard, Gauthier, Nouwen, et al., 1996).

Reference Values
Gauthier and colleagues (1993) found a SE-CPAQ mean score of 41.02 (SD = 17.50) in a sample of 65 panic-disordered individuals with agoraphobia. Table 12 (above) presents a comparison of pretreatment,

posttreatment, and follow-up SE-CPAQ means pertaining to two samples of 14 patients each. All subjects were diagnosed as panic disordered with agoraphobia. For one sample, the treatment was exposure, and for the second sample, the treatment modality was cognitive restructuring (Bouchard, Gauthier, Laberge, et al., 1996).

Safety-Seeking Behaviour Scale

Description
The objective of the Safety Seeking Behaviour Scale (SSBS) (Salkovskis, 1995a) is to assess the frequency with which patients display 10 safety behaviors when they feel very anxious or panicky. The SSBS asks them to rate that frequency on a four-point scale: 0 (never), 1 (sometimes), 2 (often), and 3 (always).

Psychometric Properties
No psychometric properties on the SSBS have been described. Salkovskis, Clark, and Gelder (1996) found a positive correlation between the Agoraphobia Cognitions Questionnaire and the SBSS. Furthermore, they found that different types of catastrophic fears (e.g., having a heart attack versus choking to death) involved somewhat different types of safety-seeking behaviors, although some of the fears (e.g., acting foolishly and losing control) were associated with the same safety-seeking behaviors.

Reference Values
No comparative data were available.

Body Sensations Questionnaire

Description
The Body Sensations Questionnaire (BSQ) (Chambless, Caputo, Bright, & Gallagher, 1984) is an 18-item scale that assesses how frightened subjects feel about experiencing certain bodily sensations associated with the arousal accompanying anxiety. The last item is an open item so that patients can indicate nonlisted symptoms and describe how they are experienced. Patients indicate on a five-point Lickert scale (1–5) how frightened they feel about experiencing each of the sensations. All

still limited. In addition, there are research data suggesting that anxiety sensitivity is also associated with the development of agoraphobic fears and avoidance (Taylor & Rachman, 1992). But, since Taylor and Rachman did not assess subjects' panic attacks, it is not clear what role panic attacks played in such relationships.

Psychometric Properties

The ASI has shown adequate internal consistency (Telch, Shermis, & Lucas, 1989) and test/retest reliability: .75 in a two-week period (Reiss, Peterson, Gursky, & McNally 1986); .73 over a three-year period (Maller & Reiss, 1992), and also good construct validity (Reiss, Peterson, Gursky, & McNally, 1986; Peterson & Heilbronner, 1987).

The structure of the ASI has been conceptualized and found to be unifactorial (Reiss, Peterson, Gursky, & McNally, 1986; Taylor, Koch, McNally, & Crockett, 1992). However, some studies suggest a four-factor underlying structure (e.g., Peterson & Heilbroner, 1987; Telch, Shermis, & Lucas, 1989; Cox, Parker, & Swinson, 1996): fear of cardiorespiratory distress and gastrointestinal sensations, fear of cognitive/psychological symptoms, fear of symptoms in public (negative social consequences), and fear of trembling and fainting. The construct of anxiety sensitivity is related to trait anxiety (e.g., $r = .12$, $p < .01$), but they differ in that anxiety sensitivity refers to fear of anxiety symptoms whereas the construct of trait anxiety taps into the tendency to respond anxiously to a wide variety of stressors, and, therefore, the propensity to feel chronically anxious (McNally, 1994). A study conducted by Schmidt, Lerew, and Jackson (1997) with a nonclinical sample found a correlation of .12 ($p < .01$) between trait anxiety and anxiety sensitivity, but only the latter predicted spontaneous panic when both variables were simultaneously regressed—results that suggest their different associations with panic. Anxiety sensitivity is viewed as a first-order factor—together with injury sensitivity and fear of negative evaluation—in hierarchical models in which trait anxiety is a second-order factor (Reiss, 1991).

Reference Values

Compared with normals/controls, anxiety sensitivity is elevated in panic disorder, as well as in other anxiety disorders (Taylor, Koch, & McNally, 1992). Table 13 (p. 124) presents reference data comparing

Table 13. Comparisons of Clinical and Nonclinical Samples on ASI

	Panic Disorder			Nonclinical Sample		
	n	Mean	SD	n	Mean	SD
Brown & Cash, 1990	50	24.76	9.41	107	19.85	9.03†
Kamieniecki, Wade, & Tsourtos, 1997	15(a)	40.47	10.88	15	16.13	10.04‡
Cox, Cohen, Direnfeld, & Swinson, 1996	216	37.44	12.24	365(b)	21.85	10.14‡
Brown & Deagle, 1992				121	18.72	8.43

	Panic Disorder			Other Anxiety Disorders		
	n	Mean	SD	n	Mean	SD
Apfeldorf et al, 1994	93	38.4	11.6	50	27.6	12.3†

*$p < .05$
†$p < .01$
‡$p < .001$
Note: (a) Sample constituted by panic disorder with agoraphobia only; (b) college student sample.

Table 14. ASI Scores of Patients with Panic Disorder with Different Degrees of Severity

PD Alone (a)			PDA Mild (b)			PDA Moderate (c)			PDA Severe (d)		
n	Mean	SD	n	Mean	SD	n	Mean	SD	n	Mean	SD
22	34.65	10.93	68	33.81	12.64	64	38.66	11.45	37	40.76	13.14*

*ANOVA was significant (F = 3.43, $p < .05$), and post hoc analyses revealed that the "PDA severe" group was significantly higher than the "PDA mild group." PD alone: panic disorder without agoraphobia; PDA mild: panic disorder with mild agoraphobia; PDA moderate: panic disorder with moderate agoraphobia; PDA severe: panic disorder with severe agoraphobia.

panic-disordered individuals with normals/controls and with other anxiety disorders.

Table 14 (above) compares ASI scores for four levels of panic-disorder symptom severity (Cox, Endler, & Swinson, 1995b).

Brief Panic Disorder Screen

Description

The Brief Panic Disorder Screen (BPDS) (Apfeldorf. Shear, Leon, & Portera, 1994) is an abbreviated version of the Anxiety Sensitivity Index (ASI) (Reiss, Petersen, Gursky, & McNally, 1986). The authors wanted

Table 15. Comparison of Panic Disorder with Other Anxiety Disorders on the BDPS

	Panic Disorder			Other Anxiety Disorders		
	n	Mean	SD	n	Mean	SD
Apfeldorf, Shear, Leon, & Portera, 1994	93	12.6	4.0	50	7.5	4.1†

*$p < .05$
†$p < .01$
‡$p < .001$

to determine which subset of the ASI items would be most useful in identifying panic-disordered individuals (with and without agoraphobia). They found four items, which make up a brief scale: (1) "It scares me when I feel shaky," (2) "It scares me when I feel faint," (3) "It scares me when my heart beats rapidly," (4) "It scares me when I become short of breath." The BPDS total scores range between 0 and 16.

Psychometric Properties
A Cronbach's alpha coefficient of .875 was obtained, indicating good internal consistency.

Reference Values
We did not find studies comparing panic-disordered samples with non-clinical samples. Table 15 (above) presents differences between samples of panic-disordered individuals and subjects with other anxiety disorders.

State-Trait Anxiety Inventory

Description
The State-Trait Anxiety Inventory (STAI) (Spielberger, Gorsuch, & Lushene, 1970; Spielberger, 1983) is a 40-item inventory designed to measure anxiety as an enduring personality characteristic (Trait subscale) and as a transient experience (State subscale). The STAI's two scales of 20 items each describe different subjective experiences. Subjects are requested to indicate on a four-point scale (1, almost never, to 4, almost always) the extent to which they feel the anxiety. Scores for each

scale range between 20 and 40, with higher scores indicating higher anxiety.

Psychometric Properties
The STAI scales have good reliability and concurrent and discriminant validity (Spielberger, 1983).

Reference Values
Table 16 (p. 127) presents reference data comparing panic-disordered individuals with normals/controls and with those with other anxiety disorders.

Beck Anxiety Inventory

Description
The Beck Anxiety Inventory (BAI) (Beck, Epstein, Brown, & Steer, 1988; Beck & Steer, 1990) is a 21-item instrument designed to measure the severity of anxiety symptoms during the previous week. Subjects use a four-point scale (0–3) to indicate the extent to which they experienced each of the symptoms.

Psychometric Properties
The BAI has high internal consistency (Cronbach alpha = .92; Beck, Epstein, Brown, & Steer, 1988), a one-week test/retest reliability of .75 (Beck, Epstein, Brown, & Steer, 1988), and adequate concurrent validity (Beck & Steer, 1990). The correlation of BAI with the STAI-Trait Anxiety Inventory (Form Y)—Trait subscale was .58 ($p < .001$), and with the State subscale, it was .47 ($p < .01$; Fydrich, Dowdall, & Chambless, 1990). Discriminant validity data on the BAI can be found in Beck and colleagues (1988). Principal-factor analysis found a structure of two factors for the BAI: the first factor assesses somatic aspects of anxiety and the second component evaluates subjective aspects of anxiety (Beck, Epstein, Brown, & Steer, 1988).

Reference Values
Even though the BAI was not designed specifically to measure panic, it is sensitive to treatment effects since its items assess anxious arousal. The BAI manual indicates that scores between 0 and 7 are considered

Table 16. Comparative STAI-Trait Data Between a Clinical and a Nonclinical Sample

	Panic Disorder			Nonclinical Sample		
	n	Mean	SD	n	Mean	SD
STAI-Trait	50	47.10	11.14	107	38.90	8.97†
Brown & Cash, 1990						
STAI-Trait				121	38.21	9.32
Brown & Deagle, 1992						
STAI-Trait	15(a)	56.67	10.01	15	34.47	8.82†
STAI-State	15(a)	46.60	9.96	15	30.87	8.82†
Kamieniecki, Wade, & Tsourtos, 1997						

*$p < .05$
†$p < .01$
‡$p < .001$
Note: (a) Sample constituted by panic disorder with agoraphobia only.

Table 17. BAI Scores for Five Types of Anxiety Disorder

Disorder	n	Mean	SD
Panic disorder with agoraphobia	95	27.27	13.11
Panic disorder without agoraphobia	93	28.81	13.46
Obsessive-compulsive disorder	26	21.69	12.42
Generalized anxiety disorder	90	18.83	9.08
Social phobia	44	17.77	11.64

Table 18. BAI Scores Over Time for Two Cognitive Therapy Modalities

						Follow-up			
		Intake		Termination		Six Month		12 Month	
Treatment	n	M	SD	M	SD	M	SD	M	SD
FCT	17	29.53	14.00	9.88	9.51	7.82	7.14	8.18	9.77
SCT	18	30.78	12.05	8.00	6.95	1 0.22	10.06	6.55	6.05

Note: FCT: Focused Cognitive Therapy. SCT: Standard Cognitive Therapy.

minimal anxiety, 8 to 15 are mild, 16 to 25 are moderate, and 26 to 63 indicates severe anxiety. Table 17 (above) presents BAI scores for panic disorder with and without agoraphobia and for other anxiety disorders (Beck & Steer, 1990).

Table 18 (above) presents reference data comparing the BAI scores of panic-disordered individuals at different stages of treatment using two types of CBT interventions (Brown, Beck, Newman, et al., 1997).

Depression Anxiety Stress Scales

Description

The Depression Anxiety Stress Scales (DASS) (Lovibond & Lovibond, 1993) is a 42-item instrument measuring symptoms of anxiety, depression, and stress over the past week. Respondents use a four-point severity/frequency scale: 0 ("did not apply to me at all") to 3 ("applied to me very much") to indicate how well each symptom described the way they felt. The scales consist of 14 items each with a range of possible scores of 0–42. The authors defined anxiety as physiological hyperarousal and fearfulness, and stress as persistent tension, irritability, low frustration tolerance, and difficulty in relaxing. Depression was defined as low positive affect, low self-esteem, hopelessness, and lack of incentive. The DASS was designed to improve empirical discriminative assessment between anxiety and depression as compared with previous scales, which typically produce very high intercorrelations between these two constructs.

Psychometric Properties

The same three factors were found in factor analyses conducted on nonclinical samples (Lovibond & Lovibond, 1995), as well as on clinical samples (Brown, Chorpita, Korotisch, & Barlow, 1997). The third factor (stress) was originally not intended by the authors, however, it emerged as general distress and a negative affect shared by both anxiety and depression.

The authors reported good internal consistency, as well as convergent and discriminant validity in nonclinical samples, with the Beck Anxiety and Beck Depression inventories (Lovibond & Lovibond, 1995). Brown and associates found similar results in 437 anxiety-disordered patients. They also reported good test/retest (two weeks) reliability for each of the three scales.

Reference Values

Table 19 (p. 129) presents reference data on the DASS.

Table 19. Comparisons of Panic Disorder with Other Anxiety and Mood Disorders on the DASS*

DASS Scale		Principal DSM-R Diagnosis					
		PA/W (n=149)	GAD (n=63)	SoP (n=59)	SiP (n=20)	OCD (n=20)	Mood (n=35)
Anxiety	Mean	15.48	11.34	11.66	5.25	9.65	10.97
	SD	8.81	8.17	8.59	6.24	7.75	7.89
Stress	Mean	18.25	22.36	17.73	12.30	18.60	22.57
	SD	9.87	9.90	10.45	9.06	7.84	8.62
Depression	Mean	11.63	14.33	13.17	4.95	16.45	25.31
	SD	10.37	9.77	10.30	5.51	12.14	10.24

*From Brown, Chorpita, Korotisch, & Barlow, 1997.
Note: PA/W: panic disorder with or without agoraphobia; GAD: generalized anxiety disorders; SoP: social phobia; SiP: simple phobia; OCD: obsessive-compulsive disorder; Mood: mood disorder, which included major depression and dysthymia. Post hoc comparisons revealed that on anxiety, PA/W group > all groups and SiP < all groups; on stress, GAD, Mood groups > PA/W, SoP, and SiP group < all groups except for OCD; on depression, Mood group > all groups, and four < all groups.

Short-Form Health Survey

The Short-Form Health Survey (SF-36) (Ware & Sherbourne, 1992) is a 36-item scale assessing individuals' perceptions about their quality of life and functioning in eight areas: (1) the extent to which their physical health limits their physical functioning; (2) the extent to which their physical health interferes with their work and other daily activities; (3) the extent to which their mental health interferes with their daily activities; (4) social functioning; (5) interference by pain with work; (6) mental health; (7) perception of their vitality; and (8) general health perception. The SF-36 score ranges between 0 and 100; higher scores reflect better health and less impairment.

Psychometric Properties
Hollifield and colleagues (Hollifield, Katon, Skipper, et al., 1997) reported high intercorrelation among the eight subscales, and principal-component analysis produced a three-factor underlying structure. Data regarding reliability and convergent/discriminant validity were not available.

Reference Values

Hollifield and associates presented data comparing panic-disordered individuals and a nonclinical sample on the degree of impairment according to three of the eight SF-36 subscales (see Table 20, p. 131).

Social Readjustment Rating Scale (SRRS)

Description

The Social Readjustment Rating Scale (SRRS) (Holmes & Rahe, 1967) is a 43-item scale designed to measure significant life changes during the last year. Different events are weighted according to the estimated amount of readjustment required to cope with them. Hence subjects are requested to recall having experienced specific life events in a particular period (usually between 6 and 12 months).

Psychometric Properties

The SRRS has variable test/retest reliability with higher values obtained within shorter periods of time (e.g., .26 − .90; Rahe, 1967). The validity of the content of the SRRS has been criticized since it is standard for different populations. Thus, it may not include the particular situations and their estimated weights, which may be more relevant for the various populations (e.g., students, the elderly, adults) (e.g., Chiriboga, 1977). Hurst (1979) suggested that the SRRS content be made population specific in order to increase the scale's ecological validity.

Reference Values

No data were available on panic-disorder samples.

Self-Monitoring Forms

Self-monitoring is a useful method of obtaining a daily record of information about various issues concerning panic and agoraphobia. Typical features of panic attacks measured through self-monitoring are frequency of the attacks; duration, nature, and severity of symptoms; and cognitive, proprioceptive, and situational cues triggering the attacks (e.g., Barlow & Cerny, 1988; Rapee, Craske, & Barlow, 1990). Typical features of the agoraphobic behaviors measured are time away from home and frequency of exposure to certain situations while away from

Table 20. Comparative Data on Impairment Between a Clinical and a Nonclinical Sample Using the Short-Form Health Survey

Subscale	Panic Disorder (n=62)		Nonclinical Sample (n=61)	
	Mean	SD	Mean	SD
Physical functioning	71.00	25.00	91.10	12.40†
Mental health	45.00	18.70	75.5	19.10†
General health	51.80	24.10	79.20	17.80†

*p < .05
†p < .01
‡p < .001

home (e.g., Mathews, Gelder, & Johnston, 1981; Margraf, Taylor, Ehlers, et al., 1987). One common measure used to monitor individuals' distress levels is the Subjective Units of Disturbance Scale (SUDS) (Wolpe, 1982). SUDS can vary from 0 (not anxious/distressed at all) to 100, which indicates maximum anxiety. Typically, individuals record their SUDS level at different times/situations.

Barlow (1988) strongly recommends the use of self-monitoring forms as a way to obtain accurate data; he considers these preferable to test scores since the latter are based on the periodic recollection of experiences and, consequently, are more likely to be distorted.

Clinicians can design their own monitoring forms for different clients or they can use forms presented in books and papers on panic, such as those by Barlow (1988); Barlow and Cerny (1988); Rapee, Craske, and Barlow (1990); Craske and Barlow (1994); Barlow and Craske (1994); and Craske (1996b). A self-monitoring form known as the "Panic Diary" is shown in Figure 2.

Behavioral Tests

Behavioral Avoidance Tests

Behavioral Avoidance Tests (BATs) are useful with panic-disordered individuals suffering from agoraphobia as they assess the confidence of agoraphobic individuals to go outside their homes, both alone and accompanied. During the BATs, patients are often asked to self-monitor and register (e.g., via tape recorder) their anxiety level (Subjective Units of Disturbance, or SUDs) at different points (Barlow, Mavissakalian, &

Panic Diary

Name: _____   Date: _____

Date, time, and duration of the panic attack	Situation in which panic attack occurred and severity of the panic	Description of the panic attack symptoms and sensations experienced	Interpretation of sensations and accompanying thoughts and images	Was this a full-blown attack? Yes/No. If No, Why not?	Your response to the panic attack. What did you do? (Specify any medication taken and dosage (mg, dose, etc.)

Figure 2. Blank Panic Diary. (Copyright F. M. Dattilio, 1996)

Schofield, 1980). In addition, the patients may be asked to self-monitor their negative automatic thoughts at the same points.

There are two general types of BATs: (1) In Standardized (S-BATs), clinicians or researchers ask all panic patients to walk through a standard course that is difficult to finish for most agoraphobics. Patients go back to where they started when they feel afraid and cannot go further. Such a course is usually divided into equal segments. This allows for comparability among different patients and for a comparison of pretreatment and posttreatment changes (e.g., Agras, Leitenberg, & Barlow, 1968; Bandura, Adams, Hardy, & Howells, 1980). (2) Individualized BATs (I-BATs) are similar to the S-BATs except that the clinician designs with the patient an idiosyncratic walking course that is relevant to his or her particular case. Hence distinct avoidance situations can be selected for different individuals (e.g., Gelder, Bancroft, Gath, et al., 1973; Mavisskalian & Michelson, 1983).

Often patients and clinicians observe and assess one type of task (typically walking); however, a multitask approach is also possible in either a standardized or individualized format (e.g., Barlow, 1988; De Beurs, Lange, Van Dyck, et al., 1991). Accordingly, individuals are requested to perform several (e.g., five) activities that are typically avoided by agoraphobics (e.g., shopping, using public transportation, going to church or theaters, walking or driving a particular distance from home).

Summary and Conclusions

Given the complexity of intervening factors in cases of panic disorder with or without agoraphobia, a comprehensive and continuous multidimensional evaluation is necessary. Experiences of panic and avoidance may differ in phenomenology across persons and over time. Accordingly, rather than using one global indicator of change (e.g., an individual's overall perception of improvement), clinicians must utilize a composite measure. An adequate assessment must provide the information necessary to make a correct diagnosis, to generate a productive case formulation, to plan treatment, and to measure progress.

Because there are various psychosocial problems that are common to cases of panic disorder, clinicians are directed to the main areas to be evaluated. The availability of psychometrically valid and reliable measurement instruments allows for a standardized assessment of such areas. However, in order to understand the role of each of these factors and the factors' interaction in specific panic cases, clinicians must conduct an ideographic assessment. This approach provides a more accurate profile of a particular patient being evaluated and treated (Nelson & Barlow, 1981). In other words, a combination of nomothetic and ideographic assessment approaches is more appropriate for developing a precise case conceptualization.

In cases in which it is suspected that other disorders are coexisting with panic, particularly Axis II diagnoses, it is advisable to use such personality measures as the Minnesota Multiphasic Personality Inventory 1 or 2 or the Millon Multiaxial Clinical Scales. Such measures may serve as a backup to the Structured Clinical Interview Scale (DSM-IV) or the Anxiety Disorder Interview Scale. They both provide clinicians with a differential diagnosis on DSM-IV, along with an indication of whether or not the patient may be exaggerating his or her symptoms.

The four general areas to be evaluated in cases of panic disorder are (1) medical status, (2) phenomenology and history of panic and agoraphobia, (3) comorbidity and history of other psychiatric disorders, and (4) predisposing and precipitating factors for panic attacks and factors maintaining the panic disorder. The assessment also involves obtaining information about how panic-disordered individuals behave on the five major response systems and their interaction: cognitive, behavioral, affective, physiological, and social. In order to tap into these different areas and response systems, clinicians should use a variety of measurement techniques: clinical interviews, self-report scales, self-monitoring, behavioral observation, psychophysiological monitoring.

A number of panic and agoraphobia assessment instruments with good psychometric properties are available to clinicians. However, given the lack of empirical evidence, it is premature to decide which instruments are more useful than others in assessing a particular area. Thus, it is very important to obtain valid and reliable information for each of the areas by using a combination of instruments.

Since one of the goals of assessment is to measure treatment response, evaluation instruments can be used for that purpose. Various investigators (e.g., Barlow, Hayes, & Nelson, 1984; Jacobson, 1988; Jacobson & Truax, 1991) have questioned the usefulness of using statistically significant changes to assess treatment efficacy in clinical practice, but have proposed instead the use of indicators of clinical changes and their maintenance in natural settings and over time. Jacobson, Follete, and Revenstorf (1984) suggested that a clinically significant improvement has to do with helping the client to return to or to achieve normal or close-to-normal functioning (e.g., the patient's score is closer to the non-clinical population's mean than to the mean of the clinical population). Researchers call this nonclinical condition end-state functioning (e.g., Mavissakalian & Michelson, 1983; Barlow, 1988).

Those involved with improving current instruments and developing new ones must establish the goal of creating normative data for clinical populations (panic disorder with agoraphobia, panic disorder without agoraphobia), other anxiety-disordered populations, and nonclinical/normal populations. The purpose will be to create reliable cutoff points so as to define the range of scores that may be considered normal and the score that marks the onset of dysfunction (Himadi, Boice, & Barlow, 1986; Jacobson & Truax, 1991). This information will also allow clinicians and researchers to determine what score variation can be considered clinically significant with regard to changes resulting from treatment, and what profile constitutes end-state functioning.

5

Treatment Strategies

This section focuses on a number of treatment strategies that involve cognitive-behavioral techniques, psychopharmacology, and psychodynamically based interventions, as well as homeopathic and nontraditional approaches to treating panic.

Psychodynamic Techniques

There are approximately 32,480 books on psychodynamic theory and the majority of them deal with some aspect of fear and anxiety (Haley, 1996, p. 89). Since much of the psychodynamic approach places heavy emphasis on the role of unconscious processes in treatment, the unconscious meanings of panic symptoms are paramount. The symbolic meaning of symptoms serves as a valuable source of information about the panic sufferer's unconscious conflicts. As it is believed that panic-disordered individuals often tend to somatize their emotions and impulses, they are encouraged to explore their unconscious associations during the course of treatment.

Once the meanings of the symptoms are analyzed and interpreted, these may be made evident to the patient's conscious ego. Then, interpretation may be utilized by the therapist to place the uncovered content into clearer focus and to lay the groundwork for working through the unconscious conflicts. Through the interpretation of such content, the patient may gain not only symptom reduction, but a more mature personality.

One area of focus in treatment is the actual panic symptoms themselves. Panic patients frequently perceive normal physical variations (i.e., feeling lightheaded, hot, or dizzy) as indications of an underlying disease or illness. Patients can easily confuse their fantasies that they are sick and desperately in need of help with reality.

An excellent book by Milrod, Busch, Cooper, and Shapiro (1997) elaborates on panic-focused psychodynamic psychotherapy. Here, the authors break down the three phases of treatment as follows:

Phase 1: In the initial phase of treatment, interventions are aimed at exploring and relieving panic attacks. The strategies used involve an initial evaluation and exploration of circumstances and feelings surrounding the panic onset. A focus may be placed on personal meanings of panic symptoms and on the further exploration of the feelings and content of these specific panic episodes. Psychodynamic conflicts that are highlighted include separation and independence, anger recognition, management of and coping with expression, and sexual excitement and its perceived dangers. The main goal of this phase is to provide some initial panic relief in order to allow for further exploration. Specific highlights include the therapist's focus on the circumstances preceding the onset of panic, the patient's thoughts and feelings during panic attacks, and the meanings of panic symptoms. With this process, the therapist is able to formulate the psychologically meaningful issues involved in the genesis of the patient's panic episodes.

Phase 2: This phase involves further exploration by the therapist in greater depth with what is termed mental configurations. This is the aspect that elicits the patient's actual panic symptoms. The theory is that the core dynamics need to be fully understood and altered. Specific dynamics must be identified with the patient in the course of treatment whether through their emergence in the transferential process or through free association. This is typically done by resolving conflicts in the transference in the process of working through. As the patient's unconscious conflicts emerge in therapy, the therapist actively seeks to uncover dynamic connections with emotional configurations that occur during panic episodes. During this process, intensification of the transference allows for increasing the work on unconscious determined patterns based on childhood relationships as they emerge in the relationship with the therapist. The essential goal then is to reduce the patient's vulnerability to panic relapse through further conscious delineation of the interpersonal emotional scripts according to which patients conduct their lives. This is a multidimensional process involving personal growth, not just symptom reduction.

Phase 3: This phase involves the move toward termination, including addressing the patient's severe difficulties with separation and independence. The idea is to permit the individual to reexperience specific conflicts directly with the therapist so that the underlying fantasy can begin to be articulated and understood, and eventually interpreted with less fear. The patient's reaction to termination must also be addressed; this may include a temporary recurrence of symptoms. Whereas psychodynamic theorists do not focus primarily on psychoeducational aspects, it is believed that cognitive-behavioral and psychoeducational techniques are often explicit in treatment, and the psychodynamic therapist may consider referrals for CBT as a follow-up to psychodynamic therapy. Milrod and Scherer (1991) suggest that the panic-focused psychodynamic approach usually provides relief of panic symptoms in approximately 12 to 20 weeks of exploratory psychotherapy. They go on to state that if agoraphobic symptoms are present, improvement may be slower, depending on the intensity of the symptoms.

A more recent form of intensive short-term dynamic psychotherapy (IS-TDP) is that of Davanloo (1990), which he uses to unlock the unconscious in a very brief time. He claims that this powerful and specific technique is the most powerful form of psychotherapy and psychoanalysis ever developed and is capable of resolving the most complex pathogenic disorders (Said & Schubmehl, 1998).

Davanloo divides his central dynamic sequence in the process of partially unlocking the unconscious into a series of phases.

Phase 1: *Inquiry*. Exploring the patient's difficulties and ability to respond to treatment.

Phase 2: *Identification of character defenses*, and dealing with transference.

Phase 3: *Challenging resistance*. Acquainting the patient with the function of his or her resistance, mobilizing the therapeutic alliance, and helping the patient turn against his or her resistance.

Phase 4: *Transference resistance.* Meeting resistance head-on, intensifying transferential feelings, mobilizing the therapeutic alliance against resistance. Starting partial unlocking of patient's unconscious.

Phase 5: *Direct access to the unconscious: Partial unlocking of the unconscious.* Breaking through the complex transference feeling.

Phase 6: *Systemic analysis of the transference*, leading to the resolution of the residual resistance. This is extremely important for individuals suffering from panic disorder.

Phase 7: *Dynamic exploration into the unconscious.*

The psychodynamic approach works best with individuals who are intelligent and are able to use introspection and insight in developing personal growth.

The following is a case example of a man with panic disorder who was treated via a short-term psychodynamic approach (Said, Rossi, Van Oyen, & Went, 1998).

Case Example: A Dream of a Storm

Clayton, a 64-year-old man, was referred to a psychiatrist by his family physician for the treatment of panic attacks. This was the first episode of panic that Clayton admitted experiencing, although he did report having intermittent periods of anxiety throughout his life. Clayton, who was retired, was home alone during a summer afternoon reading a magazine when he felt autonomic symptoms—lightheadedness, some dizziness, and an increased heart rate, as well as an increased respiration rate, which led to a fear of loss of control. His symptoms were so disabling that he thought that he was having a heart attack and he called a friend, who took him to the emergency room of a nearby hospital. Clayton's wife was at work.

After a thorough medical examination, the emergency room physician administered an injection of protriptyline and referred him to his family physician. His physician gave Clayton a thorough examination, including a full blood profile and an electrocardiogram, switched the medication to alprazolam, and scheduled another appointment for a week later. Two days later, Clayton underwent another panic attack, and so was referred to a psychiatrist.

The psychiatrist conducted a standard evaluation, including taking a clinical history and exploring some of the circumstances and feelings surrounding the panic onset. It was at this point that Clayton had reported that the initial attack had occurred while he was sitting at home reading a magazine during a summer rainstorm. He recalled being distracted by the sound of the rain on the roof, and then suddenly feeling lightheaded. At first, he thought that he just was having a dizzy spell or had not eaten enough for lunch. However, very quickly his heart rate increased, along with his respiration, and a sudden feeling of terror and anticipation of loss of control overwhelmed him. The only emotion that he was able to express was fear, which seemed unrelated to the article that he had been reading.

It was after visiting his family physician that Clayton recalled a dream in which his house was flooded by a torrential rainstorm, and his wife drowned. He remembered feeling powerless to help her and was overwhelmed with guilt. This created anxiety for him, which sparked panic attacks on the following day. It was at that point that Clayton returned to his family physician, who referred him for psychiatric treatment after listening to Clayton's description of the dream.

In further exploration of significant incidents in his life, Clayton reported that his father had died of a heart attack when Clayton was about 10. Clayton, the youngest of three children, had two sisters, five and eight years his senior. Clayton reported an uneventful life, although he recalled tough times during the difficult postdepression years.

Therapy continued to explore dream content and any notion of separation anxiety, as well as anger recognition. It was during the course of this exploration that the following information was uncovered.

Clayton was raised in a small town in a mountainous area in the Northeast. When his father died, his mother tried her best to feed the family and take care of her children. But employment was not easy to find for a woman in the 1930s and Clayton recalled the family's struggle to make ends meet.

It seems that a prominent doctor in town had been helpful to Clayton's mother and the family by providing money from time to time and doing them special favors. Clayton later divulged that the doctor had taken sexual advantage of Clayton's mother, as well as of his two sisters, who were young teenagers at the time. Clayton became aware of this activity because the doctor would frequently visit his mother in her room with the door closed, as he also occasionally did with Clayton's sisters. Not surprising, this was an issue that was never openly discussed among the family members. It apparently was something that Clayton had blocked out and uncovered only during the course of treatment. Clayton recalled that the doctor generally visited on rainy days, when Clayton's mother usually was sent home early from her job at the Garden Mart. Clayton remembered that many times his sisters would lock themselves in their rooms and cry themselves to sleep.

Further exploration uncovered the fact that Clayton felt powerless in the face of what was taking place, knowing that his mother and sisters endured the sexual abuse because they needed the money the doctor gave them in return. Moreover, the doctor was a powerful man of great influence and the family was afraid of antagonizing him. The unspoken agreement in the house was never to discuss the issue and Clayton had been harboring that secret all of his life.

Apparently, the summer rainstorm had uncovered feelings of powerlessness and loss of control. The fact the Clayton had been alone and his wife, whom he depended on, was out of the house at work was a contributing factor. The following night's dream of a rain-induced flood in his home was symbolic of the intrusion of the doctor who had sexually abused Clayton's mother and sisters. The symbolism of the water had a sexual connotation, provoking an anger reaction coupled with fear of loss of control.

Once this aspect was uncovered, therapy focused on working through some of the issues of guilt and feelings of loss of control and powerlessness. Transferential issues also focused on the analyst, who was an older male physician, eliciting anger reactions from Clayton during the treatment. In the process of uncovering information, a heavy use of dream content enabled the analyst to establish the framework for Clayton to divulge his tightly kept secret. As the process of working through continued, Clayton reported a reduction in anxiety and the absence of any future panic attacks. His medication was used sparingly during treatment, titrated to a subclinical dose, and eventually discontinued.

This case is a typical example of how unconscious conflicts about past traumas, anger, and dependency can be worked through in a short-term focused approach.

Cognitive-Behavioral Techniques

A great deal of the professional literature has focused on the use of CBT and its effectiveness in treating panic and anxiety disorders (Beck, Emery, & Greenberg, 1985; Barlow, 1988; Dattilio & Salas, 1999). Most specifically, exposure-based treatments have been quite successful in reducing panic (Barlow, 1988), particularly when used in concert with pharmacological interventions (Zitrin, Klein, & Woerner, 1978). Cognitive-behavioral treatment focusing on panic control through education, cognitive restructuring, interoceptive exposure, and breathing retraining has been reported as successful in most cases in both individual and group formats (Telch, Lucas, Schmidt, et al., 1993).

Most recently, brief treatments of panic attacks in emergency situations have used exposure instruction with relative effectiveness (Swinson, Soulios, Cox, & Kuch, 1992; Dattilio, 1995). In one study, 33 patients with panic attacks were seen in two emergency room settings; 40 % of the patients had been diagnosed with the Structured Clinical Interview Schedule (SCID) as meeting the criteria for panic disorder with agoraphobia. Patients were randomly assigned to two groups receiving either reassurance or exposure instruction. Outcome measures demonstrated significant improvement over a six-month period for those in the exposure group. Those in the reassurance group showed no improvement on any measure, and, in fact, reported increased symptomatology (Swinson, Soulios, Cox, & Kuch, 1992). The specific treatment in this group involved informing patients that the most effective way to reduce their fear was to confront the situation in which the attack occurred. Patients were advised to return to the situation as soon as possible after the interview and to wait until their anxiety decreased. Although this approach improves on the use of pharmacological interventions, it still falls short of providing the individual with any specific set of coping techniques, especially for dealing with future panic episodes. It also relies on extinction procedures and appears to require more time for reducing symptoms and may not always be practical, depending on the circumstances in which the individual experienced the attack.

There are a number of additional CBT techniques that have proved to be more satisfactory alternatives in the treatment of panic. These techniques provide individuals with specific coping mechanisms to apply during future episodes or attacks, as well as with the opportunity to improve their ability to control and prevent panic attacks.

Controlled Breathing

Very early studies on anxiety refer to the use of progressive muscle relaxation and controlled breathing, as well as carbon-dioxide inhalation (Wolpe, 1958; Lazarus, 1963, 1964). These techniques are based on the premise that a state of relaxation and a state of anxiety cannot coexist, and so are viewed by some as being all that is necessary to put a stop to recurrent panic attacks (Lum, 1981; Clark, Salkovskis, & Chalkley, 1985).

The concept of controlled breathing is an offshoot of the hyperventilation hypothesis, which contends that prior to panicking, people commonly hyperventilate (Hibbert, 1984), meaning that they tend to breathe through their mouths, take short shallow breaths of air, or sigh frequently. With diaphragmatic breathing, one form of breathing retraining for counteracting hyperventilation, individuals are instructed to breathe through their noses normally and to count the number of breaths while at rest, keeping the frequency to 8 to 12 times per minute. They are also told to place both hands over the abdomen while breathing, and to notice the movement of the diaphragm. The goal is to slow the respiration rate to 8 to 12 times per minute. They are instructed to practice the exercise during both panic and nonpanic periods (Clum, 1990).

If, during a severe panic attack, the diaphragmatic method does not enable the individual to obtain a full breath, which is often the case, then the alternative of breathing into a paper bag or cupped hands may be used to increase the level of carbon dioxide (Dattilio, 1990). Another alternative is to exhale through the mouth as much as possible, and then slowly to inhale through the nose, repeating the process several times. While practicing these techniques, distraction may be used to divert one's attention from the panic symptoms to enhance the positive effects of the breathing exercise.

Breathing retraining is a technique that is typically coupled with the reinterpretation of interoceptive cues using cognitive restructuring and stress inoculation techniques.

Biofeedback Treatment

Biofeedback is a treatment modality aimed at producing instrumental conditioning of, and voluntary control over, autonomic nervous system responses experienced as involuntary or automatic (Schwartz & Olson, 1995; Salas & Dattilio, 1997). Biofeedback is widely used for a variety of psychophysiological disorders. Even though it has not been commonly used in treatment protocols of outcome studies with panic-disordered cases, we have found it to be very useful as an adjunct to CBT. Specifically, biofeedback has been used with panic cases with three different, complementary purposes.

Psychophysiological Awareness and Decatastrophization
Panic-disordered individuals are frequently confused about the origin of their panic attacks. Many are not aware of the physiological changes accompanying their threatening automatic thoughts and emotional experiences, and experience such changes (e.g., heart-rate acceleration) as coming "out of the blue," which, in turn, is usually interpreted in a catastrophic fashion. Through biofeedback, individuals develop insight into how their feared physiological changes are connected to their thoughts and emotions. Also, biofeedback can be used to teach panic-disordered individuals about the physiological consequences of using substances (e.g., heart-rate acceleration as a result of consuming caffeine) or performing certain physical activities (e.g., jogging, changing postures). That awareness reduces misattributions about the origin of such bodily changes and reduces catastrophization as the individual understands the benign nature of his or her physical experiences (Wells & Dattilio, 1992).

Various biofeedback modalities can be employed, but we most frequently use galvanic skin response (GSR)/electrodermal response (EDR) thermal and heart-rate feedback since these are more sensitive to emotional changes and commonly feared sensations in panic-disordered individuals (e.g., heart-rate changes, cold hands, flushed face).

Relaxation Training

Biofeedback-assisted relaxation has been widely used to enhance the relaxation response. In our protocol with panic cases, we usually combine progressive muscle relaxation and biofeedback as part of our relaxation training. We tape the relaxation instructions used during the training session, and then use biofeedback to improve those responses (e.g., muscle tension, skin temperature) that need to change the most. Biofeedback not only helps patients to perceive the physiological differences between being tense and being relaxed, but also facilitates the acquisition of relaxation skills. Usually, one or two consecutive sessions are required for biofeedback aimed at improving relaxation response. Most of the training occurs at home where patients practice progressive muscle relaxation on a daily basis with the purpose of improving their relaxation skills and cultivating a stable low arousal level.

Respiratory Control Training

As previously mentioned, it is widely accepted that an important proportion of panic-disordered individuals are chronically stressed and present with a condition of chronic mild hyperventilation, even during resting conditions (e.g., Ley, 1985b; Clark, Salkovskis, & Chalkley, 1985; Holt & Andrews, 1989). It is also known that most people hyperventilate severely once the panic attack starts (e.g., Salkovskis, Warwick, Clark, & Vessels, 1986; Hibbert & Pilsbury, 1988). Consequently, training panic-disordered patients in respiratory control has been a standard component of CBT protocols (e.g., Clark, 1986; Ley, 1987a: Dattilio & Berchick, 1992; Craske, Meadows, & Barlow, 1994). Typically, breathing control is taught initially in vivo and then through an audiotape that describes a breathing pattern incompatible with hyperventilation: deep and slow diaphragmatic breathing. Patients are instructed to practice with the tape at home until they are able to start slow regular breathing without the aid of the tape. After they learn how to produce the appropriate breathing, they are instructed to apply such skills to voluntarily induced hyperventilation. The habituation produced by repeated practice and the self-efficacy developed by practicing the controlling symptoms of hyperventilation typically reduce the anxiety related to such symptoms.

In addition to training with audiotapes, biofeedback assistance can also be used to accelerate the acquisition of a good breathing pattern and breathing control. Individuals obtain from the computer monitor precise feedback regarding their thoracic and diaphramatic breathing rates and the amplitude used to regulate their breathing. Frequently, patients spontaneously convey to us how valuable the technique has been to their self-confidence in controlling the initial symptoms of panic and learning to relax better. Usually, two to four breathing biofeedback sessions in a two- or four-week period, combined with home practice using audiotapes, are sufficient to produce significant changes in the resting breathing pattern and respiratory control skills. The home-practice audiotape can usually be made during the instrumental sessions so that individuals can experience continuity in the style of relaxation training.

The latest computerized biofeedback equipment allows for the very rich and detailed feedback of physiological changes, which facilitates motivation and self-regulatory skill acquisition. It also allows the researcher and the clinician to store the sessions' data, which not only can be used to conduct studies, but may also be available to the therapist and the patient for evaluating treatment progress. We use this technique as a valuable tool to help us to deliver faster and more effective treatment results.

Case Example: Using Breathing Biofeedback

Figures 3–5 represent the grafted breathing of a panic-disordered 26-year-old woman with a 10-year history of panic disorder with agoraphobia and a history of separation anxiety as a child. Within the CBT treatment package, she received three 20-minute sessions of breathing-biofeedback–assisted relaxation, one week apart. In addition, she was instructed to practice a form of progressive muscle relaxation at home via audiotape for 10 minutes a day.

A Focus-1000 biofeedback system was used to aid the client in breathing retraining. She was instructed to control the bouncing rhythm of a ball, which was presented on a computer screen. The goal was to make the ball jump over the line in the patttern of a bell-shaped curve, which was depicted on the screen. As the patient learned to control the

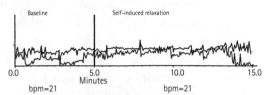

Figure 3. Diaphragmatic and thoracic breathing rate during baseline and self-instructed relaxation before receiving breathing biofeedback training.

Note: BPM = Breaths per minute

Figure 4. Diaphragmatic and thoracic breathing rate during the third breathing biofeedback session.

Note: BPM = Breaths per minute

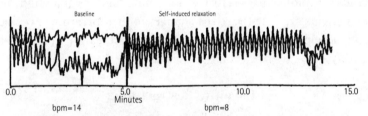

Figure 5. Diaphragmatic and thoracic breathing rate during baseline and self-instructed relaxation after three weekly biofeedback sessions and home practice of progressive muscle relaxation.

Note: BPM = Breaths per minute

bouncing ball, she also learned to produce a deep and slow diaphragmatic rhythm of breathing. Although the frequency and depth of the breathing were not measured directly by the computer software, we were able to count from the monitor her breaths per minute during the various conditions. Also, the differences in such variables can easily be observed visually on the graphs.

Figures 3 and 4 present the patient's thoraxic and diaphragmatic breathing patterns before and after three breathing-biofeedback treatments. In each of the two assessment sessions, there was a five-minute baseline when she was completing the panic questionnaires, and 15 minutes of self-induced relaxation (no feedback from the monitor). Figure 5 shows the thoraxic and diaphragmatic breathing patterns that were produced during the third biofeedback training session.

Figure 3 demonstrates how the patient exhibited a mild hyperventilation during baseline. Her breathing pattern was mainly thoraxic, fast (21 breaths per minute [bpm]) and shallow. Figure 3 also shows that her breathing pattern did not change from baseline to self-induced relaxation. This performance suggests that she did not know how to breathe in a more relaxing way. Figure 4 shows how the patient learned deep and slow (6 bpm) diaphragmatic breathing by controlling the feedback from the computer screen. Finally, Figure 5 depicts the patient's performance after she received breathing retraining. At baseline, she was breathing at 14 bpm and deeper than the pretraining baseline. Upon self-induced relaxation, she slowed her breathing to 8 bpm and increased the depth of her breaths. She also reported being a bit more at ease throughout the day, even when she was not deliberately relaxing.

This graphic display provides some idea of the effectiveness and importance of biofeedback-assisted breathing and relaxation training. When patients are able to see the changes in their breathing graphically, this often helps them to learn to control their breathing patterns more effectively.

Cognitive Restructuring

The CBT model of panic contends that, very often, an individual's threatening misinterpretation of bodily sensations plays an integral role in the escalation and maintenance of panic symptoms (Argyle, 1988; Beck, Emery, & Greenberg, 1985; Dattilio, 1987; Ottaviani & Beck, 1987). Consequently, part of the treatment consists of correcting misappraisals of bodily changes involving an overestimation of perceived danger and an underestimation of the capacity for coping (Dattilio, 1987, 1990; Greenberg, 1989). The goal is to help panic-disordered individuals to formulate a more accurate explanation of their symptoms.

Cognitive restructuring starts by assisting the person to identify the sequence and reciprocal influence of bodily changes, catastrophic attributions (automatic thoughts), anxiety, and further sensations during panic attacks. In our clinic, we use the SAEB system discussed earlier (Dattilio, 1994b) to facilitate such awareness. With this new information, the panic-discordered individual can get a glimpse of the factors involved and the processes that occur during the panic sequence. In this respect, individuals can challenge their beliefs that they are helpless victims of an illness or an uncontrollable catastrophe. A second phase consists of educating people who suffer attacks about the nature of their panic and anxiety. This helps them to develop a more objective view of the disorder, as well as of their role in maintaining and controlling their panic attacks. Emphasis is placed on the following concepts and principles: anxiety/fear as a defense reaction to the perception of threat; the role of thoughts/ beliefs, feelings, bodily changes, and behaviors in panic, and the reciprocal influences among them; the physiology of panic; the cognitive nature of their anticipatory anxiety; the role of avoidance and confrontation of aversive stimuli; the role of cognitive distortions and selective attention toward physically threatening cues; and risk factors for panic. Also, the concepts of fear of emotions and of fear of bodily changes are addressed. This phase can be accomplished through different complementary methods, such as didactic presentations, videotapes, and suggested readings.

The next phase focuses on helping people to apply such concepts and principles to their actual experiences of anticipatory anxiety, panic, and phobic avoidance. This phase involves training individuals in self-monitoring and the clinician's use of Socratic questioning (rather than didactic presentations) to help them to analyze their anxiety/panic in terms of its components (e.g., bodily sensation, automatic thoughts) and processes (sequence of events). Also, their beliefs (e.g., attributions, outcome expectations) are rated in terms of subjective units of credibility (SUCs, on a scale of 0 to 100); their cognitive distortions are identified (e.g., emotional reasoning, catastrophizing), challenged, and reformulated; and, again, their credibility on the new beliefs is continuously rated. This third phase of cognitive restructuring can be accomplished through various means: (1) by examining patients' recent anxiety/panic episodes from a new perspective, and (2) by instructing individuals to conduct behavioral experiments designed to test their catastrophic attribution and predictions, and to help in the reformulation of distorted beliefs. Part of the experiment is conducted in the clinician's office (via interoceptive exposure exercises) and part in exposure assignments in *in vivo* settings. Although the emphasis and the form of cognitive restructuring vary at different points during treatment, the technique is used throughout the entire program.

The client is presented with a therapeutic exercise whereby he or she is instructed to follow the therapist in taking successive short breaths of air, inhaling and exhaling, for approximately two to three minutes. This procedure serves to reproduce the symptoms of panic by activating the autonomic nervous system and disrupting the balance of oxygen and carbon-dioxide levels, sometimes causing hyperventilation as well (Dattilio, 1990). Symptom induction allows the therapist to obtain a direct report of the client's thought processes as the attack develops and to assist the client in controlling the attack through progressive breathing and thought restructuring. The goal is to reproduce the type of situation that may precipitate an attack and then show the client that he or she can "turn on" as well as "turn off" the attacks.

Once the symptoms have been induced, the therapist records the sequence of events that have occurred, paying particular attention to the specific symptoms experienced, the automatic thoughts that occurred, and the emotional reaction that resulted. Figure 3 provides an example of how to track the client's panic sequence during an attack using the SAEB system (Dattilio, 1994b). In response to the initial symptom, a spontaneous increase in heart rate, the automatic thought is overreactive in the sense that it is assumed that "something is wrong" or that the client "could faint."

It is essential that all clients who are candidates for this technique receive medical clearance prior to the exercise to ensure that the technique is not contraindicated by an existing medical condition. The therapist can then begin to intervene with the deescalation techniques by collaboratively focusing with the client on the initial symptoms.

In the case presented in Figure 6, a spontaneous increase in heart rate followed by the thought, "Something is wrong," or "I'm going to faint," translates into fear. By identifying the early onset of symptoms in the panic cycle, the therapist can aid clients in the deescalation of symptoms—having them downplay the severity of the symptoms by altering their misinterpretations. For example, in Figure 6, Rosemary had developed a pattern of responding to an increased heart rate by perceiving it as dangerous and a sure sign that something was wrong. In having clients restructure their thoughts, they are asked to consider an alternative response that may involve a less catastrophic implication. For instance, "Just the fact that I have an increase in heart rate doesn't mean that this is necessarily dangerous or that something is wrong. It is probably just benign autonomic activity, which will last for a limited time." This cognitive response is supported by having the client log each attack and review the log for reassurance that since nothing dangerous occurred in the past, it is unlikely to occur in the future. Patients are then taught controlled breathing in order to regulate their oxygen intake and reduce autonomic activity.

The purpose of this type of restructuring is to lessen the likelihood that the individual's automatic thoughts are fueling the subsequent increase in symptoms and emotional reaction and to persuade the person that his or her fear ("I might faint") is unsubstantiated. This point can be reaffirmed with cognitive correction via factual information (e.g., in order to faint, one must experience a decrease in blood pressure, whereas blood pressure increases with increased heart rate and anxiety). In addition, this serves to improve the patient's perceived sense of bodily control, which reduces the intensity of threat and danger.

This type of thought correction is followed throughout the entire panic cycle and then reinforced by virtue of reexposure to symptoms through the use of the panic-induction exercise. It is the combination of the artificial induction of symptoms (e.g., purposely increasing heart rate), the reinterpretation of these symptoms (e.g., "It won't hurt me"), deescalation of the catastrophic thoughts (e.g., "This won't last forever"), and the eventual reduction of symptom severity that makes the technique effective. In addition, follow-through by having the client expose himself or herself to real-life situations is an important component of treatment so that the ability to generalize the techniques to a variety of situations can develop.

This technique is usually well received by panic sufferers, particularly after they have overcome their initial apprehension about raising their autonomic activity level. With those clients who do not benefit from the intervention (e.g., become too overwhelmed or are unable to increase their autonomic activity level), it is recommended that the same technique of cognitive restructuring be used without the symptom-induction exercise.

Exteroceptive Exposure

Exteroceptive exposure, also referred to as *in vivo exposure*, consists of systematic confrontation with agoraphobic situations. Exteroceptive exposure is typically programmed in a progressive manner, from the least to the most fearful stimuli. Hence an individualized hierarchy of feared situations is constructed based on the person's self-report; also, clinicians' observations in behavioral avoidance tests have been used for the same purpose. Confronting each feared situation is rated using a SUD scale (e.g., 0–10). At each step in the hierarchy, the individual's exposure to the feared situation is maintained until the anxiety has subsided (Marks, 1987). Exposure seems to be more effective when one's attention is focused on internal (bodily sensations) and external (situation) phobic stimuli, and distraction and other forms of avoidance are prevented (Craske, Street, & Rowe, 1989). Usually, a combination of long exposure (e.g., two to four hours a day) with repeated practice is used for optimal results. Research indicates that daily exposure and spaced exposure (e.g., once per week) are equally effective over both the short term and long term, as well as with regard to their dropout and relapse rates (Chambless, 1990). Exposure should be practiced until the individual consistently feels confident in his or her ability to deal with previously feared situations with no signs of subtle avoidance.

In vivo exposure can be implemented as a therapist-directed (intense therapist contact) or a self-directed technique (manualized programs with minimal therapist contact). Both have proved effective (e.g., Ghosh & Mark, 1987; Mathews, Gelder, & Johnston, 1981). However, self-directed in vivo exposure does not seem appropriate with severe (home-bound) cases of agoraphobia (Holden, O'Brien, Barlow, et al., 1983). In our clinic, we frequently combine both techniques: initially, we use therapist-directed exposure and then, as the individual progresses, we switch to self-directed exposure. In some cases, the self-directed exposure phase includes an intermediate step of involving the assistance of a support person (e.g., spouse, parent, friend) before moving to solo exposure.

It is important to enhance generalization of exposure gains by helping patients take credit for the symptom reduction they accomplished when confronting the phobic situation. That is, if the panic-disordered individual learns to feel relaxed in a previously feared situation only because he or she became habituated to the situation, the person's attribution for safety will continue to be external (e.g., "This situation is familiar to me, therefore, it now feels safe"). As a consequence, the generalization to a new, unfamiliar situation will be limited. Thus, clinicians can use exteroceptive exposure not only to induce habituation, but also as an opportunity for patients to practice their new coping skills and new attitude toward their panic symptoms (e.g., constructive self-instructions, diaphragmatic breathing, safety behavior/signal prevention). In this way, using in vivo exposure as a guided mastery treatment can increase patients' self-efficacy to control panic symptoms (Williams & Zane, 1989; Williams, 1990; Van Hout, Emmelkamp, & Scholing, 1994).

Case Example: Using Introceptive Exposure and the SAEB System

Following is an excerpt from an actual treatment session in which symptom induction, deescalation procedures, and controlled breathing were used with Rosemary, a 32-year-old emergency room nurse who suffered panic attacks. Take note of how the SAEB System is implemented quite effectively with this patient during the process of assessment and treatment.

Therapist: Rosemary, I'd like you to begin to breathe in a special way by inhaling and exhaling only through your mouth, very quickly, almost as you would if you were out of breath—like this [therapist demonstrates method of controlled breathing]. All right! Now try it along with me—short staccato breaths [Rosemary mimics the same procedure].

Therapist: Great! Now let's try it for real. I am going to say "go" and I want you to begin breathing along with me in the manner that we just practiced. Once we start, I am going to discontinue, but I want you to continue on for about…oh, maybe a minute and a half to two minutes, or for as long as you can, nonstop. I have a glass of water here since your mouth may become dry at the point at which we stop the exercise. Okay? Are you ready?

Rosemary: Yes, I guess!

Therapist: Let's begin…

[Therapist and Rosemary begin the exercise together. Throughout the exercise, the therapist supports Rosemary in her exercise by breathing with her simultaneously for short periods and keeping track of the time.]

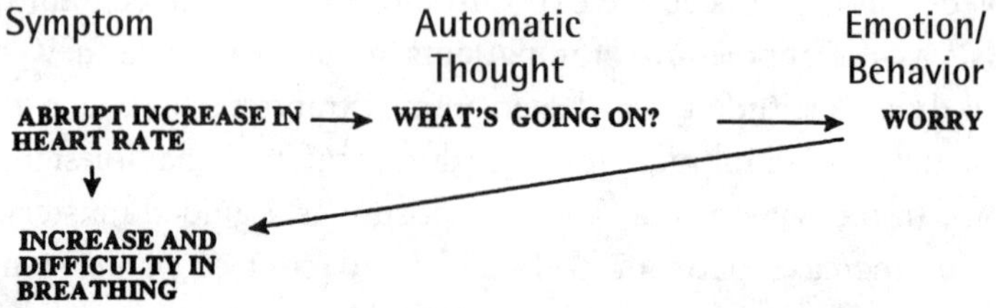

Symptom	Automatic Thought	Emotion/ Behavior

ABRUPT INCREASE IN → WHAT'S GOING ON? → WORRY
HEART RATE

↓

INCREASE AND
DIFFICULTY IN
BREATHING

Figure 6. Rosemary's panic sequence: Phase 1.

Rosemary: (Only 45 seconds into the exercise, breathing very heavily) I can't do this anymore! My heart is starting to race like crazy.

Therapist: Okay, what are you feeling right now?

Rosemary: Just my heart pounding.

Therapist: Anything else?

Rosemary: Well, I don't like not being able to breathe real well—I sort of enjoy breathing normally!

Therapist: What's going through your mind as you say that to me and experience these sensations?

Rosemary: I am thinking to myself, I am going to have one of those attacks—it never fails—I just don't trust my body—I want to leave, run away.

Therapist: Let's try and go just a little further with the breathing to see if you experience any other symptoms.

Rosemary: Sure, whatever you say. You're the doctor!

Therapist: Rosemary, try to remember that this is a diagnostic test designed to help both of us learn to control your panic. It's not meant to give you a hard time.

Rosemary: I know—I just hate having these damn attacks!

[Rosemary resumes the breathing exercise.]

Rosemary: (As another 50 seconds pass) Oh no!—I have to stop—I'm getting worse.

[Begins to cry] I didn't want to do this because of what might happen.

Therapist: Okay, just try to calm down and tell me what's happening.

Rosemary: Help me, please! I feel like I am out of control.

Therapist: What are you experiencing, Rosemary?

Rosemary: I am feeling lightheaded and tingling in my hands...they feel numb...oh God, I hate this! What's wrong with me? I am losing it! [Crying]

Therapist: All right, Rosemary, just begin to breathe slowly with me now. Let's calm ourselves down. Close your eyes and just breathe slowly and continuously, inhaling slowly through the nose and exhaling slowly through the mouth so that we slow everything back down to your normal resting state.

[Several minutes pass as Rosemary does this.]

Therapist: How do you feel now?

Rosemary: Better, but still a little dazed—like I'm in a fog.

Therapist: All right, well, that should pass in a little while. Let's talk about the experience that you just had while it is fresh in your mind.

Rosemary: I didn't like it. It was almost as bad as what I had in the car the other day.

Therapist: Well, actually that's kind of good, since it provides us with some insight into what you experience during an attack. So, let's try to reconstruct what just went on with you and see whether or not there is some connection to what occurs each time you experience an attack.

Rosemary: So, we're just going to talk, no more breathing?

Therapist: Yes, no more breathing, at least for now! Now, when we first began the exercise, you stated that you felt your heart pounding.

Rosemary: Correct!

Therapist: So, is it fair to say that this is usually the initial symptom?

Rosemary: Yes.

Therapist: All right now, do you remember a few minutes ago when we began doing the exercise and your heart rate began to increase?

Rosemary: Yes.

Therapist: What thoughts went racing through your mind at that point?

Rosemary: Probably "What's going on? What's happening?"

Therapist: Okay, and then do you remember what you felt...or did?

Rosemary: Well, I began to really worry.

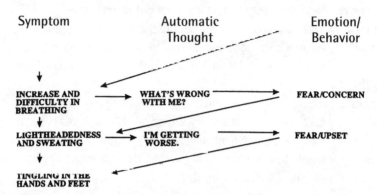

Figure 7. Rosemary's panic sequence: Phase 2.

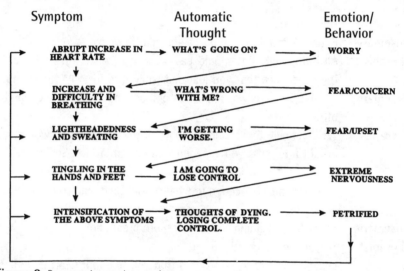

Figure 8. Rosemary's complete panic sequence.

Therapist: Great—so we have the initial sequence of what occurred with you during the first few seconds of the attack. Let's get this down on paper: [See Figure 6.]

Therapist: So, what do you think so far—does this look accurate to you?

Rosemary: Yes, very accurate. The more that I think about it, that's exactly what has been happening to me each time.

Therapist: Okay then, let's continue. So next, we have what?

Rosemary: Ah, I am not really sure.

Therapist: Well, let's go back and look at those Beck Anxiety Inventories that you filled out and also at what we captured on paper during the panic induction.....All right, we have marked here, "increase and difficulty in breathing" and "lightheadedness and sweating." Do you agree?

Rosemary: Yes, this seems right.

Therapist: Okay—now we need to attach the thought and emotion-slash-behavior to each of these.

[See Figure 7.]

The process is then continued all the way through to the last symptom that Rosemary can recall experiencing, which, in this case, was a tingling in the hands and feet. Vectors are then drawn from these last symptoms to all aforementioned symptoms, automatic thoughts, and emotions/behaviors to depict a continuous cycle as in Figure 8. [See Figure 8.]

As can be observed, this figure depicts the escalation process of the panic cycle in this particular case involving cognitions and affect as well as behaviors. The connection is demonstrated via the vectors drawn. Vectors are also drawn downward from each sensation in order to indicate the sympathetic chain that occurs autonomically in this process, aside from the escalation caused by thoughts, emotions, and behaviors. This eventually leads to the completion of the entire diagram (Figure 8).

This technique has a number of therapeutic effects aside from allowing the panic sufferer to see the sequence of events graphically. It also allows for the individual breakdown of each symptom so that the patient and therapist can both intervene at various levels, particularly when attempting to restructure specific catastrophic misinterpretation.* It may also be easier for the therapist and patient to collaboratively rewrite new cognitive interpretations and substitute alternative emotions and behaviors.†

Paradoxical Intention

Paradoxical intention, originally developed by Frankl (1984), is much like symptom induction in that it involves a behavioral prescription for

---

*This complete intervention is portrayed in detail on videotape: Dattilio, F. M. (1996), SAEB.
†Excerpt reprinted with permission from Dattilio, F. M. (1994).

clients to perform responses that seem incompatible with achieving the goal for which they are seeking help. The specific difference, however, is that in paradoxical intention, patients are asked to exaggerate their anticipations rather than behaviorally to induce the symptoms by deliberately hyperventilating. For example, individuals who experience panic attacks and fear that they may die suddenly or become "overwhelmed" would be instructed to "go ahead and let themselves die" or do whatever they fear they might do (Dattilio, 1987). After several attempts, they often discover that they are unable to achieve the feared response, and their anxiety diminishes. At this point, many patients are able to perceive the ridiculous or irrational aspect of their apprehensions, which is strongly encouraged by the therapist. They are then instructed to repeat this same procedure in selected settings at graded levels of panic-evoking situations until they have few or no symptoms. The technique also differs from symptom induction and deescalation in that there is no deescalation of symptoms and no instruction on the use of controlled breathing as an anxiety-reducing agent. In fact, it poses the opposite approach to the patient, with the reliance on the paradoxical focus itself as the trigger in reducing anxiety (Dattilio, 1987; 1994a).

Paradoxical intention has at times been rather loosely defined in the literature, particularly since it has been utilized by therapists of varying theoretical orientations who conceptualize it quite differently (Dell, 1981; Efran & Caputo, 1984; Ascher, 1984; Dowd & Trutt, 1988; Sexton, Montgomery, Goff, & Nugent, 1993). More specifically, the debate appears to center around whether or not the "intention" referred to is the patient's or the therapist's. This issue is fully discussed by Dowd and Trutt (1988) and the intention was clearly defined earlier by Frankl (1975) as being the patient's. Thus, the technique of paradoxical intention may fall more clearly within the bounds of a cognitive intervention, since it first forces a behavioral change, which is followed by a restructuring of cognition upon reflection on the implication of the behavioral change. This point has been challenged, however, by others (Bandura, 1977), who argue that the behavioral change precedes the restructured cognition.

In the case example below, the technique is described in detail.

Case Example: A Physician on Overload

Jack, a 46-year-old, married physician, had experienced dozens of panic attacks, sometimes three attacks per day within a two-month period, prior to referring himself to psychological treatment. A comprehensive physical, including a cardiovascular and neurological examination by two colleagues, yielded negative results and Jack concluded that psychotherapy was the best alternative, particularly because he preferred not to rely on medication, even though he had often prescribed medication for his patients for similar symptoms.

Jack's first panic attack occurred quite abruptly while he was on a hunting trip in the Canadian mountains, a trip that had been planned almost a year in advance. The week before the trip, Jack carried an unusually heavy work load, doubling up on his patient schedule in order to prepare for 10 days away from his busy practice. Consequently, Jack was on overload, and his fast-paced life came to a screeching halt on the drive to Canada.

It was during his first day in the wilderness that Jack had his initial symptoms—many of the typical characteristics of panic, along with a feeling of "floating outside of his body" (a common panic symptom). His second attack took place 12 hours later, and then a third attack after a 24-hour interval. His attacks occurred in different places, with each new attack more intense than the previous one. Jack, as a physician, first considered all of the medical problems that might cause such symptoms. When he was unable to come up with a satisfactory explanation, he checked into a hospital in the closest Canadian town and sought consultation with the emergency room physician. After a thorough physical and neurological examination, including blood and platelet studies, a thyroid scan, and an electrocardiogram, revealed nothing abnormal, Jack returned home and referred himself to a clinical psychologist.

What Jack had experienced was a typical example of panic disorder. One-hour sessions were conducted once a week in a clinic office. The initial session involved a detailed behavioral analysis designed to acquire the information necessary for treatment. As many data as possible were gathered about the nature of his panic attacks through questions regarding Jack's previous experiences with anxiety, and whether he had a history of emotional or behavioral problems. In the second and third sessions, a detailed hierarchy was developed, indicating the specific anxiety-producing situation that elicited attacks for him (e.g., traveling away from home). He was instructed to rate the amount of anxiety that each situation would produce, using a scale ranging from very little or no anxiety (0) (e.g., walking in the neighborhood) to the most intense anxiety-producing situation he might face (100) (e.g., traveling out of the country).

Once the hierarchy was developed, in the fourth session the therapist instructed Jack to expose himself directly to the least-feared situation and to allow himself to become anxious without attempting to interfere with his anxiety. If he found himself wanting to avoid it physically (by leaving) or cognitively (by imagining himself being somewhere else), he was to concentrate on making his anxiety worse. If his anxiety intensified and he felt his usual symptoms of tightness in the chest, sweatiness, and shortness of breath, he was to exaggerate those symptoms as much as possible. This is the premise on which paradoxical intention is based. The patient is requested to do the opposite of what he or she might be inclined to do (i.e., avoid the attacks) by seeking help or taking medication. It was explained to Jack that deliberately intensifying the symptoms would eventually reduce his anxiety and weaken his attack, since his symptoms had no medical etiology and, therefore, were based on a catastrophic misinterpretation of bodily sensations.

Each time Jack attempted to exaggerate his attacks, he was unable to do so. Consequently, his anxiety and panic sensations diminished significantly. The same method was repeated during sessions 5–10, through the hierarchical levels, until Jack no longer had panic attacks or feared that an attack might occur spontaneously. The six one-hour follow-up sessions involved repeated exposures, even though no symptoms were present.

Figure 9 depicts how Jack's panic attacks quickly declined after exposure treatment and were still nonexistent six months after treatment

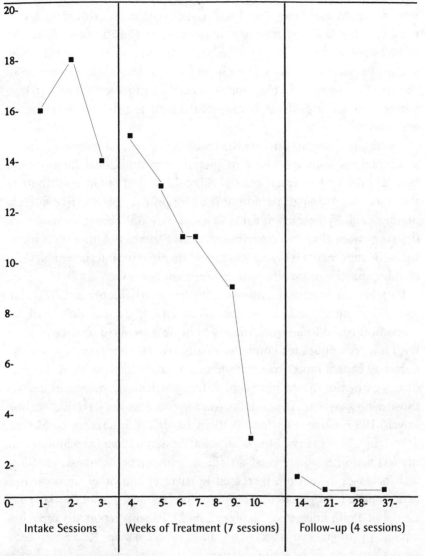

Figure 9. Jack's panic attacks.

with no residual symptoms. This is believed to be a direct result of the paradoxical technique since no other insight-oriented therapies were used. The therapist also maintained a rather formal and subdued atmosphere throughout treatment so that no other variables (e.g., client–counselor relationship) would be construed as creating change.

Essentially, it is important for therapists to educate clients on the nature and properties of anxieties, helping them to understand that anxiety is limited and benign and will not hurt them regardless of its intensity. This was particularly important in Jack's case since his knowledge of the body's metabolism was extensive. Also, the client should be taught the actual mechanics of the technique so that he or she clearly understands that both the actual exposure to the feared situation and the use of the paradoxical intent are the key to reducing symptoms.

Finally, it is important that the therapist conduct a thorough behavioral analysis with the client to identify any additional factors (e.g., marital problems or interpersonal difficulties) that might contribute to the disorder. Although paradoxical intention may be effective in eliminating panic symptoms in some cases, it may not always focus on underlying issues that can contribute to panic attacks. A more schemata-focused approach involving cognitive therapy or interpersonal skills training may be more effective if symptoms continue.

Paradoxical intention appears antithetical to the other CBT treatments for panic, such as symptom induction, deescalation, and the relaxation-based techniques, mainly because it seems to provide patients with few techniques for coping with anxiety. However, certain individuals may benefit more from paradoxical treatments than others because of the extinction-based philosophy. It is particularly recommended for those who may experience relaxation-induced anxiety (Heide & Borkovec, 1983; Cohen, Barlow, & Blanchard, 1985; Lazarus & Mayne, 1990), in which many of the traditional anxiety-reducing techniques are ineffective. Such side effects as tingling, numbness, dizziness, paradoxical increases in tension, increased heart rate, and other untoward reactions have been reported with relaxation-based treatment (Borkovec & Grayson, 1980; Edinger & Jacobsen, 1982). Patients reportedly often lose interest in progressive muscle relaxation or fall asleep. Relaxation techniques can even evoke seizure activity or traumatic memories, which may undermine the intention of the treatment (Kiselica & Baker, 1992).

Paradoxical intention would also be recommended for patients who appear resistant to techniques that involve actual symptom induction, as well as for patients with a history of cardiovascular disorders. Even though paradoxical intention encourages the symptoms to worsen, there is no direct induction of symptoms (e.g., overbreathing); thus, the likelihood of cardiovascular stress is reduced. It is, therefore, suggested as an alternative treatment when induction is contraindicated and when an expedient intervention is required, such as with crisis situations.

Symptom induction, deescalation, breathing retraining, and paradoxical intention are all nonpharmacological techniques that may be invoked for the rapid amelioration of panic symptoms in emergency and crisis situations. In combination with exposure and/or pharmacological interventions, these techniques may prove to be the most efficacious (Brown, Rakel, Wells, et al., 1991).

Nontraditional Approaches

Eye Movement Desensitization and Reprocessing

A new method that has shown benefit in the treatment of traumatic memories and has recently been explored as a potential intervention in panic disorder is Eye Movement Desensitization and Reprocessing (EMDR) (Shapiro & Forrest, 1997).

Developed by Francine Shapiro (1989), EMDR is an integrative exposure and cognitive reprocessing procedure that was initially used for treating traumatic memories.

In her 1995 book, Shapiro explains that while walking through the park one day in May 1987, she noticed that some disturbing thoughts suddenly disappeared. She also noticed that when she deliberately brought these thoughts back to mind, they were not as upsetting or as valid as they had been previously. Shapiro began to pay close attention to her behaviors and discovered that when disturbing thoughts came into her mind, her eyes spontaneously started moving very rapidly back and forth in an upward diagonal. Again, the thoughts disappeared upon doing this, and when she brought them back to mind, their negative charge was greatly reduced. Shapiro then began making the eye movements more deliberately while concentrating on a variety of disturbing thoughts and memories. She found that these thoughts also disappeared and lost their charge. Subsequently, Shapiro began to try the eye movement on other people and found that it had the same positive effects.

This serendipitous discovery is similar to the one made by the founder of the speed-reading technique, Evelyn Wood. Wood developed her revolutionary method of speed reading after she had accidentally dropped a book on the ground. She picked it up and, as she brushed the dirt from the page, noticed that she had quickly retained the contents of the page by following the brushing motion of her hand (Frank, 1990). This led to her eventually developing one of the most effective speed-reading programs in the world.

Shapiro initially developed EMDR while working with some 70 people over the course of about six months, with refinements added over the past 10 years. Consequently, she was able to develop a standard procedure that consistently succeeded in alleviating patients' complaints. Since the primary focus of EMDR was on reducing anxiety, this became the targeted population. Shapiro has reported encouraging results of EMDR in the treatment of posttraumatic stress disorder (PTSD) (Shapiro, 1996, 1998a). Recent controlled studies show that 84–90% of trauma victims who have PTSD improved after the equivalent of three 90-minute sessions (Marcus, Marquis, Sakai, 1996; Rothbaum, 1997; Scheck, Schaeffer, & Gillette, 1998). Case series (Lazrobe, Kite, Triffleman, et al., in press) by other investigators support the notion of EMDR as a powerful treatment tool for PTSD (Wolpe & Abrams, 1991; Marquis, 1991).

In contrast, other studies yielded less favorable outcomes with Vietnam veterans with PTSD (Boudewyns, Stwertka, Hyer, et al., 1993). There are significant problems with the methodology of these studies, however. For example, researchers used one or two applications in only one or two sessions of EMDR as opposed to the full range of treatment that is prescribed in EMDR training. In a more recent study, Carlson and colleagues (Carlson, Chemtob, Rusnak, et al., 1998) compared the effectiveness of two psychotherapeutic interventions for PTSD using EMDR and biofeedback-assisted relaxation on a randomized controlled-outcome group. The researchers found that at posttreatment and/or nine months' follow-up, combat veterans diagnosed with PTSD who received EMDR treatment improved much more than did veterans in routine clinical care or in biofeedback-assisted relaxation treatment alone. Seventy-five percent of the EMDR group no longer had PTSD.

Sanderson and Carpenter (1992) also tested the contribution of eye movement to the effects of a simplified version of EMDR. They compared EMD with Image Confrontation, a procedure that purportedly differs from EMD only in that it requires subjects to keep their eyes closed and motionless. The two procedures were equally effective in reducing anxiety levels among phobic subjects. Note, however, that the EMD procedure applied in this study was akin to an imaginal flooding procedure with the addition of eye movement rather than the EMDR procedure introduced by Shapiro. Moreover, the overall time spent on EMD and on Image Confrontation was extremely brief, making it unlikely that differential treatment effects would be observed. Both groups received only seven applications of imaginal exposure, with or without eye movement, lasting 20 seconds each.

Acierno, Tremont, Last, and Montgomery (1994) attempted to address some of the procedural limitations in the aforementioned studies—namely, the simultaneous assessment of cognitive, physiological, and behavioral effects of EMDR—by using a different design. They applied a repeated within- and between-session tripartite assessment in a conceptual replication of Shapiro's 1989 study with a multiphobic individual. The results failed to produce clinically significant intra- and intersensory improvements beyond those produced by the control procedures on all dependent measures. The overall results did not support the effectiveness of EMDR. The results of this study may have been due to the fact that the procedure was flawed since the researcher used EMD instead of EMDR. This exception suggests that when EMDR is used in enough sessions, and in the manner that is prescribed, it is likely to be more effective (Shapiro, 1998). Such was the case in a more recent study that investigated a 15-month follow-up of the effects of EMDR on a population of PTSD individuals (Wilson, Becker, & Tinker, 1997). Initial treatment effects for both PTSD and partial-PTSD participants were substantial and were maintained over a 15-month period.

The method's popularity is growing, causing considerable controversy among clinicians and researchers. Most of the criticism pertains to the lack of construct validity (Kazdin, 1992) of EMDR; that is, the lack of clarity about causal relationships between the intervention components and the treatment outcomes.

It was fairly recently that Goldstein and Feske (1994) reported on the use of EMDR in the treatment of panic disorder. They initially selected seven panic-disordered subjects who were patients at an anxiety disorder clinic. The patients were treated with EMDR for memories of past and anticipated panic attacks and other anxiety-evoking memories of personal reference. Standardized report inventories and behavioral monitoring instruments were employed to measure changes with treatment. After only five sessions of EMDR, subjects reported a considerable decrease in the frequency of panic attacks, fear of experiencing a panic attack, general anxiety, fear of body sensations, depression, and other measures of pathology. These results sparked the authors' further investigation of the effectiveness of EMDR for panic.

In a subsequent study, the same authors (Feske & Goldstein, 1997) randomly assigned 43 outpatients diagnosed with panic disorder to six sessions of EMDR. A control group was assigned to the same treatment, but with the omission of the eye movement and with a waiting list. Posttest comparisons showed EMDR to be more effective in alleviating panic and panic-related symptoms than the waiting-list procedure. Compared with the same treatment without the eye movement, EMDR led to a greater improvement on two of five primary outcome measures at posttest. Unfortunately, however, EMDR's advantages had dissipated three months after treatment. Consequently, this fails to firmly support the eye-movement component of the treatment of panic disorder (Feske & Goldstein, 1997). Shapiro (1998) notes that Feske and Goldstein removed part of the treatment package in the research protocol, which may have made a crucial difference in the maintenance of effectiveness (e.g., self-control imagery, attention to physical stimuli, and log reporting). Had these been included in the study, they might have made a difference in the treatment outcome. This was the issue of debate regarding the efficacy of eye movement in the Feske and Goldstein (1997) article.

In summary, while there are solid empirical data on EMDR's efficacy for PTSD, much more work is necessary before it can be considered a viable alternative for treating panic.

EMDR Intervention Procedure

An eight-phase approach incorporating a complex methodology, EMDR requires that the patient engage in imaginal recall of the disturbing event and focus on associated affect, cognitions, and sensations while engaging in bilateral rhythmical stimulation (e.g., eye movement, tapping, or auditory tones). For a more detailed description, see Shapiro (1995).

After each set of stimulations, whose length depends on the client's feedback, is an eye-movement set, which usually lasts approximately 20 seconds; the patient then briefly reports on any change in the image or concurrent experiences and discusses the resultant cognitions, affect, and proprioceptive sensations. He or she then engages in the next set of eye movements (or shoulder tapping, etc.), during which he or she focuses on any new, spontaneously generated material. This cycle of imaginal exposure in conjunction with eye movement, followed by the patient's feedback, is continued until the patient no longer generates relevant associations, is feeling comfortable, and reports that the original memories fail to elicit discomfort.

In the case of panic, the EMDR procedure is maintained, but the standardized protocols are modified. There must be a standardized protocol for panic. In the study by Goldstein and Feske (1994), subjects received one 60-minute information-gathering session followed by five individual 90-minute EMDR sessions over a period of two weeks. During the initial session, the therapist identified relevant anxiety-prolonging memories, such as the first and the worst panic attack, life events that the subjects identified as related to the panic disorder, and anticipated panic episodes. Treatment started with the memory that elicited the highest level of discomfort.

The following is an excerpt from a session with a patient being treated with EMDR.

Case Example: Unidentified Stress

Jake, a 42-year-old warehouse supervisor, submitted to treatment after being referred by his physician. Jake had begun having unexplained panic attacks. His family practitioner, an osteopath, was reluctant to prescribe anxiolytic medication and referred him for CBT.

During the intake interview, a thorough history was taken and cognitive-behavioral analysis was conducted in an attempt to link Jake's panic symptoms to some type of psychological stressor. He had been cleared medically and it was determined that his symptoms were a result of stress. Surprisingly, however, Jake did not feel that he was stressed and he reported having a very satisfying life. He had a good job and had been happily married for more than 20 years. He said he had many friends and hobbies and enjoyed each day that life brought him.

Even though no specific stressor or trauma was identified, Jake was treated with a traditional course of CBT. He was taught deep progressive muscle relaxation and deescalation techniques. Jake worked collaboratively with the therapist and successfully alleviated his panic symptoms in only seven days.

Despite his rapid success, Jake remained troubled by his panic symptoms, and within six weeks, they returned, more intense than before. He had always been a "commonsense" type of guy and needed some sort of explanation for anything that happened. What disturbed Jake was that he was unable to identify any stress in his life, particularly leading up to the day that he experienced his initial attack. It was hypothesized that this was one factor that contributed to the return of his symptoms. On one occasion, Jake recalled this scenario: he had been standing in line at a local bakery, waiting to be served, when he felt an abrupt increase in his heart rate and an immediate sense of lightheadedness. He was overcome by a queasiness in his stomach and felt compelled to leave the store. His first thought was that he had the flu or a virus; however, his symptoms abated immediately when he left the bakery, with no residual sensations. Later, he thought that perhaps some aroma in the bakery had made him feel ill or that he even might be allergic to yeast or other baking supplies.

Unable to determine the etiology of Jake's attacks, the therapist presented the case at a clinic staff meeting, where it was suggested that the use of EMDR be considered. Because the therapist's knowledge of EMDR was limited, one of the senior staff members, who was fully trained on levels I and II of EMDR, offered to assist in several sessions.

With Jake's agreement, both his therapist and the senior staff clinician began to educate Jake on the rationale of EMDR and to explain its history and philosophy. Since a detailed patient history had already been obtained, the initial 90-minute session consisted of establishing a hierarchy that was similar to that which Wolpe had proposed in his early work with systematic desensitization (Wolpe, 1958). The range of the hierarchy was from 100 SUD (subjective units of discomfort), the worst panic episode that Jake experienced, to 10, which pertained to a situation that produced little anxiety or panic symptoms.

Treatment began with the memory that elicited the highest

level of discomfort, which for Jake was his initial panic attack while standing in line at the bakery. He was asked to focus specifically on the negative cognitions and the body sensations eliciting the emotion of fear. Once this was achieved, he was instructed to focus on the therapist's two fingers (index and forefinger), which were placed directly in front of Jake's face at a comfortable distance (approximately 12 to 14 inches). The therapist then began to move his fingers back and forth across Jake's line of vision. Once tracking was established, the speed of the therapist's movements was increased with the hand traveling approximately 12 inches on each sweep. Jake concentrated on this exercise, which consisted of 24 bidirectional, saccadic eye movements. At the conclusion, Jake was instructed to close his eyes and rest. Before the therapist could instruct Jake to "blank" the image out of his mind, he began to have autonomic symptoms, which included increased heart rate, sweating, and shortness of breath. When therapist inquired about what was going through Jake's mind, Jake burst into tears and began to describe a motorcycle accident that he had forgotten about and that had occurred some 20 years earlier.

In the early 1970s, Jake had been riding his motorcycle in Philadelphia when it began to drizzle. The rain fell quickly, making the hilly cobblestone street very slick. He had just crossed an intersection at the top of a hill where there was a set of trolley-car tracks when his Harley-Davidson slipped on the wet trolley tracks, causing him to lose control and to slide down the hill and end up under the front end of an oncoming trolley car. Jake lay trapped, with his leg pinned under the trolley car, for almost 20 minutes waiting for an ambulance. As he lay on the cobblestone street, passing in and out of consciousness owing to the excruciating pain, his eyes remained focused on the horizon of light-brown cobblestones, associating them in a remote way with the pain and agony of the accident. Apparently, he had repressed this image for 20 years until it was elicited by the EMDR exercise.

Jake realized that while he was waiting in line at the bakery, his eyes met the horizon of dozens of freshly baked loaves of Vienna bread on the racks. It dawned on him that this scene paralleled the earlier memory of lying in the street in pain with nothing but a horizon of brown, curved cobblestones, and that these resembled the loaves of bread arranged in a symmetrical pattern. This connection appeared to be the key to Jake's difficulty in overcoming his panic. He admitted that he never adequately dealt with the trauma of his accident and had subsequently given up riding a motorcycle.

The essential role of EMDR in this case pertained to the processing involved. Not only did it serve to uncover the trauma, but it allowed Jake to process it as well.

Virtual Reality and the Treatment of Panic Disorder with Agoraphobia

A new alternative to standard in vivo exposure for individuals who have panic with agoraphobic onset is known as virtual-reality exposure (VRE), which integrates real-time computer graphics, body-tracking devices, visual displays, and other sensory input devices to immerse a participant in a computer-generated virtual environment. Virtual-reality exposure is potentially an efficient and cost-effective treatment for anxiety disorders that has been gaining attention in the literature (Rothbaum, Hodges, Watson, et al., 1996). It was shown to be successful in reducing the fear of simple phobias in the first known control study on the treatment of a psychological disorder (Rothbaum, Hodges, Kooper, et al., 1995).

Although the use of virtual reality with panic disorder has not been studied, it is likely that its application for this disorder would be helpful.

The technique provides a new type of human–computer interaction in which users no longer are simply passive observers of images or stimuli on a computer screen, but become active participants in a computer-generated, three-dimensional, virtual world. New graphics and display technologies provide the user with a sense of presence or immersion in the virtual environment. The user is essentially presented with a computer-generated view of a virtual world that changes in a natural way with motions of one's head. A head-mounted display is most commonly used to create the virtual environment. Such displays consist of a separate screen for each eye, together with some type of display optics and a head-tracking device. A computer processes visual images and displays scenes consistent with the direction in which the user is looking within the virtual environment. For some environments, users may also hold a second position sensor that allows them to manipulate objects in the virtual environment. Virtual-reality exposure is a potentially efficient and cost-effective treatment for anxiety disorders. Although its use with panic has not been fully explored, it has been successful in reducing the fear of height in the first known controlled study of VRE and the treatment of psychological disorders (Rothbaum, Hodges, Kooper, et al., 1995). Outcome was assessed on measures of anxiety, avoidance, attitudes, and distress. Group differences were found on all measures, with the VRE group significantly improved at posttreatment, whereas the control group failed to show change. The efficacy of VRE therapy for fear of flying was also supported in a recent case study (Rothbaum, Hodges, Watson, et al., 1996).

Virtual-reality exposure was designed to be a component of a comprehensive treatment package and is recommended at that point in therapy when exposure therapy would be introduced. The treatment package includes a menu of virtual environments that can be used for agoraphobic patients that would be comparable to in vivo exposure situations (e.g., public places, open spaces).

The use of VRE has promise for panic disorder as well, particularly for those panicking individuals who experience agoraphobia or more elaborate forms of avoidance. Although the technique has not been perfected, it holds great promise for the future and is likely to be studied more aggressively in the next several years.

Thought Field Therapy

Among some of the latest nontraditional treatments for panic is a relatively new method known as Thought Field Therapy (TFT), which was developed by Roger Callahan (1996), and was originally called the Callahan Technique.

The development of TFT began around 1979 as a treatment for specific phobias. Since that time, it has been utilized to treat a variety of problems, including addictions, PTSD, depression, and panic disorder. This easy-to-apply technique involves algorithms or therapeutic recipes developed by Callahan over a number of years. According to Callahan, the procedures themselves were actually discovered through the unique TFT causal diagnostic procedures that address what Callahan believes to be the basis of fear and anxiety disorders. The technique has its origins in the bodily energy system, which Callahan claims has been well documented for centuries—the same system addressed by various meridian therapies, such as acupuncture.

Callahan reports that his initial application of this technique took place with Mary, a middle-aged woman who had such a severe case of hydrophobia (fear of water) that she was unable even to look at water on television without becoming extremely anxious. She also had a history of nightmares involving water, which began during her childhood. Callahan treated Mary for approximately a year and a half with traditional methods, such as systematic desensitization, cognitive therapy, rational-emotive therapy, hypnosis, and relaxation therapy. This treatment enabled her to sit by the side of a swimming pool, but with no reduction in her level of anxiety. During this period, Callahan began to explore the notion of the bioenergy system and the effect it might have on anxiety. Mary had complained about feeling a sensation in her stomach during therapy, something she had difficulty describing. Callahan assumed that this might have something to do with a disruption in Mary's stomach meridian. This meridian begins directly under the eyes and proceeds down the body and through the stomach, ending at the tip of the second toe on each foot. Therefore, it was Callahan's guess that if he tapped under Mary's eyes several times, the disruption in that meridian would be alleviated and there would be a shift in her experience of anxiety. Consequently, he proceeded to tap under Mary's eyes for approximately a minute—whereupon Mary exclaimed, "It's gone," referring to the "awful feeling" in her stomach. Astonished by her response, Callahan decided to put her case to the test. He claims that he used to have to drag Mary to the pool. After using this technique, however, she actually ran to the pool with enthusiasm. As Mary did not know how to swim, Callahan became apprehensive that she might jump into the pool and drown, and shouted nervously, "Mary, look out." She stopped, laughed, and said, "Don't worry, Dr. Callahan, I know that I don't know how to swim. I'm not going to jump in." Callahan claims that this was an important moment for him as he realized that this treatment did not cause people to act impulsively. He admits that, at first, he did not know what was going on, but, realizing that the procedure had eliminated Mary's fears and that her nightmares about water had disappeared, he recognized that something positive had occurred and that he was on track to an expedient cure for phobias. He also realized that he had to do further research before he could help clients with problems more complex than Mary's, but after assessing the application of the technique more thoroughly, he was able to develop his theories of how he could access certain meridian systems to reduce anxiety.

Callahan maintains that a core aspect of TFT methodology is the requirement that the patient think about or "attune" to the problem. If the specific psychological problem is not "attuned" at the time that treatment is being delivered, the treatment will accomplish nothing. However, if the patient thinks about a particular problem, and is able to feel negative emotion at that time, then tapping directly under one or both orbits of the eyes (approximately one inch below) can, in many instances, alleviate anxiety. The tapping, it should be noted, should not be strong enough as to cause pain. Callahan also recommends that one should then tap underneath the arm (approximately four inches under the armpit), which helps to reduce anxiety further. He recommends five or six taps at this location and then five or six taps right below the collarbone next to the sternum, which further facilitates the process. Individuals have reported a decline in the way they feel when thinking about their particular fear or anxiety after being tapped on these acupuncture points.

While tapping under the eyes, under the arm, and under the collarbone appears to help many people, Callahan contends that some have a block that makes treatment difficult. He refers to this block as "psychological reversal" and has devised a specific treatment for alleviating this condition as well. In this case, the patient is directed to tap on the side of the little finger of either hand while saying, "I accept myself even though I have this problem." Callahan has now discontinued the use of the affirmation in conjunction with the tapping on the side of the hand, however, Gallo (1998) believes that Callahan made this change in his method, which involves discontinuation of the psychological-reversal affirmation in response to various investigators who have claimed that TFT is at least partly a cognitive therapy that directly attempts to change the belief of the patient. Callahan asserts that TFT is not cognitively oriented.

Callahan, who was trained as a behaviorist, used traditional behavioral methods for years. Therefore, with TFT, he also utilizes a SUD scale (subjective units of discomfort) to assess the intensity of an individual's fear or anxiety level. He suggests a rating of 1 to 10, with 10 the highest level of distress. This is a major aspect of the assessment procedure. During assessment, TFT relies on a basic philosophy that is a mechanism for addressing the energy system, believed to be the fundamental cause of all negative emotion. Callahan states that his diagnostic procedure requires a yearlong training program in order to develop proficiency. Actually, the basic training takes only a few days, but the practitioner is offered telephone support for a year, as it takes time to learn how to do the procedure well.

The diagnostic procedure involves pinpointing specific energy sources and addressing specific fears, depression, and so on. It is called Thought Field Therapy because it actually addresses the thought field of a particular problem, such as panic. Callahan asks patients to think about their specific distress in its worst state—usually a 10 on the SUD scale. The client is then asked to rate the SUD (1–10) with regard to how he or she feels at the present moment while thinking about the problem, which does not necessarily have to be a 10 SUD.

Callahan believes that, in some cases, anxiety involves a process of "self-sabotage," or psychological reversal, and he addresses this in treatment when indicated. He believes that much of his success is attributable to the fact that he addresses psychological reversal immediately and has the patient correct it. Such correction involves tapping on the psychological-reversal spot on the outside edge of the hand, midway between the wrist and the base of the little finger, or at the point of impact if one were to administer a karate chop. Callahan states that psychological reversal is not a treatment for a psychological problem, but rather a procedure to eliminate a block that precludes treatment effectiveness. According to Gallo (1998), while the psychological-reversal treatment removes the block to other treatments, he has also found that, in many situations, simply utilizing the psychological-reversal treatment has resulted in a reduction of the identified problem itself.

Callahan admits that the tapping procedure may seem very strange, but it is based on methods of ancient acupuncture. He has found that when anxiety is addressed in the proper fashion and the right order, very often individuals can quickly reduce their levels of anxiety and fear. He claims that the treatment either succeeds or does nothing at all, and that TFT algorithms work best with phobias as opposed to more extensive anxiety disorders, which require the TFT causal diagnosis. Nevertheless, he urges people who suffer from panic disorders to attempt simple algorithms for the condition since "it won't hurt, and it might help." Even though he is less specific about the success rate for panic disorder, the basic theory is still applicable to anxiety disorder in general.

The following case scenario may provide some insight into how TFT would be applied to a case of panic attacks.

Case Example: A Memory of Trauma

Kate,* a 40-year-old woman married for the third time, entered therapy on the recommendation of her sister who had been treated earlier for physical-abuse trauma and social phobia. Kate was experiencing generalized anxiety and frequent, severe panic attacks, often several times a day, involving tension, tachycardia, difficulty breathing, and fear of losing her mind, or even dying. Kate was also phobic of driving and was anxious as a passenger. She had a history of alcohol abuse and was increasingly relying on alcohol to manage her anxiety.

In describing her first panic episode, Kate nervously related an event to the therapist that had occurred 10 years earlier. She and her second husband, whom she referred to as "the love of my life," were attending a work-related social event. As Kate was mingling with her colleagues, she noticed that a woman who was sitting next to her husband had her hand between his legs. The woman had been drinking heavily, and so had Kate's husband. "I was humiliated! I thought he'd get up and leave, but he didn't!" Kate said emphatically.

Almost matter-of-factly, Kate continued, "We got into a huge argument that night at home. We had both been drinking and my husband got so mad that he took a gun and put it to the

---

*Reprinted in part with permission from: Gallo, F. (1997). A no talk cure for trauma: Thought field therapy seems to violate all the rules. *Family Therapy Networker* (*MD*), March/April, 65–74.

back of my head and threatened to shoot me. All I can remember is yelling 'No!' He then backed off and I ran into the bedroom. Then he shot himself." Kate described the sound of the shot and said, "I heard a shot and came around the corner......and I couldn't believe it." She added in a monotone, "Him, there, in a pool of blood." Kate called 911 and the police and ambulance arrived a few minutes later. Initially, the police arrested her for murder before determining what had happened. Shaking her head in disbelief, Kate sighed, "There was a lot of confusion. I kept saying 'What am I going to do? What am I going to do?'" Her family lived in Pennsylvania, more than 2,000 miles away. Kate had a panic attack that night because, she recalled, when her sister finally returned her telephone call, she had to coach Kate how to breathe. Apparently, Kate was so upset that she was unable to talk over the telephone. Since that incident, Kate has had panic attacks and has never truly overcome the trauma that she experienced. She had never sought treatment as she believed that she could deal with the situation on her own.

The TFT therapist described the method of intervention for trauma relief and subsequent panic symptoms. It was explained to Kate that this technique was similar to acupuncture in the sense that she would learn to tap on points of her body that are believed to affect the body's bioenergy system. Since Kate was familiar with acupuncture, she understood some of the thinking behind TFT and felt that the therapy might be worth a try.

The initial step in working with Kate was to help her identify a target for treatment, an important link in the chain of events that holds a trauma together. Often this is the most painful moment, or an aspect of the experience that represents the entire trauma. Some individuals are easily treated upon thinking about the trauma as a totality, while others need to approach the event in a step-by-step, linear fashion.

In this case, the therapist began to inquire at what point Kate wanted to begin. In TFT, this is especially important for patients who feel violated and need to maintain control over the process. Also, securing the individual's permission and piquing his or her interest help to establish a strong working alliance.

Thought Field therapists believe that when one thinks about the entire memory, whether it be a trauma or an episode of panic, it often has different aspects. For example, in this case, there were a number of scenarios: Kate's husband holding the gun to her head, the argument, the moment she found him dead, and the way the police treated her when they arrived on the scene. Kate was asked to think about the events on a 10-point scale, with 10 being the worst level of distress and 1 being no stress at all. Next, Kate was asked to rate each event as she thought about it. Kate designated 10 as being the point at which she came around the corner and found her husband lying on the floor.

Kate was then guided through the initial stages of TFT algorithm, or what is known as a therapeutic recipe. This involved having her tap several times with two fingers at the following acupuncture energy meridian points in sequence: the inside edge of one eyebrow at the bridge of her nose (a point along the bladder merdian); on the bony orbit directly under one eye (the stomach meridian); four inches under an armpit (the spleen meridian); and under her collarbone, next to the sternum (the kidney meridian). This sequence of events was that derived by Callahan, who used a specific muscle-testing diagnostic procedure with a wide array of individuals who suffered from various traumas. This sequence, sometimes with some minor variations, has been found to be highly effective, and it is seldom necessary to use the diagnostic procedure itself with traumatized individuals.

This first series of tapping, which required less than one minute, was followed by the therapist's asking Kate to rate the same scene on the subscale and determine whether or not it had decreased in intensity from its original designation of 10.

Kate stated that she was still able to visualize the scene, however, she didn't feel the same fear that she had initially felt and she now rated it a "5."

The therapist then took her through the next step of the algorithm, which is known as the nine gamut treatments (9G). This step requires approximately 10 seconds to complete. It involved having Kate tap repeatedly at a point on the triple heater meridian, between the little finger and the ring finger knuckles on the back of her hand, while moving her eyes in various directions, humming, and counting. This 9G concept was also derived by Callahan from his muscle-testing procedure, and he considers it an essential aspect of the TFT algorithm architecture. Apparently, it usually produces additional relief or seems to tune in other aspects of the psychological problem that requires treatment.

Once again, Kate was asked to rate her level of distress while visualizing her husband lying on the floor. With no trace of surprise, she reported, "It's gone! It's now down to 1." Kate was asked subsequently to identify any remaining distress. She rated the moment when her husband held the gun to her head and designated that once again as a level of 10. Within seconds, using the same sequence as before, Kate's distress was gone. "There's no fear when I think about it. Not the old butterflies. I'm not getting them." Kate paused and then stated, "It's there, I can see it clearly, however, I don't have the same fear that was associated with it before." Kate contended that she had never been able to think about this scene prior to treatment and was truly astounded at the result.

The therapist then asked Kate to search for any other scenes from the series of events that still were distressing for her. She said that the incident in which the police treated her as a suspect was a particular image that disturbed her. The same sequence was repeated using the trauma algorithm with slight changes to incorporate her anger toward the police. Kate was also directed to tap on the radial aspect of her little fingernail (the heart meridian), since this is said to be beneficial in the treatment of anger. She subsequently reported that the anger was gone and she was able to rationalize that the officers were only doing their job.

Finally, Kate was asked to think about the argument that she and her husband had had just before the event. She rated this once again as a 10 because of her feelings of guilt. Within a few minutes of applying the same sequence of taps, the distress decreased from units of 10 to 6 and then to 4, 2, and eventually to 0.

Since it was the therapist's feeling that the basic trauma sequence was insufficient to alleviate all of Kate's guilt feelings, the "recipe" was adjusted to include the inside tip of her index fingernail (the large intestine meridian), another point identified as relevant in the treatment of guilt.

By the conclusion of this session, Kate was quite calm and relaxed, with a pleasant glow on her face.

A follow-up session with Kate the next week showed that memories of her husband's death no longer bothered her; she was feeling much less anxiety and the frequency and intensity of her panic had diminished significantly. However, the panic attacks had not been eliminated completely, and thus the therapist followed up by inquiring of Kate what might have triggered her subsequent attacks. Kate stated that her anxiety was compounded after her brother-in-law died of a heart attack following a argument that she had had with him over money. On the day that he died, Kate's panic attacks resumed and intensified. It is believed that this event, not only significant in and of itself, stirred up the unresolved trauma about her husband's death.

Once again the therapist proceeded with the trauma algorithm, having Kate tap on various meridians, which eventually eliminated her distress when recalling any of the images of the events.

At the conclusion of treatment, the therapist and Kate experimented with sequences of points, deriving an individually tailored algorithm that she herself could use to alleviate any anxiety and panic occurring before the next session.

At the third session, Kate reported that all of the traumas had been resolved and that she had even fewer instances of panic during the past week. Any residual symptoms lasted only seconds and were much less intense. Kate had successfully used the algorithm she learned in the past sessions to alleviate her residual anxiety. The resolution of panic symptoms apparently varies depending on the individual; some require repeated treatments over time, including self-treatment or what would be considered homework exercises.

Follow-up consisted of one contact one month posttreatment

and four additional monthly contacts. Kate reported doing quite well, stating that none of the traumatic events bothered her and the nightmares that she had been having were gone. She said she was panic-free and was able to drive without feeling any anxiety.

Fred Gallo, an expert on TFT, reports that results such as Kate's are quite common. The technique is best for experiences of trauma, and much of its success depends on the skills of the therapist, as well as on the specific follow-up procedure.

Despite the growing popularity of TFT, no controlled outcome studies have demonstrated its effectiveness. Hence research is needed to validate empirically its effectiveness for psychiatric disorders. Empirical validity is still the bedrock of acceptance in the scientific community, and for this reason, the efficacy of TFT remains questionable. Clinicians using TFT should exercise the technique with caution.

Interpersonal Psychotherapy

Interpersonal Psychotherapy (IPT) is a nondirective, but focused approach recently proposed as an alternative or adjunct to CBT strategies with panic (Van Rijsoort, 1997). Originally devised to treat depression, it since has been proposed as an alternative in the treatment of panic disorder. It focuses primarily on identifying and modifying those interpersonal problems that are thought to be responsible for episodes of depression. In addition, a major focus is on specific difficulties that individuals have in forming or maintaining relationships and that lead to symptoms of anxiety or depression.

The strategies of IPT are somewhat vague, however, they essentially involve three phases of treatment. Initially, the individual is diagnosed with the disorder using a medical model that is explained to the patient in detail. A major problem or a focus area associated with the onset of the disorder is identified and an explicit treatment contract is established with the patient. In the interim phase, the focus of treatment is primarily on major and current interpersonal problems with which the individual is struggling around the symptoms of anxiety. The third and final phase involves the patient's feelings about the termination of treatment, a review of the progress made, and an outline of the remaining work.

To date, there have been two empirically related studies in which IPT was compared with CBT. One, conducted by the National Institute of Mental Health (NIMH), was a large multisite study of the effectiveness of CBT and IPT for treating depressed outpatients (Elkin, Shen, Watkins, et al., 1998). In all treatment situations utilized in the study, it showed significant change from the pretreatment to posttreatment phases and found no significant differences between IPT and CBT.

Additionally, Fairburn and colleagues (Fairburn, Jones, Peveler, et al., 1991) compared IPT and CBT for the treatment of bulimia nervosa and at the end of treatment found IPT to be the less effective of the two. Eventually, however, IPT caught up and was as effective as CBT 12 months and six months later. This finding suggests that IPT may have a delayed effect, but nonetheless maintains a powerful effect that may be comparable to that of CBT.

As a result of these findings, researchers at Universiteit Maastricht in the Netherlands have used IPT as an alternative treatment for panic disorder without agoraphobia. The major theory contends that panic disorders are associated with the fear of addressing interpersonal issues and that individuals become "stuck" in the anticipatory phase of anxiety. The object of treatment thus is to help people face the issues that they are avoiding and to resolve their problems with a hope that their panic symptoms will dissipate.

The theory states that role disputation and transition are the two main interpersonal problems that mark the onset of panic disorder. Interpersonal deficits appear to be the central focus of this modality for panic disorder; this is in association with the fear of interpersonal interaction.

The following case study illustrates how IPT is used in the treatment of panic.

Case Example*: Difficult Family Relationships
Ms. B., a 61-year-old, married woman, and a grandmother, reported having had a panic disorder since the death of her father 20 years earlier. She would experience panic attacks on and off, with their frequency having escalated to one attack every two

---

*This case was adapted from a presentation given by Van Rijsoort at the European Congress of Behavior and Cognitive Therapies, October 1977, Venice, Italy.

weeks by the beginning of treatment. The patient began to avoid situations where she expected that she might have a panic attack. She also tended to be very dependent on others, which became more pronounced with the intensity of her panic.

Her specific fear of fainting and choking was a major concern, together with the anticipation that she might die of a heart attack while alone. Ms. B., the eldest of eight children, when younger had been given the responsibility by her mother for raising her siblings. Her relationship with her mother was characterized by a fear of being manipulated. She described her mother as an egocentric woman who never said anything positive to her. Her relationship with her father, whom she considered a warm and loving man, was much better. His unexpected death at an early age was a great shock to Ms. B. Her mother died approximately six years before Ms. B. entered treatment.

Ms. B. had never learned to take her own needs seriously and always tried hard to take care of others first. She also tended to avoid anything that would turn out negatively and so would proceed with caution when embarking on most activities.

The initial phase of treatment involved the therapist's exploring the interpersonal problems that contributed to Ms. B.'s panic disorder. It became evident that there were many conflicts in the family, particularly over the issue of inheritance when her mother died. Apparently, the mother had willed money only to her sons. Ms. B. was furious over this and, with the support of her sisters, initiated a lawsuit to contest the will. She lost the suit, which reinforced the dissension in the family, causing her to lose contact with one of her brothers. Another brother died during the course of the suit, creating a great deal of emotional turmoil for Ms. B. While telling this story to the therapist, she became extremely emotional, but stated that she felt relieved that she could talk about it and found comfort in the fact that someone took a serious interest in her life. Subsequently, this conflict became the focus of therapy.

The intermediate phase of treatment focused on the exploration of different options and on handling the conflicts that were stressing Ms. B. A great deal of emphasis during treatment was also placed on helping her become more aware of her feelings and of what she really wanted out of the conflict. It was determined that Ms. B. was inclined to avoid direct confrontations, and that, if she wanted to feel better, she needed to start talking about her anger at and her sadness about her siblings. The therapist also helped Ms. B. to prepare for confrontations via assertiveness training. Role playing was used in preparation for the confrontations with her siblings. She also talked about her anger regarding the brother who had died. Confidence building was another aspect of treatment and was achieved through specific exercises for reducing her dependency on others.

The final phase of treatment involved reviewing the effects of the above with Ms. B. Focus was also placed on emphasizing and reinforcing her self-confidence and encouraging her to continue practicing her confident, self-assertive attitude. At this point, she reported an absence of panic attacks during the last four weeks of therapy and was urged to continue taking risks and doing things that caused her anxiety.

The results of this case study indicated a decreased response on the Fear Survey Questionnaire and the Symptoms Checklist-90 (SCL-90), as well as for state anxiety on the State Trait Anxiety Inventory (STAI). This was attributed directly to the treatment.

The Universiteit Maastricht researchers infer that Ms. B. became more independent and self-confident, which directly contributed to the reduction of her panic and avoidance. No form of exposure therapy was encouraged. There also was no emphasis on specific interoceptive cues of panic or techniques for the reduction of autonomic symptoms. The only aspect of the treatment that was similar to behavioral techniques was the reinforcement of Ms. B.'s exposure to those things that she feared, as well as the assertiveness training. From the IPT perspective, when interpersonal problems are addressed and the dilemmas are solved, panic and avoidance lessen. It is also believed that the solving of interpersonal conflicts generalizes to the symbolic conflict represented by panic, which leads to eventual self-exposure and anxiety reduction. However, no systematic empirical evidence is available to support such an assumption.

The technique has only recently been introduced as a potentially effective intervention for treating panic disorder. Until more empirical outcome studies are conducted, its effectiveness remains unknown.

Stress Control—a Large-Group Didactic Approach

A relatively new approach to treating anxiety has been developed by a group of clinicians at the Glasgow Community and Mental Health Services in Scotland (White, Keenan, & Brooks, 1992.)

Stress control is a two-hour succession program utilizing CBT techniques that are designed as a pragmatic alternative to coping with the anxiety. This program was established to accommodate the large number of anxiety-disordered patients referred to primary-care services by alternative sources. The therapy sessions employ a strong didactic approach that combines elements of traditional group therapy and a more innovative, educational forward/self-help package.

The aim of the stress-control program is to teach patients about the nature of anxiety and the method for controlling it in a didactic setting. The long-term goal is to turn the individual into his or her own therapist, providing him or her with the education and skills necessary to overcome anxiety. Patients are explicitly told that they do not have to speak if they do not want to while participating in the groups. Any contribution is optional. They are also instructed not to discuss personal problems during the group sessions, but primarily to absorb the didactic information that is presented to them. They are also informed that stress control is a complete therapy and that no further help is available upon completion of the course. The participants are given a detailed 154-page booklet, which is divided into information and treatment sections that provide information on anxiety and summarize the content of each session of the course. In addition to the discussion of anxiety management, information on the control of panic is included. The booklet also acts to generate realistic expectations and to aid in the retrieval of information discussed during sessions.

All patients are assessed individually prior to the course. The Anxiety Disorders Interview Schedule for DMS-IV (Barlow, DiNardo, et al., 1985) is used for research projects and a shorter, 40-minute clinical interview for routine clinical work. If suitable, patients are given the booklet, assessment forms, and other information at the time of the interview. Stress control is considered the treatment of choice for patients with DSM-IV principal diagnosis of generalized anxiety disorder, panic disorder (with or without agoraphobia), and social phobia. This method is routinely used as an adjunct to individual therapy for those suffering from PTSD, OCD, major depression, or dysthymia.

The group typically involves approximately 20 individuals, but has been as large as 40 to 60 individuals. The clinicians who developed this program suggest that the larger the group, the better, as that often allows an immediate reconceptualization of the problem and self-perception (White, Keenan, & Brooks, 1992).

The group process utilizes the following format.

Session I.   The nature of anxiety:
              Introduction to the course.
Session II.   Controlling your body:
              Progressive muscle relaxation based on the protocols of Bernstein and Borkovec (1973). A cassette is supplied for home use.
Session III. Controlling your thoughts:
              The nature of anxious thinking, identification, and monitoring of the automatic thoughts. Based on the cognitive approaches of Beck, Emery, and Greenberg, (1985) and Meichenbaum (1977).
              Controlling your thoughts; controlling anxious thinking and rational reprisal.
Session IV.   Controlling your actions:
              Exposure, finding hidden problems, problem solving.
Session V.   Controlling your panic attacks:
              CBT based on Clark, Salkovskis, and Chalkley (1985), and including respiratory control.
Session VI.   Controlling depression, insomnia, and the future:
              Cognitive-behavioral advice, including stimulus response, paradoxical intention, and cognitive and behavioral rehearsal.

The format of the typical session is outlined in the following.

- Review: discussion of previous sessions and homework.
- Education: therapist talks in detail about session topic (e.g., nature of negative self-statements, avoidance, etc.).
- Therapy: based on a lecture format, this involves teaching specific skills to be used to deal with the session topics (e.g., progressive relaxation, rational reprisal).
- Intermission.
- Workshop: patients are given the opportunity to practice the skills learned earlier (e.g., carry out technique to identify automatic thoughts, breathing exercises to help control panic).
- Review of session.
- Homework assignment relating to the session topic.

Stress control has been shown to be an effective treatment for generalized anxiety disorder in terms of both clinical outcome and cost efficiency (White, Keenan, & Brooks, 1992). White, Keenan, and Brooks (1992), in a comparative treatment-outcome study of generalized-anxiety-disorder patients, found a few differences among cognitive (CT), behavioral (BT), combined (CBT), and placebo–subconscious retraining (SCR) conditions of the therapy. Results of the process measurement and the unexpected improvement of patients in the placebo versions strongly suggest the importance of nonspecific factors (White, 1993; White, Brooks, & Keenan, 1995).

In a recent study with panic-disordered patients, 90% of the patients at posttherapy and 70% at six-month follow-up were panic-free and coping better on a range of measures (White, in press).

Although only one outcome study has been performed on the use of this approach in the treatment of panic disorder, it remains a promising alternative. There is good evidence that a large-group didactic anxiety-management program is a clinically and cost-effective approach to the treatment of the many chronically anxious patients referred to psychology outpatient clinics. The authors feel that this approach has further potential in the treatment of other types of disorders as well, and in the preventive treatment of patients with diagnoses of mixed anxiety and depression.

A more systematic assessment of outcome with other anxiety disorders, including panic, is under way, while a complete self-help version has been shown to be useful in the treatment of heterogeneous anxiety-disordered patients (White, 1997, 1995, in press).

Group Treatment

Group psychotherapy has gained increasing attention as an alternative treatment for panic disorder. Group formats vary in their approach from cognitive to interpersonal and psychodynamic modalities. Regardless of the modality, however, it is important that the therapist be properly trained in the treatment of panic disorder.

The research suggests that there is some support for the use of group therapy as opposed to individual treatment. Toseland and Siporin (1986) reviewed 32 studies in which clients were randomly assigned to individual or group treatment. The same modality and techniques were used with all subjects in both the group and individual formats. The results obtained in 75% of the studies demonstrated that the group format was more effective in 25% of the studies. Nowhere was it found that individual treatment was more effective than group treatment.

But even though group may be more effective, patients often prefer individual treatment. Among their reasons might be a feeling of embarrassment about letting others in on one's secrets, as well as the irrational fear that being exposed to individuals who are worse than themselves might exacerbate their condition. They also may fear that they will find out that they themselves are worse off than others in the group, and so avoid it.

Despite the avoidance by some patients of group treatment, research suggests that individual therapy is more beneficial when followed up by group therapy (Zuercher-White, 1997).

Panic disorder was treated in groups of four to five patients in a study by Telch and colleagues (Telch, Lucas, Schmidt, et al., 1993). The groups met for 12 sessions (each an hour and a half long) in an eight-week period. Clients were assessed at baseline, posttreatment, and six-month follow-up. On the basis of several outcome measures, it was found that 85% of the clients resolved their panic attacks, significantly more than those in untreated control groups. Full recovery was recognized in 63% to 80% of the clients who were exposed to treatment.

It was also reported that group CBT appears to be the most effective treatment for panic attacks (Evans Holt, & Dei, 1991). These researchers conducted a brief, intensive, two-day group in a formal workshop setting. Information was provided to clients, along with instructions in stress management and other techniques to gain mastery, including in vivo exposure and flooding techniques. Participants were also asked to set goals and were encouraged to be functionally independent. Outcome measures during posttreatment suggest that 48.6% of subjects were totally free of symptoms, with 36.5% improved enough to allow them to function normally.

Telch and associates (Telch, Lucas, Schmidt, et al., 1993) conducted a study that resulted in a greater proportion of panic-free subjects after being treated with group CBT as compared with treatment controls.

Typically, group treatments involve four to nine members per group and often have multiple leaders. Group treatment can be divided into segments and may last 12 to 16 weeks. Alternatives may involve two-hour open-ended group sessions. Other types of group treatment include medication support groups and consumer-run self-help groups.

In general, group psychotherapy may be considered at least as effective as individual treatment. In a detailed description of the specific group format for panic disorder, Zuercher-White (1997) outlines the work of a 14-session panic group that meets weekly for two hours per session, and works primarily from a CBT perspective.

Pharmacotherapy

As mentioned earlier, pharmacotherapy has been the medical treatment of choice in most settings involving acute anxiety or panic, particularly because many of the pharmacological agents, but especially the benzodiazepines, act so quickly (Liebowitz, Fyer, & Gorman, 1986). As you may recall, the refinement of the diagnostic criteria for panic originated partly in the early work of Donald Klein on the use of tricyclic antidepressants.

Currently, there exists some debate in the professional literature over the use of medication versus a nondrug treatment for panic. Some clinicians believe that medication should be used essentially for blocking panic attacks and that formal CBT methods are useful only when the individual has agoraphobia. Others, however, feel that medication should be used when functional therapies fail or when a person is believed to have a panic disorder that is attributable to an inherent chemical imbalance. What makes this issue moot is that there are data to support both perspectives, as well as the belief that maximum results will be achieved by a combination of CBT with medication. For a more detailed explanation and review of the current literature, see, for example, Barlow (1988) and McNally (1994). It would be prudent, however, to use the least invasive procedures, especially in light of some of the addictive potential of the benzodiazepines.

Table 21 (pp. 190–195) lists the various medications commonly used in the treatment of panic symtoms, together with their classifications, recommended doses, and effective actions.

Anxiolytic Compounds

Benzodiazepines

Probably the most common antipanic medications are the benzodiazepines. These have long been touted as the fastest-acting, most effective medication for blocking panic. They are also probably the most frequently distributed by physicians and hospital emergency rooms for patients complaining of panic attacks. Although discovered in the 1920s, two of the first benzodiazepines did not become popular until the early 1960s: diazepam (Valium) and chlordiazepoxide (Librium). Both of these compounds were considered low-potency benzodiazepines. The literature on the use of these medications for the treatment of panic is quite extensive, and it suggests that low-potency benzodiazepines are effective in reducing panic attacks if prescribed in high doses (Noyes, Anderson, Clancy, et al., 1984).

However, this poses a problem, because the drugs are highly sedating, and also may promote drug dependency.

In reaction to this criticism, a new classification of the compound known as high-potency benzodiazepines was developed in the late 1970s/early 1980s. These compounds are often five to 10 times more potent than diazepam, which allows them to bind with great efficiency at benzodiazepine receptor sites. They also possess anxiolytic properties, but are much less sedative than equivalent doses of the low-potency benzodiazepines. As with the other benzodiazepines, the high-potency benzodiazepine's synergistic effect with other compounds is very good,

Table 21. Medications Commonly Used in the Treatment of Panic Symptoms

Agent	Approved Indications	Dose Range (Average)	Rate of Onset	Half-Life (Hrs.)	Rate of Elimination	Side Effects
Benzodiazepine Anxiolytics						
Librium (chloradiazepoxide)	Anxiety Alcohol withdrawal Preoperative sedation	10–40 mg (5–10 mg (t.i.d.–q.i.d.)	Intermediate	Long acting	Slow	Fatigue Dizziness Weakness Drowsiness Ataxia
Valium (diazepam)	Anxiety Alcohol withdrawal Convulsive disorders	4–40 mg (2–10 mg b.i.d.–q.i.d.)	Rapid	Long acting	Slow	Same as above
Serax (oxazepam)	Anxiety Anxiety associated with depression Alcohol withdrawal	10–20 mg t.i.d.–q.i.d.	Intermediate	Short	Rapid	Same as above
Tranxene (chlorazepate dipotassium)	Anxiety Alcohol withdrawal Convulsive disorders (adjunct)	7.5–60 mg t.i.d.	Intermediate	Long acting	Slow	Same as above
Ativan (lorazepam)	Generalized anxiety Anxiety associated with depressive symptoms	1–6 mg daily	Intermediate	Intermediate	Rapid	Same as above
Centrax (prazepam)	Anxiety	20–60 mg (30 mg daily)	Slow	Long acting	Slow	Same as above
Xanax (alprozolam)	Generalized anxiety	0.5–6 mg (0.25 mg t.i.d.)	Rapid	Intermediate	Rapid	Same as above

Agent	Approved Indications	Dose Range (Average)	Rate of Onset	Half-Life (Hrs.)	Rate of Elimination	Side Effects
Benzodiazepine Anxiolytics						
Paximpam (halazepam)	Anxiety	60–160 mg (20–40 mg t.i.d.–q.i.d.)	Intermediate	Long acting	Slow	Same as above
Klonopin (Clonazepam)	Myclonia Antipanic	.25–3 mg daily	Slow	Long acting	Slow	Same as above
Nonbenzodiazepine Anxiolytics (Azaspirone)						
Buspar (buspirone)	Generalized anxiety	15–30 mg (5 mg t.i.d.)	Slow	Short	Rapid	Dizziness Headache Nausea Nervousness
Hypnotic Benzodiazepines (Insomnia)						
Dalmane (flurazepam)	Sleep Sedation	15–30 mg	Rapid	Long	Moderate	Drowsiness
Halcion (triazolam)	Sleep Sedation	0.125–0.25 mg	Rapid	Long	Moderate	Drowsiness Anterograde amnesia
Restoril (tamazepam)	Sleep Sedation	15–30 mg	Rapid	Long	Moderate	Drowsiness
Prosom (estazolam)	Slow Sedation	1.0–2.0 mg	Rapid	Long	Moderate	Drowsiness
Doral (quazepam)	Slow Sedation	7.5–30 mg	Rapid	Long	Moderate	Drowsiness

Table 21. Medications Commonly Used in the Treatment of Panic Symptoms *(continued)*

Agent	Approved Indications	Dose Range (Average)	Rate of Onset	Half-Life (Hrs.)	Rate of Elimination	Side Effects
			Nonbenzodiazepine Hypnotic (insomnia)			
Ambien (zolpidem)	Slow Sedation	5–10 mg	Rapid	Long	Moderate	Drowsiness
			Tricyclic Antidepressants			
Tofranil (imipramine)	Depression Enuresis	75–250 mg (75 mg daily)	Slow	Long acting	Slow	Drowsiness Dry mouth Constipation Lightheadedness
Norpramin (desimpramine)	Depression	100–200 mg Adults	Slow	Long acting	Slow	Same as above
Pamelor (nortriptyline HCL)	Depression	25–150 mg (25 mg t.i.d.–q.i.d.)	Slow	Long acting	Slow	Same as above
Elavil (amitriptyline) [endep]	Depression	75–250 mg (75 mg daily)	Slow	Long acting	Slow	Same as above
*Anafranil (clomipramine)	Obsessive-Compulsive	75–250 mg (150 mg daily)	Slow	Long acting	Slow	Same as above
Sinequan (doxepin)	Depression	75–250 mg (100 mg daily)	Slow	Long acting	Slow	Same as above
Desyrel (trazodone HCl)	Depression	50–300 mg (50–100 mg daily	Slow	Intermediate	Slow	Drowsiness Dizziness Nervousness Fatigue

Agent	Approved Indications	Dose Range (Average)	Rate of Onset	Half-Life (Hrs.)	Rate of Elimination	Side Effects
		Nontricyclic Antidepressants				
Prozac (fluoxetine)	Depression	20–40 mg (daily)	Slow	Long acting	Intermediate	Headaches Dizziness Anxiety Nausea
Wellbutrin (bupropion HCl)	Depression	50–150 mg	Slow	Intermediate	Intermediate	Seizures
Ludiomil (maprotiline HCl)	Depression	75–150 mg (75 mg daily)	Slow	Long acting	Slow	Dry Mouth Drowsiness Dizziness Nervousness
*Zoloft (Sertraline)	Depression	50–200 mg (daily)	Slow	Short acting	Intermediate	G.I. Upset Nausea Headaches
*Paxil (Paroxetine)	Depression	20–100 mg	Slow	Intermediate	Intermediate	Insomnia, Agitation, Tremor, Anxiety, Nausea, Diarrhea, Dry Mouth
Effexor (Venlafaxine)	Depression	37.5–200 mg	Slow	Intermediate	Intermediate	Same as above
*Luvox (fluvoxamine)	Depression	50–300 mg	Slow	Intermediate	Intermediate	Same as above
*Serzone (nefazodone)	Depression	100–500 mg	Slow	Intermediate	Intermediate	Same as above
Celexa (citalopram)	Depression	20–40 mg	Slow	Intermediate	Intermediate	Same as above
Remeron (mirtazapine)	Depression	15–45 mg	Slow	Long acting	Intermediate	Weight gain Sedation Somnolence

*Antiobsessional agents.

Table 21. Medications Commonly Used in the Treatment of Panic Symptoms *(continued)*

Agent	Approved Indications	Dose Range (Average)	Rate of Onset	Half-Life (Hrs.)	Rate of Elimination	Side Effects
Monoamine Oxidase Inhibitors (MAOI)						
Parnate	Major depression	30–60 mg (50–100 mg daily)	Slow	Intermediate	Intermediate	Drowsiness Dizziness Nervousness Fatigue
Nardil	Depression	15–90 mg (15 mg t.i.d.–q.i.d.)	Slow	Long acting	Slow	Dizziness Drowsiness Sleep disturbance
Antihistamines (Off-Label Used as Anxiolytics)						
Atarax, Vistaril (hydroxazine)	Antihistamine Anxiolytic Narcotic potentiator	10–50 mg	15–30 min. oral 5–10 min. IM–parenteral 1–3 min. IV–parenteral	~4 hrs.	6–10 hrs.	Sedation Ataxia Incoordination Dry mouth Double vision
Benadryl (diphenhydramine)	Antihistamine Sleep medication	25–100 mg	~45 min. initial oral		6–10 hrs.	Same as above
Calcium Channel Blockers (Antihypertensives)						
Tenormin (Atenolol)	Antihypertensive	25–100 mg	1–1½ hrs. PO	8–12 hrs.	16 hrs.	Same as Inderal
Catapres (Clonidine)	Antihypertensive	0.1–3 mg	3–5 hrs. PO 8–12 hrs. patch	12–16 hrs ~72 hrs.	16 hrs. 40–60% in 24 hrs.	Dry mouth Constipation Drowsiness/sedation

Agent	Approved Indications	Dose Range (Average)	Rate of Onset	Half-Life (Hrs.)	Rate of Elimination	Side Effects
Beta-Adrenergic Blockades						
Inderal (Propranolol)	Antihypertensive	10–80 mg	1–2 hrs. PO 3–5 min. IV	4–6 hrs.	<12 hrs.	Slow pulse Wheezing Cold extremities Depression

making them user friendly and relatively safe in case of an overdose. They are, however, lethal if combined with alcohol or high doses of antidepressant medications.

Among the most popular of these high-potency benzodiazepines is alprazolam (Xanax) (Ballenger, Burrows, DuPont, et al., 1988), the first high-potency benzodiazepine described as having antipanic efficacy. Its rapid onset of action and its tolerance rate provide a very positive side-effects profile and it has become an attractive alternative to many of the tricyclic antidepressants. There is also much less drowsiness associated with taking it. Alprazolam has proved its effectiveness in many outcome studies, the most prominent of which is the collaborative study conducted by the Upjohn Co. in 1992 (McNally, 1994).

One of the problems with alprazolam, aside from its addictive potential, is that the benefits completely vanish once the drug is withdrawn. In fact, it is reported that some patients are actually worse after their medication is discontinued as the frequency and intensity of panic attack may increase (Rachman, 1990). As with most of the benzodiazepines, there is also difficulty with withdrawal, which is particularly a problem when higher doses are taken for long periods.

Two other high-potency benzodiazepines that have become popular are lorazepam (Ativan) and clonazepam (Klonopin). According to the literature, both of these compounds produce rapid, significant, and equivalent reductions in the frequency and intensity of panic attacks. One of lorazepam's negatives is that, in some studies, 25% of the panic patients receiving it developed a major depressive episode, although their panic attacks ceased (Lydiard, Howell, Laraia, et al., 1989).

Clonazepam is probably the newest benzodiazepine on the market. One of its positive aspects is that its half-life is greater than that of alprazolam; also, it requires fewer daily doses than does alprazolam and some of the other benzodiazepines. It is considered, as well, to be one of the least addictive benzodiazepines available at the present time.

Nonbenzodiazepine Anxiolytics
Buspirone (Buspar) is an azaspirodecanedione derivative that apparently binds to serotonin and dopamine receptor sites in the brain and functions as a nonaddictive anxiolytic. Even though this is a very attractive quality, buspirone has yielded disappointing effects in panic trials. Clin-

ical trials suggest that it is more effective for generalized anxiety states as opposed to panic (Robinson, Shrotriya, Alms, et al., 1989).

In addition to buspirone, a number of azaspirones used in Europe include ipsapirone, gepirone, and tandospirone.

Some individuals have used buspirone for the residual effects of anxiety once the panic has subsided and benzodiazepine treatment has been titrated. Buspirone is also a treatment of choice during anxiety treatment when alcohol or substance abuse has been identified as a dual diagnosis.

Beta-adrenergic Blockades

Beta-blockers are often used in treating some of the peripheral vascular effects of anxiety, including lightheadedness, shakiness, and tachycardia. While their usefulness is minimal, some believe that their effects are sufficient to reduce those symptoms that are most threatening during panic (Kathol, Noyes, Slymen, et al. (1980). The results have been mixed at best (APA, 1998). Two such compounds in common use are propranolol (Inderal) and atenolol (Tenormin).

Two major studies underscore the ineffectiveness of beta-blockers with panic, and, in some cases, they have worsened the outcome as compared with exposure treatment (Noyes, Anderson, Cleary, et al. 1984; Hafner & Milton, 1977). Consequently, the literature remains somewhat ambiguous with regard to their level of effectiveness.

Calcium Channel Blockers

Verapamil (Calan, Isoptin)

Very little is known about the true effectiveness of calcium channel blockers for panic. Their main attributes are their antihypertensive and antiarrhythmic properties, which aid significantly in reducing panic in some cases, particularly when the symptoms are pronounced. Successful results have been achieved with regard to complaints of palpitations and hyperventilation.

Only one study to date suggests that calcium channel blockers have a clinically significant effect in reducing the frequency of panic attacks as compared with placebos (Klein & Uhde, 1988). Consequently, these compounds may be used for atypical cases of panic when only limited symptoms are displayed and/or when patients do not respond to other agents.

Antidepressants—Tricyclics

One of the first classes of medications to be used in the treatment of panic and anxiety was the tricyclic antidepressants. These psychotropic medications have been tested more thoroughly than any other drug class in the treatment of panic disorder and agoraphobia.

A number of tricyclics currently on the market are used in the treatment of panic and anxiety, including the following.

Imipramine (Tofranil)

Donald Klein was the first to document the beneficial effects of imipramine in the treatment of panic as a result of his landmark study and a number of empirical outcome studies that tested its effects on panic in agoraphobic patients (Klein, 1964). It was tested alone and compared with nonpharmacological treatments, including behavior therapy (Klein, Zitning, Woerner, & Ross, 1983). The results suggest that the combination of the two is the most efficacious.

Overall, most studies have shown that imipramine benefits panic-disordered potents with agoraphobia, at least when combined with exposure treatments. There is some question about the direct effects of imipramine and whether or not it acts more to reduce depressive symptomatology, thereby creating only a secondary benefit for panic. It is also felt that imipramine directly alleviates anticipatory anxiety, thus mitigating the effect of panic (Brown, Rakel, Well, et al., 1991).

Imipramine has been found to be more effective in the long run in treating panic, particularly where there is depression. Normal doses begin at 75 mg and may be increased to 150–250 mg per day. Side effects include some peripheral vascular effects, dry mouth, and sedation.

Desipramine (Norpramin)

Desipramine hydrochloride (Norpramin) is a tricyclic antidepressant that has received mixed reviews as to its effect as an antipanic drug. Kalus and associates (Kalus, Asnis, Rubinson, et al., 1991) reported that a placebo was found to be significantly better than desipramine. While the latter has been known to have some effect on panic patients, its effectiveness when used alone is very poor. Desipramine works best when combined with exposure and behavior therapy. Normal dosing starts at 25 mg and may be increased up to 300 mg per day, as needed— usually for individuals who have coexisting depression. Side effects may include orthostatic hypotension. Of the secondary amine tricyclics, it is generally the best tolerated (i.e., it has the fewest side effects).

Serotonin Reuptake Inhibitors

Clomipramine

Clomipramine (Anafranil) is a tertiary amine tricyclic that potentially blocks the reuptake of both serotonin and norepinephrine. This compound is a "chemical cousin" of imipramine, and is approved only for the treatment of obsessive-compulsive disorder.

Clomipramine appears to be effective in the treatment of panic disorder when combined with self-exposure and is noted for markedly reducing general anxiety. As one of the more serotonergic compounds, it has a greater antipanic efficacy than some of the noradrenergic compounds.

The usual dose for adults starts at 25 mg daily, and is gradually increased to approximately 100 mg during the first two weeks of administration. Doses can be increased over subsequent weeks to a maximum of 250 mg per day.

One of the down sides of clomipramine hydrochloride is its anticholenergic and sedative effects, and the fact that it may also cause moderate orthostatic hypotension.

Selective Serotonin Reuptake Inhibitors

Fluvoxamine (Luvox)

Fluvoxamine is a unicyclic antidepressant that selectively blocks the reuptake of serotonin. Although it has received more notoriety with regard to obsessive-compulsive disorders, it has recently been looked at as an effective treatment for panic attacks. A study by Den Boer and Westenberg (1990) found that fluvoxamine markedly reduced self-monitored panic attacks and subsequently diminished agoraphobic avoidance behavior. Other studies have supported this, particularly that by Black and colleagues (Black, Wasner, Powers, & Gabel, 1993), who compared fluvoxamine with a placebo and CBT, and got superior results.

The dose usually begins at approximately 50 mg per day, and is quickly titrated to 100 mg. This usually continues for one week, and then is increased to a maximum of 300 mg per day. Side effects may include headache, gastrointestinal problems (nausea, diarrhea, etc.), and sexual dysfunction.

Fluoxetine (Prozac)

Fluoxetine is a selective 5-HT reuptake inhibitor that reportedly is effective in many types of anxiety disorders, particularly OCD and panic. Other studies have suggested that patients have become panic-free after seven weeks of fluoxetine treatment (Gorman, Davies, Steinman, et al., 1987).

The normal starting dose for panic is 10 mg per day, in the morning, although some patients have been known to be able to tolerate only 10 mg every other day, as a starting dose. A liquid concentrate is also available that can be given in doses as low as 2–4 mg per day for panic disorder. Typically, doses do not exceed 80 mg per day. Indications are also very strong for its use with OCD and major depression, which often require a dose of 60–80 mg.

Fluoxetine is probably one of the most widely prescribed drugs in the world and has been touted as one of the antidepressant medications that are safe enough to be taken during pregnancy (Lydiard & Ballenger, 1987; Goldstein, 1995). More recently, fluoxetine has demonstrated effectiveness in low doses (5 mg per day) (Schneier, Liebowitz, Davies, et al., 1990).

Serotonin N Reuptake Inhibitor

Nefazodone HCl (Serzone)

Nefazodone, an antidepressant unlike the selected serotonin reuptake inhibitors, was originally designed for the depression of patients with associated symptoms of significant anxiety. It works presynaptically (5-HTZa) and as an antagonist postsynaptically. It has proved to have some effect on symptoms of anxiety and agitation during periods of major depression (Fawcett, Marcus, Anton, et al., 1995).

Doses usually begin at 50 to 100 mg, with titration up to 300 mg. Common adverse effects include some dry mouth, somnolence, nausea, and dizziness. Nefazodone may be an excellent alternative when patients have difficulty tolerating the tricyclic antidepressants or the selective serotonin reuptake inhibitors. Unfortunately, there is a lack of research supporting its effectiveness as an antipanic medication.

Monamine Oxidase Inhibitors

As an alternative to the antidepressants, the monamine oxidase inhibitors (MAOIs) have also been successful with individuals who suffer from panic associated with atypical depressive features, which include reverse vegetative symptoms. Monamine oxidase is an enzyme that deactivates monamines, such as serotonin, norepinephrine, dopamine, and tyramine.

The MAOIs phenelzine (Nardil), isocarboxazid (Marplan), and tranylcypromine (Parnate) are all antidepressants and are considered by many psychiatrists and psychopharmacologists to be good blockers of panic attacks. Doses range from 20 to 90 mg (Parnate, 20–60 mg; Nardil, 30–90 mg).

One of the deadly side effects of MAOIs is that consumption of any foods containing tyramine (such as aged cheese or red wine) while taking these drugs may result in a hypertensive crisis and death.

Some researchers believe that high doses of MAOIs and benzodiazepines are extremely effective in the early treatment of panic disorder (Sheehan, Ballenger, & Jacobsen, 1980). Like the tricyclic antidepressants, MAOIs have a latency of onset of action of approximately one month before any therapeutic effects are observed.

Other compounds, such as β-adrenergic blockers, have also been used to treat panic, with increasingly effective results.

Table 1 lists all medications that are prescribed for the treatment of panic.

Titrating Medication and Relapse

As with many medical conditions, panic is a relapsing, remitting disorder that is often precipitated by stressful life events. According to the literature, from 30% to 90% of individuals with panic disorder relapse within one year of the discontinuation of treatment (Roy-Byrne & Katon, 1987). Consequently, it is important to proceed with caution in titrating medications and combining adjunctive psychotherapeutic techniques in order to decrease the tendency toward relapse and withdrawal.

Typically, individuals are maintained on medication for six to 12 months subsequent to the stabilization and reduction of panic symptoms. It is beyond this point that gradual titration of the medication can be considered. Tricyclic antidepressants should be tapered by 25 to 50 mg every one to two weeks. Monamine oxidase inhibitors should be tapered by 10 to 15 mg (one tablet) weekly (Katon, 1992, p. 98).

Benzodiazepine therapy is a bit trickier during titration, particularly with panic-disordered individuals, because of its withdrawal effects. Rebound effects are particularly likely with compounds such as alprazolam. The recommendation for avoiding rebound effects is to treat panic disorder for at least six months and eventually to taper benzodiazepines slowly over the course of two months. If symptoms recur, readjustment to the stabilizing dose is recommended (Lydiard, 1988). It is important to note that the immediate cessation of benzodiazepines at higher doses may have deleterious effects, including the onset of seizure activity.

Katon (1988) recommends some additional strategies for dealing with difficulty in benzodiazepine titration. He suggests that the addition of carbamazepine at 400–800 mg daily will decrease benzodiazepine withdrawal symptoms, even if the benzodiazepine is tapered rapidly over four to seven days. The addition of a tricyclic antidepressant at therapeutic levels of 100–300 mg will also decrease the likelihood of rebound panic attacks with the tapering of benzodiazepines.

The combination of CBT techniques and pharmacological agents has been most successful in treating panic disorder. When pharmacological agents are used in conjunction with nonpharmacological techniques, it is recommended that a multicomponent treatment package be used, such as that described by Craske and Barlow (1990b). This program has four major components: (1) education and corrective information concerning the nature, etiology, and maintenance of panic; (2) CBT techniques aimed at helping the patient identify, monitor, and alter faulty appraisals of threat that contribute to panic; (3) slow diaphragmatic breathing as a way to reduce or eliminate physical symptoms that often trigger panic attacks; and (4) interoceptive exposure exercises designed to reduce patients' fear of somatic sensations through repeated exposure to feared bodily sensations. It is suggested that the program might be utilized in emergency settings as well.

Homeopathic Treatments

The word "homeopathic" is derived from the root *homeo*, which means "similar"; the suffix *pathein* means "illness."

Even though homoepathic treatments lack empirical evidence as effective interventions in the treatment of panic, we felt that it was important to include them in this section for several reasons. For one, many individuals have turned to homeopathy as an alternative to traditional medicine because of the untoward side effects caused by some of the compounds used to treat panic. Furthermore, additional research is being conducted on homeopathic remedies, both in the United States and elsewhere, owing to their increasing popularity. Therefore, it is our belief that clinicians should become more familiar with the properties and use of such remedies since it is likely that they will be employed more frequently in the future as an alternative to pharmaceuticals.

Homeopathic treatments adhere to the philosophy that the symptoms that one develops represent one's own way of fighting illness. Homeopathic remedies are derived from plants, flowers, animals, and minerals. The basic premise is to use such natural resources to restore the patient to a natural state of health. According to this philosophy, one's natural state is a healthy one and everyone has the ability to return to that state. Although some clinicians do not support the use of these remedies without psychological treatments, they often can be helpful as an adjunct to therapy. Clinicians should be aware of their properties, since some patients who arrive for treatment may be already using them.

Natural Herbs and Roots

In recent years, natural remedies have been the focus of much attention in the treatment of psychiatric disorders. Even though homeopathic remedies have been around for thousands of years, the spotlight now has been turned on their use as alternatives to traditional medicine and psychotherapy. Actually, of course, many modern medicines are derived from plants and roots.

Among a number of calming agents are four that have been receiving a great deal of attention in the media, particularly for the treatment of panic and anxiety: kava, tyrosine, melatonin, and St. John's wort.

Kava

The kava root (known scientifically as *Piper methysticum*) was first introduced to the West by Captain James Cook during his voyage to the South Seas in 1768. The actual origin of kava remains unknown, but it has been used by the Oceanic people of the Pacific islands, such as Micronesia, Melanesia, and Polynesia, for centuries. Kava drinkers report a pleasant sense of tranquility and sociability, and often also sedative and anxiolytic effects upon consuming larger amounts.

It is believed that the pharmacological actions of kava are due primarily to kavalactones or kava alpha-pyrones, which are found in the fat-soluble portion of the root. Kava extracts have been shown to exert significant benefits with regard to anxiety and panic, and possess no addictive potential (Connor & Vaughan, 1999).

Clinical Studies. Several European countries have approved kava preparations for the treatment of nervous anxiety, insomnia, and restlessness on the basis of detailed pharmacological data and favorable clinical studies.

In one double-blind study on anxiety, 29 patients were assigned to receive kava extract three times daily while another 29 patients received a placebo. Therapeutic effectiveness was assessed using several standard psychological measurement instruments. In this four-week study, those taking the kava extract evinced a statistically significant reduction in their symptoms of anxiety, including feelings of nervousness and somatic complaints, such as heart palpitations, chest pains, headache, dizziness, and gastric irritation. No side effects were reported with the kava extract (Lehman, Kinzler, & Friedman, 1996).

A more impressive placebo-controlled study involved 101 subjects diagnosed with anxiety at 10 different medical centers. Subjects were diagnosed with an array of anxiety disorders, including agoraphobia, specific phobia, and generalized anxiety, and were monitored using the Hamilton Anxiety Scale and the Adjective Mood Scale. The placebo group received a sugar pill three times a day while the clinical group received concentrated kava extract containing approximately 70 mg of active kavalactones three times daily. Subjects in the kava group demonstrated marked improvement in anxiety symptoms over the control group with eight weeks of treatment. In addition, the kava was tolerated quite well by the subjects, with few effects (Volz & Kieser, 1997).

Two additional studies have shown that, unlike benzodiazepines, alcohol, and other drugs, kava extract is not associated with depressed mental function or impairment in driving or in the operation of heavy equipment. It appears that kava actually improves mental function and, at the recommended levels, does not promote sedation (Singh & Blumenthal, 1997).

Even though there have been no studies to date assessing kava's true effectiveness with panic disorder, an investigation of its use in treating panic is under way (Dattilio, in progress).

Dosage. The dosage of kava preparations is based on the level of kavalactones. On the basis of clinical studies using pure kavalactones or kava extracts standardized for kavalactones, the recommendation for anxiolytic effects is 45–70 mg of kavalactones three times daily. For sedative effects, the same daily quantity (135–210 mg) can be taken as a single dose one hour before retiring. The substance comes in tablet form and also in a 125-mg spray.

Potential Adverse Effects. Although side effects are rare among users, they can occur, especially when kava is taken on an empty stomach and in very high doses for extended periods. The most common side effects are nausea and other gastrointestinal problems, headaches, dizziness, rash, and insomnia. Symptoms disappear with its discontinuation or use in dosages below 150 mg. Kava is not recommended for pregnant or lactating women.

Tyrosine

Tyrosine is a precursor of the neurotransmitters norepinephrine and dopamine. These neurotransmitters regulate mood, among a number of other functions. Tyrosine acts primarily as a mood elevator. A lack of

adequate amounts of tyrosine may lead to a deficiency of norepinephrine in the brain, which can result in depression and sometimes anxiety
(Wolf & Masnaim, 1983).

Tyrosine attaches to iodine atoms in the body to form active thyroid
hormones. Consequently, low plasma levels of tyrosine have been associated with hypothyroidism, which may produce symptoms that are
commonly found in panic disorder. Symptoms of tyrosine deficiency can
also include low blood pressure; low body temperature, such as cold
hands and feet; and restless-leg syndrome.

Supplemental L-tyrosine has been used for stress reduction, and research suggests that it may be helpful for chronic fatigue and narco-
lepsy. It has been used to help people suffering from anxiety, depression,
allergies, and headaches, as well as those undergoing withdrawal from
certain drugs, although there is very little literature to support its effectiveness for panic.

Individuals taking MAOIs, commonly prescribed for depression, must
strictly limit their intake of any foods containing tyrosine and should
not take any supplements containing L-tyrosine, as this can lead to a
sudden and dangerous hypertensive crisis. Also, individuals who have
a history of hypertension should avoid tyrosine.

Dosage The dosage for tyrosine is much like that for the other amino
acids. The starting dose is usually 500 mg daily, with an upper limit of
2,500 mg.

Potential Adverse Effects. Although tyrosine is not addictive, its side
effects may include irritability, headaches, constipation, nausea, and
stomach upset. Tyrosine is also not recommended for pregnant women.

Melatonin

Melatonin is basically a hormone that is produced by the pineal gland
in the brain. This gland contains pigment cells similar to those found
in the eyes, and reacts to periods of light and dark as transmitted to it
through the eyes and optic nerves. Because the pineal gland is responsible for indicating sleep as well as waking states, it has been called the
body's internal clock. Melatonin is produced primarily at night during
sleep. When darkness sets in, the gland produces a surge in melatonin

that goes to all parts of the body. In counterpoint, the pineal gland slows melatonin production when light hits the retina in the morning.

Melatonin is used primarily for individuals who have difficulty with sleeping, but it may also be used for those with anxiety (Connor & Vaughan, 1999). Although the benefits have not been substantiated, some have used it for difficulty with sleep as a result of anxiety. Those who experience panic attacks at night may consider the use of melatonin to reduce fitfull sleep patterns or early-morning awakenings. Melatonin aids in beginning the advancement of the REM sleep phase. It is an ideal agent because it is safe, is not habit forming, and does not cause grogginess or hangover effects in the morning. However, its long-term effects are largely unknown. There are no current studies demonstrating the effectiveness of melatonin in treating panic disorders.

Dosage. Recommended doses are 1 to 5 mg at bedtime; however, the therapeutic effect and proper dose vary among individuals. It is recommended that melatonin be taken 30 minutes to two hours before bedtime for best results. It is available in tablet form.

Potential Adverse Effects. Melatonin is probably one of the least toxic compounds. Only 10% of users are likely to experience side effects. If they do occur, they usually include nightmares, headaches, morning grogginess, mild depression, and low sex drive.

Melatonin is not recommended for pregnant or lactating women, or for individuals with immune system disorders.

St. John's Wort

The extract of the flowering plant known since ancient times for its medicinal qualities, St. John's wort (*Hypericum perforatum*) has become one of the fastest-growing nonmedical supplements for the treatment of depression. Its attraction is its mild to moderate relief of depression, along with virtually none of the negative side effects that are associated with the antidepressant compounds. Extracts of the plant are inexpensive (about 25 cents a day) and available without a prescription. *Hypericum* is also said to have fewer side effects than aspirin.

A number of studies have explored the use of St. John's wort in treating mild to moderate depression. It is thought that it demonstrates a neuroepinephrine and serotonin-reuptake-inhibiting effect. It is also thought that it acts on the cortisol system by inhibiting the cytokine interleukin-6 and other cytokines excreted by cells of the immune system.

Some believe that St. John's wort may also be effective for individuals who experience anxiety—namely, panic—along with depression (Müller & Rossal, 1994; Connor & Vaughan, 1999).

Dosage. Recommended doses are 300 mg upon rising, followed by a second 300-mg dose three hours later, and a final dose of 300 mg in another three hours. Some find that taking two 300-mg doses at breakfast and the third at lunch works best for them. It can also be used at bedtime for difficulties in sleeping.

Potential Adverse Effects. Side effects are minor, but may include stomach upset or nausea. They can be reduced by taking capsules with meals. St. John's wort is also not recommended for pregnant women or for those who are lactating.

Combined Treatments

As stated previously, no modality of treatment has a patent on cure. Therefore, it is our belief that no one modality can be all things to all people. Thus, clinicians need to remain open to using what works in a particular situation. In addition, a combination of treatment modalities may prove to be the best approach—most commonly, some form of CBT combined with medication. Although there are limited data available on the efficacy of combined treatments for panic, they remain the treatment of choice. Most studies support the combination of antidepressants and traditional exposure therapy (Telch & Lucas, 1994). Consider, for example, the use of relaxation methods. Regardless of the fact that these involve progressive relaxation training or biofeedback, much of the research literature suggests that adding coping-skills training augments the effectiveness of treatment (Jannoun, Oppenheimer, & Gelder, 1982).

The efficacy of both CBT and pharmacological interventions in the treatment of panic disorder with and without agoraphobia has been well established. Furthermore, the efficacies of each treatment approach alone seem to be comparable (e.g., Conttrux, Note, Cungi, et al., 1995; Klosko, Barlow, Tassinari, & Cerny, 1990). However, each approach has its strengths and its drawbacks. The main limitation of pharmacotherapy is the possibility of relapse when the medication is discontinued; relapse rates of 50% or higher are typical (Marks, Swinson, Basoglu, et al., 1993; Spiegel, Bruce, Gregg, & Nuzzarello, 1994). The tendency to relapse has been reported even when the dosage, especially of benzodiazepines, is tapered very slowly (Marks, Swinson, Basoglu, et al., 1993), and with a longer maintenance period before drug discontinuation (Wardle, Hayward, Higgitt, et al., 1994; Spiegel, Bruce, Gregg, & Nuzzarello, 1994). Another limitation of medications is that most people became dependent on them after prolonged use, and consequently suffer withdrawal symptoms when the treatment is terminated. A review of the literature indicates that some panic patients will not accept medications as a viable treatment alternative, and that others cannot tolerate the side effects, leading to dropout rates of 15% to 28% (Craske, 1996a).

The main limitation of CBT interventions is that, in some cases, the anxiety is so severe that the panic-disordered individual cannot focus on learning the new skills necessary to overcome the disorder. A second limitation is that CBT requires individuals to take an active role in their recovery, which includes engaging in a series of anxiety-provoking assignments. Approximately 10–30% of panic patients either reject CBT or discontinue treatment altogether (Barlow, Craske, Cerny, & Klosko, 1989; Clum, 1989; Craske, 1996b; Craske, Brown, & Barlow, 1991; Sharp, Power, Simpson, et al., 1996).

Rationales for Combining Treatments

In a search for more effective treatments of panic disorder, researchers and clinicians have explored the use of combined treatment components and treatment approaches. The main reason for combining intervention techniques has been to reduce the length of treatment, to reduce relapse probability after discontinuing medication, to enhance patients' compliance with CBT assignments, and to deal more effectively with complex cases. Although many combinations are possible, we are limiting our discussion to combinations of CBT with pharmacotherapy because of the scarcity of studies employing other modalities, as well as the proven effectiveness of CBT. Most studies have compared combinations of psychosocial treatment components (e.g., cognitive restructuring plus exposure) with pharmacotherapy (e.g., antidepressants, high-potency benzodiazepines) versus psychosocial treatment alone and medication alone.

Advantages of Combined Treatments

As mentioned previously, although panic attacks can be treated effectively with either CBT alone or pharmacotherapy alone, the general thrust is to combine these interventions, particularly for panic patients who suffer frequent and disabling panic attacks (Craske, 1996b; Spiegel & Bruce, 1997). It has been found that without CBT, panic patients treated only with drugs are usually unprepared for managing their anxiety and the bodily sensations that accompany the discontinuation of the medication (APA, 1998). For example, in a study conducted by Otto and colleagues (Otto, Pollack, Sachs, et al., 1993), it was found that 76% of patients who received a combination of alprazolam or clonazepam and CBT were able to stop drug use, whereas that result was observed in only 25% of the medication-alone group. Similar findings have been reported for other recent studies (Spiegel, Bruce, Gregg, & Nuzzarello, 1994; Hegel, Ravaris, & Ahles, 1994). Hence CBT provides panic patients on medication not only with a new insight and skills to overcome their anxiety, but also with an internal understanding of the therapeutic gain that facilitates less dependence on drugs.

CBT Format

Cognitive-behavioral interventions for panic typically are made up of three main components: exposure to interoceptive fear cues, cognitive restructuring, and breathing control. The cognitive component of CBT can take different forms (e.g., rational-emotive-behavior therapy, stress inoculation training, paradoxical intention). However, preliminary research suggests that Clark and Salkovskis' (1987, 1995) cognitive model—which is an adaptation of the standard Beck-Emery-Greenberg (1985) model, and focuses on the correction of catastrophic misinterpretation of bodily and emotional changes—is more effective than other types of cognitive interventions (e.g., Beck, Sokol, Clark, et al., 1992; Chambless, Goldstein, Gallagher, & Bright, 1986). When the treatment target is the agoraphobia aspect of the disorder, a new component is added to the treatment package: exposure to exteroceptive cues (e.g., movie theaters, traffic jams), which is typically delivered in a prolonged, graduated, and in vivo format.

A number of studies have demonstrated that cognitive restructuring alone and pure exposure are similarly effective in treating panic. This equality of effectiveness refers not only to the nature of the changes, but also to the rate of change over time. Preliminary results suggest that cognitive restructuring enhances the durability of treatment gains resulting from exposure (Chambless & Gillis, 1996). Also, at three-month follow-up, the combination of in vivo exposure and cognitive restructuring has been noted to be superior to exposure alone or to exposure plus relaxation (Michelson, Marchione, & Greenwald, 1989). However, not all studies indicate that a combined treatment (interoceptive exposure plus Clark–Salkovskis' cognitive therapy) for panic is superior to the two approaches when employed separately (Margraf & Schneider, 1991).

Drug Types

As mentioned previously, four types of medications have demonstrated comparable effectiveness in reducing panic symptoms: tricyclic antidepressants (TCAs), selective serotonin reuptake inhibitors (SSRIs), monoamine oxidase inhibitors (MAOIs), and benzodiazepines (APA, 1998).

In the past, it was not uncommon for general physicians and psychiatrists to prescribe benzodiazepines for panic disorder. However, there is no convincing evidence that adding benzodiazepines to an empirically validated CBT format (e.g., Barlow & Cerny, 1988, pp. 151–170; Clark & Salkovskis, 1987, pp. 120–150) significantly improves the treatment outcome for panic, either acutely or in the long run. In fact, a number of studies suggest that most panic sufferers can derive similar benefits from short-term therapy and support, without the need for medication (Catalan, Gath, Edmonds, & Ennis, 1984; Shapiro, Struening, Shapiro, & Milcarek, 1983). Probably, the most attractive feature of benzodiazepines is that they reduce anxiety quickly. Hence they are most effective with highly anxious patients, although their benefits usually are not transferred to a drug-free state, thus limiting the therapeutic gain significantly (Spiegel & Bruce, 1997). In view of the cumulative evidence on benzodiazepine withdrawal and relapse, Barlow (1988) does not recommend its use at any time during panic-disorder treatment unless an overwhelming need for immediate relief is apparent. In this case, the therapist can contract with the patient for a rapid withdrawal (e.g., three weeks of drug use).

An alternative to benzodiazepines has been the selective use of TCA, whose withdrawal effects are more manageable (Andrews, 1982). There are some studies that suggest that beneficial effects can be attained by combining antidepressants with in vivo exposure (Telch & Lucas, 1994; De Beurs, Van Balkom, Lange, et al., 1995). A recent meta-analytic study found no differences in the amelioration of panic between the use of antidepressants plus exposure in vivo and of exposure alone and antidepressants alone. However, combining the interventions proved superior to either medications alone or exposure alone for depression and background anxiety, which suggests that antidepressants enhance the impact of in vivo exposure (Van Balkom, Bakker, Spinhoven, et al., 1997).

A more recent study involved a randomized double-blind placebo-controlled clinical trial with 326 subjects carefully screened for a diagnosis of panic disorder (Barlow, Gorman, Shear, & Woods, 1998). Subjects received either imipramine or cognitive-behavior therapy (CBT), or a combination. The results indicate that both treatments were significantly better than placebos, and individual CBT and imipramine worked approximately equally well at the end of acute treatment and after six months of maintenance. Response to placebos was short-lived. Among those completing treatment, imipramine produced a higher-quality response. Six months following treatment discontinuation, more patients responding to imipramine whether combined or not with CBT, had deteriorated as compared with those responding to CBT alone or to CBT combined with placebos, where subjects tended to retain their gains.

These investigators conclude that there seems to be little advantage in combining drugs and CBT, and each individual treatment works approximately equally well immediately following the treatment and during maintenance. Follow-up data after termination indicate that CBT is more durable.

Recently, the American Psychiatry Association (1998) recommended

SSRIs over the other three classes of drugs for panic disorder. The recommendation was based on a comparison of the efficacies of the medications and of their adverse side effects. In preliminary studies, a combination of the SSRI paroxetine and cognitive therapy was superior to cognitive therapy plus placebo (e.g., Oehrberg, Christiansen, & Behnke, 1995). Further research is needed on the effects of combinations of SSRIs with CBT as compared with their separate gains.

Additional Psychosocial Treatment Components

Two factors that may enhance the benefits of the essential treatment components are relaxation and spouse participation.

Relaxation

There has been some controversy over whether or not relaxation alone is sufficient in treating panic disorder (Margraf, Barlow, Clark, et al., 1993; McNally, 1990; Clark, Salkovskis, Hackmann, et al., 1994). Recent studies have compared relaxation with other treatment methods, with surprising results (Clark, Salkovskis, Hackmann, et al., 1994; Öst, 1988). The treatments in this classification included EMG-biofeedback (Canter, Kondo, & Knott, 1975; LaBoeuf & Lodge, 1980), heart-rate biofeedback (Rupert & Holmes, 1978), and progressive relaxation (Canter, Kondo, & Knott, 1975). The controversy appears to center on the belief that with most patients the relaxation response is slow in onset, particularly during states of high anxiety, and that many who attempt to relax in the face of high or chronic anxiety are unsuccessful (Raskin, Bali, & Peeke, 1980). Barlow and colleagues (Barlow, Crase, Cerny, & Klosko, 1989) found that the addition of Öst's (1987) applied relaxation to a combination of interoceptive exposure and cognitive therapy as a treatment for panic did not enhance the outcome as compared with the same combination without applied relaxation.

Spouse Participation

It is well known that panic disorder may have an impact on the marital and family dynamics. In many cases, the spouse or another family member can play an important role in maintaining the disorder by being overly protective, critical of attempts to change, and a source of distress.

In such instances, the incorporation of the person in the treatment program may improve treatment compliance. The spouse (or other family member) can be a source of encouragement and support for the exposure-based procedure and in enduring the typical ups and downs in the process of recovery. There is some evidence that participants in a spouse-accompanied treatment group responded better than did the non–spouse-accompanied group at posttreatment and at one- and two-year follow-ups (Barlow, O'Brien, & Last, 1984; Cerny, Barlow, Craske, & Himadi, 1987; Himadi, Cerny, & Barlow, 1986).

Other Psychological Components

The standard treatment techniques for panic disorder focus on the symptoms themselves, with the immediate goal of reducing those symptoms. However, in many panic-disorder cases, it is also important to address the patient's underlying interpersonal dynamics. The idea of considering the patient's social systems during treatment has been underscored in the literature, particularly regarding marital and family treatment (Barlow, 1988). An example of such a dynamic is presented in Chapter 7 in the case of Susan. As you will see, during their work, it became clear to her therapist that serious marital conflicts were contributing to Susan's sensation of being trapped, and that they also played a role in contributing to her distress and the manifestation of autonomic activity. When Thorpe and Burns (1983) conducted a survey of stresses related to panic attacks in a population of panic-disordered individuals, they found that marital and family difficulties were high on the list of stressors and were viewed as potential roadblocks to maintaining gains in treatment. Thus other CBT techniques and intervention modalities can be added to the treatment package after, or while, overcoming the agoraphobic avoidance, and if the patient is taking medication, after or during drug discontinuation. The goal is to reduce the patient's vulnerability to relapse and to promote an end-state functioning level. Among the techniques that may be part of long-term follow-up interventions are couples therapy, family therapy, assertiveness training, and problem-solving and stress-inoculation training that teaches the patient how to deal effectively with daily stressors and emergencies.

Conclusion

Overall, study results suggest that no treatment modality can be all things for all panic patients. Hence clinicians need to remain open to using different pure or combined approaches, depending on the situation. Although not all patients need combined treatment, in some cases, it may be necessary. It is not clear as to which type of panic-disordered individual responds better to CBT alone, to medication alone, or to a combination. Whereas most people benefit from the combination of CBT and medication, many have recovered from panic disorder through the use of psychoanalytic or interpersonal approaches combined with some cognitive or behavioral techniques. What is important for clinicians to remember is to use what works and to remain sensitive to the patient's needs.

6

Self-Help Interventions

Support Groups

A distinction must be made between group psychotherapy and support groups. Support groups typically are groups of individuals who have been through treatment and need to rely on group meetings as booster sessions. These groups usually are conducted by a trained professional or a paraprofessional and are designed primarily to support patients in utilizing what they have learned in the course of treatment. Although such issues as backsliding and stumbling blocks are often discussed, emphasis is placed on a support system as opposed to any specific intervention or treatment.

Quite often, recovered panic-disordered individuals will form their own patient support groups and conduct them primarily as leaderless groups. These may be beneficial to some degree, but a potential caveat is that untrained professionals may face difficulties depending on the condition of other group members. These groups are not recommended unless there is professional supervision and it may behoove clinicians to have their patients avoid groups that are not so monitored.

Typically, support sessions are conducted on a monthly basis. Members may attend to talk about achieving their goals or to celebrate their successes. Generally, they can attend group meetings as long as sessions are available. Group support systems are recommended for individuals who have had serious relapses, but only after they have reentered treatment. Some support groups may also involve the spouse or other relatives of a person with panic disorder and these can be very helpful to family members in their struggle to understand panic.

It is important to remember that support groups are not a substitute for effective treatment, but are designed to complement treatment.

Family/Spousal Support

Even though panic is an individualized disorder, it undoubtedly has a ripple effect on the families. However, little research exists on the role of relationships and their contribution to panic disorder. Marital and family difficulties were ranked high on their lists of stressors by panic-disordered subjects who were surveyed by researchers Thorpe and Burns (1983). Clearly, this may play a major role in accelerating the treatment process as well. Much of the professional literature supports the concept of educating spouses and family members to the treatment of panic and contributing to their understanding of why and how the disorder develops (Barlow, 1988). What is more, it is important for treating clinicians to coach spouses and immediate family members on their roles in the treatment process. This should be executed with care and only after it has been determined that the patient's spouse or other family member is not facilitating an unhealthy dependency that may be enabling the patient's disorder, particularly since research has indicated that marital relations play a key role in the development and maintenance of panic and agoraphobia (Goldstein & Chambless, 1978; Wolpe, 1970). Further studies have focused on the relationship characteristics of agoraphobics and their partners (Epstein & Dutton, 1997; Epstein, Dutton, Dattilio, & Vittore, in press) and suggest that agoraphobics are in more maladjusted marriages than are other couples; however, agoraphobics differ from other groups in that their degree of marital maladjustment falls in the middle between that of highly distressed and of nondistressed couples (Arrindell & Emmelkamp, 1986; Lange & Van Dyck, 1992).

Unfortunately, little in the literature addresses the benefits of including the spouse in treatment, and the results of doing so are mixed (Himadi, Boice, & Barlow, 1986; Barlow, O'Brien, & Last, 1984, Arnow, Taylor, & Agras, 1985).

Spouses are often trained by the treating clinician on how to coach their partners through difficult periods, as well as how to support the recovery process in general. Clinicians can and should take the opportunity to address any relationship issues that may be contributing to the panic cycle (e.g., overprotectiveness, dependency) and assess the need for further conjoint therapy. Since no research studies are available on the use of marital or family therapy alone or with medication for the treatment of panic, no conclusions can be drawn about the efficacy of the approach.

Bibliotherapy

An adjunct technique that has proved very helpful with anxiety-disordered individuals is bibliotherapy. In fact, assigned readings may be helpful regardless of the type of therapy employed, since they can supplement the treatment process. Some studies actually show that bibliotherapy alone is as effective as eight sessions of group or individual CBT (Gould, Clum, & Shapiro, 1993; Lidren, Watkins, Gould, et al., 1994).

As a behavioral technique, bibliotherapy serves as a continuous reinforcement of many of the principles and concepts regarding coping skills promoted in therapy. Literature designed for clients may also help those who are suffering from panic to feel less isolated and to become aware that others experience the same symptoms and struggle with the same reactions.

A number of excellent self-help books are available to panic sufferers, including *Don't Panic* by Reid Wilson (1986) and *Coping with Panic* by George Clum (1990). Both were written by professionals skilled in the use of CBT, and so would provide excellent supplemental reading and supportive aids to many of the techniques described in this chapter. Appendixes A and B list a number of such books, with asterisks indicating our preferences among the recommended readings. Those in Appendix B would be of particular interest to patients, who should be directed to read these books as they are receiving treatment, and may even benefit from them after the termination of therapy.

Although many self-help books are written by individuals who themselves are recovering or who have recovered from panic disorder, we recommend that the reader be skeptical of the author's credentials. Panic and axiety can be serious disorders and it is essential that any suggested treatment be approved by a trained professional.

Homework

Homework is a very important aspect of any modality, particularly the CBT treatment of panic. Many of the coping skills that are taught in treatment require practice to become part of the person's repertoire of skills. Homework assignments that include breathing exercises and cognitive coping skills are necessary in order for the panic-disordered individual to learn how to respond effectively when spontaneous panic attacks occur. In our opinion, homework is what gels the effects of that which is learned during the course of treatment. Since the therapeutic hour is usually limited to a fraction of time in a person's life, homework assignments serve as an extension outside of the therapy session and bridge the gap between treatment sessions.

Recording information on such forms as the "Weekly Panic Log," which was developed by the Center for Cognitive Therapy in Philadelphia (reprinted in Dattilio & Berchick, 1992) is also vital in allowing both the client and the therapist to track the occurrence of the client's panic attacks. The use of the Panic Diary developed by Dattilio (1996) shown in Figure 2 is demonstrated in Figure 10 for Susan (discussed in Chapter 7).

In addition, practice exercises may utilize audiotapes or videotapes of the therapy sessions, particularly for demonstrating relaxation methods and breathing exercises.

Last, homework is also a prelude to the eventual coping skills that will be used in relapse prevention and should be strongly emphasized in any treatment regime despite the noncompliance common among patients.

Whereas homework assignments vary during the course of treatment, typical assignments may include practicing methods of progressive muscle relaxation training, breathing exercises, practicing challenging automatic thought statements during periods of automatic activity, self-exposure to stimuli that may cause autonomic arousal, and/or recording catastrophic thought statements.

Name: _Susan_   **Date:** _2/12_

Date, time, and duration of the panic attack	Situation in which panic attack occurred and severity of the panic	Description of the panic attack symptoms and sensations experienced	Interpretation of sensations and accompanying thoughts and images	Was this a full-blown attack? Yes/No. If No, why not?	Your response to the panic attack. What did you do? (Specify any medication taken and dosage (mg, dose, etc.)
2/12	Driving home from work (10)	Increased heart rate Increased breathing Lightheadedness; fear	Felt afraid Thought I was going to die I am losing control	Yes	Pulled the car over to the side and waited until symptoms stopped. I also cried.
2/15	Waiting in line at the department store to pay for items.	Heart began beating fast Lightheadedness	Felt like I was losing control and needed to "get out."	Yes	Ran out of the store and left packages behind.

Figure 10. Susan's Panic Diary.

Self-Help Approaches

Despite the reported effectiveness of some self-help treatment programs, the topic continues to be viewed with skepticism by clinicians and researchers (Ghosh & Marks, 1987; Ghosh, Marks, & Carr, 1988). Most self-help programs typically offer self-instruction techniques involving CBT interventions, namely, exposure treatment. These programs tend to address the agoraphobic aspect as opposed to the panic.

Although we accept the use of bibliotherapy as a support system to professional treatment, we caution the encouragement of self-help programs, particularly for anyone who has not had professional help.

Relapse Prevention

Panic relapse after treatment usually occurs as a result of the discontinuation of skills practice and exposure, as well as of poor follow-up in therapy. In fact, often treatment is ended abruptly by the patient when his or her symptoms remit.

It is essential that clients contract with the therapist to complete their treatment and to include all of the follow-up visits. Those visits should focus on a skills check and anticipation of the use of techniques in the event of a spontaneous recurrence of panic symptoms. Other issues that should be addressed are the psychosocial and internal stressors that may trigger panic. Therapists can often prepare patients for potential relapse by educating them on the reasons why relapse occurs and having them accept the possibility that it may indeed occur. A specific outline for steps to be taken should be reviewed in advance in the event that a patient backslides. In fact, it is often suggested to patients that they note these steps on an index card and keep it with them so that they can refer to it if they experience any early symptoms of panic.

Reverse role playing may also be used, in which the therapist acts out the role of the person relapsing and requests that the patient coach him or her in a step-by-step fashion on how to reduce the symptoms. This serves to reinforce all of the skills taught and to identify any pitfalls that might be encountered during the process.

Finally, it is also recommended that patients be instructed not to delay in contacting the therapist for booster sessions when they are finding it difficult to cope on their own. It is often the delay that facilitates the return of the panic cycle in full force.

The Therapeutic Relationship

Finally, some mention should be made of the therapeutic relationship. Regardless of the modality of treatment used or the specific techniques implemented, the therapeutic relationship is always a central mechanism in making an intervention effective (Dattilio, Freeman, & Blue, 1998).

In our opinion, it is essential that the therapist treating panic disorder always remember to remain compassionate and mindful of the struggle endured by panic-disordered patients. Despite the etiology, their symptoms are real to them and present a threat. It is the genuineness and warmth of the treating clinician that add an interpersonal quality to the treatment approach, which, it is hoped, will make the difference.

7

Panic Disorder with Agoraphobia—
An In-Depth Example

The Case of Susan

Susan, 42 years old, had been married for 10 years and had two children. She also worked full-time as an advertising executive. Susan presented with symptoms of panic attacks for which she was diagnosed by her family physician and prescribed alprazolam (0.5 mg) on an as-needed basis. As she did not like to take medications, her physician also referred her for psychotherapy, so that she could learn how to regulate her anxiety and control her attacks on her own.

Susan initially submitted to a two-hour intake procedure in which she was administered the structural clinical interview scale of DSM-IV, along with the Beck Anxiety Inventory (BAI), Beck Depression Inventory (BDI), and a number of other panic questionnaires.* She also provided a full history, which, for the most part, was unremarkable and devoid of any medical problems or major mental illnesses. During the intake process, Susan informed the therapist that she had undergone an extensive medical evaluation by her family physician, which included an electrocardiogram, an electroencephalogram, and a complete blood profile, all of which produced negative results. Susan's symptoms were evidenced in an increased heart rate, breathlessness, sweaty hands,

---

*These included the PASQ (Panic Attack Symptom Questionnaire) and the MI (Mobility Inventory).

scared feelings, and lightheadedness. She said that she had been experiencing severe attacks three times per week. The most recent attack, which she reported during the initial session, had occurred during a meeting with clients while at work. Her first sensation was of "feeling scared." A particular problem with Susan was her inability to convey the exact sequence of her symptoms or of what was happening to her both cognitively and affectively. She also described the urge and need to leave the situation each time she experienced an attack; in her most recent attack, this desire to leave jeopardized a very important business meeting. She also said that she had begun to avoid public places or situations that might bring on an attack or make escape difficult for her.

Susan's history of panic attacks dated back almost seven years prior to her seeking treatment, when she ventured outside of the home to enter the workplace. This was while the children were very young, and it was decided that she would obtain employment in order to help with the family expenses, as well as to fulfill some of her own goals. Susan reported that getting started on her career was rather difficult, but that she had come a long way in the past seven years and had developed quite a level of expertise. The number of advertising accounts under her supervision had increased and she had begun to enjoy an increasingly successful career in the three or four years she had been employed by her firm. But this also created some ambivalence for her. Susan was uncertain why her success created problems, but she did know that her symptoms were getting worse and posing an obstacle to her continued success. She felt debilitated and almost paralyzed at times by her symptoms, which had inspired her to consult her family physician.

After the initial intake session, the therapist established a rapport with Susan, while simultaneously developing a conceptualization as to how she viewed her disorder and her symptoms. The way she put it was that she experienced random symptoms that seemed to "all run together." She also admitted that her panic symptoms were extremely frightening, and that at times she felt as though she were losing control.

The first treatment session focused on an attempt to identify the initial symptoms that occurred during each panic attack in order to develop more insight into the sequence of her attacks, as well as the automatic thoughts, emotions, and behaviors that accompanied the symptoms. It is not uncommon for panic victims to experience an initial symptom that sets the stage for the subsequent autonomic activity. For Susan, her increased heart rate sympathetically induced an increase in respiration, which culminated in sweating and an elevated body temperature. Part of the difficulty in assessing Susan's symptoms was that she reported a vague recollection of the sequence of symptoms and described them as simply a "blur in her mind." This is not uncommon with panic victims who experience a number of symptoms. It was decided to attempt to structure Susan's recollection by focusing on a recent event in which she experienced panic and to help her to reconstruct her attack by using the SAEB system (Dattilio, 1990, 1994b, 1995, 1996) described in Chapters 4 and 5. This was reconstructed by using Susan's recollection of her most recent attack, which had occurred in the previous week. Susan recalled, "I was at my office and we were having a meeting. We were sitting around the conference table with other salespeople and managers, discussing a new account. All of a sudden, I just started feeling scared and my heart started to beat faster and I got all sweaty and, I don't know, everything sort of ran together." One of the thoughts that Susan recalled was that her coworkers might recognize that she was having a problem, but were perplexed as to what it was. Susan was able to identify that the first sensation that she experienced was an increase in her heart rate and that this was a consistent symptom that initiated most of her attacks. What troubled her more was the sensation of being out of breath, or "breathless" as she called it, and feeling the need to leave the room.

Upon implementing the SAEB system with Susan, it was discovered that she was unable to recall clearly her particular sensations because of what she referred to as a "memory blur." At this point, it was obvious to the therapist that he might have to consider using a symptom-induction exercise in order to obtain the full breadth of exactly what symptoms Susan experienced, along with her particular automatic thoughts, emotions, and behaviors.

What was surprising, however, was that, despite her experiences of panic, Susan was always able to function and to engage in verbal exchanges with clients or colleagues without visually displaying her distress. Nonetheless, Susan feared that she might appear incoherent to others. When a reality check was utilized by asking Susan if anyone ever noticed any peculiarity about her physical appearance, she admitted that no one had ever said anything to that effect. This was a first step in helping Susan to recognize some of the cognitive distortions that accompanied her panic and the first move toward restructuring some of her beliefs about the effects and outward display of her symptoms. This is an extremely important aspect of assessment and treatment since cognitions have been well documented as playing an important role in both the escalation and modulation of panic (Kenardy, Evans, & Oei, 1988).

At this point, the therapist decided to educate Susan to the principles of anxiety and panic and explain her problem in an integrative framework. The therapist started with the CBT theory of panic, describing some of the potential underlying causes of panic, which included physiological and interpersonal aspects.

Susan was reminded that everyone possesses a built-in alarm system, which is referred to as the anxiety response—a part of the survival mechanism. An analogy would be a building that contains a fire alarm to alert inhabitants to impending danger. In humans, the danger may be physical or psychological. It was important to explain to Susan that in the process of evolution, any organism that failed to develop such a warning signal was unable to defend itself against danger or harm. Therefore, the survival mechanism is something that we all need to help keep us alive.

It was explained that as intricate as our bodies and brains are, sometimes sensations are mistriggered. Also, some individuals have a tendency to misinterpret bodily sensations catastrophically, depending on the manner in which they react to certain stimuli. Some stressors may affect the body's alarm system, including anything from general fatigue to the onset of an illness or even early signs of a menstrual cycle. Quite often, too much caffeine in a cup of coffee or certain foods that contain stimulants (e.g., monosodium glutamate) can set off the alarm system, evoking autonomic symptoms. In addition, some of the underlying issues were addressed by explaining to Susan that treating the symptoms alone was insufficient. It was stressed that it was important to get to any underlying conflicts that might be stressing her and contributing to the manifestation of symptoms. To emphasize this point, the analogy of a skin rash was used, for which a topical agent may provide some symptomatic relief, and yet may miss the etiology of the irritation, particularly if it arises from a systemic disorder. Analogies such as this are often helpful in aiding patients to understand that sometimes the underlying issues have to be confronted in order to keep the symptoms from recurring. The relapse of symptoms in panic disorder is common, especially when the underlying dynamics are not addressed properly.

Once it was felt that Susan understood how panic and anxiety work, the therapist began to share with her some of the treatment options. The use of medication was discussed, as well as several of the CBT strategies that are said to be effective in treating panic disorder (see Chapter 5). This psychoeducational component is extremely important so that the patient has a good understanding of exactly what is happening in his or her body and is no longer mystified by the attacks. Susan was then introduced to the use of the panic diary (see Figure 2), which is designed to help the patient keep track of his or her panic attacks during the week. The therapist described the use of the diary to Susan so that she was clear as to its purpose.

When Susan inquired about some of the specific mechanisms of the treatment, she was told about the use of progressive muscle relaxation and breathing retraining via controlled breathing and was given a self-instructional audiotape to help her carry out these exercises. It was suggested that she listen to this tape for approximately 20 minutes each day and to try to follow along with the program. This particular tape adhered to the relaxation format described by Borkovec, Grayson, and Cooper (1978). It was also suggested that at the next session, the therapist would propose a diagnostic strategy designed to better assess the specifics of Susan's panic symptoms and would utilize the SAEB system to track her symptoms, as well as her automatic thoughts, emotions, and behaviors. As a homework assignment, Susan was instructed to complete the panic diary without any attempt to mediate her panic symptoms. She was advised that, if she should experience a panic attack, she should try her best to ride it out, but also attempt to record as much as she could in the panic diary in order to establish a baseline. She was also instructed to bring her diary to the next session and to be prepared to engage in a special breathing exercise.

Session 2

At the second session, Susan told the therapist that she had had a rather rough week. She spontaneously produced her panic diary, which indicated that she had had two major panic attacks during the week. She

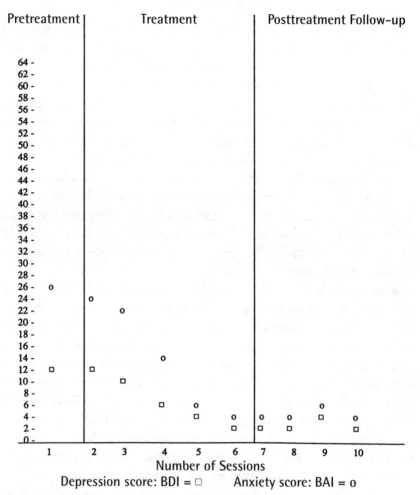

Figure 11. Susan's levels of anxiety and depression.

had also completed the Beck Anxiety Inventory with a score or 26 (severe) and the Beck Depression Inventory, which indicated a low score (12) (see Figure 11).

Susan reported that she had had a panic attack while driving home from work during which she initially experienced an increased heart rate, along with increased breathing, lightheadedness, and a general sense of fear. She stated that she was simply taking her normal route home, when suddenly she began to breathe heavily and her heart began to race. She recalled becoming hysterical and entering into a state of full-blown panic (see Figure 12).

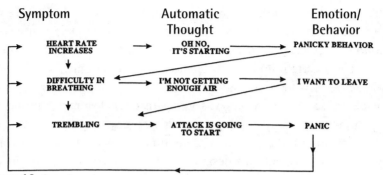

Figure 12. Susan's panic sequence.

When asked what went through her mind at the point, Susan mentioned "feeling afraid." "I didn't know what was going to happen to me and so I just became afraid." The therapist noticed that in her panic diary, Susan had indicated that she felt as though she were losing control, but when asked directly, she stated that she had maintained control despite the fact that she had experienced a full-blown panic attack. She did pull her car to the side of the road until some of her symptoms subsided, but when asked what she did to cause them to subside, she explained that she "cried herself out" until she "got herself together." Interestingly, "getting herself together" involved some cognitive self-talk that would come out in the subsequent sessions. Susan did state that it was important that she get home and so she forced herself to continue driving until she reached her driveway safely.

Susan's second attack that week came while she was in a department store and she experienced the same symptoms while standing in line to pay for some items. She stated that once her heart began beating fast, she felt lightheaded and left the store abruptly, leaving the packages behind. When asked once again what went through her mind, she stated simply that she felt as though she were losing control and felt compelled to get out. When questioned in detail, she said that she felt afraid, but was unable to pinpoint any specific thoughts.

The therapist explained to Susan that part of the conceptualization process actually involved an initial step to treatment. At this point, he began to introduce the concept of utilizing an induction exercise that involved breathing that was somewhat different from the one she had practiced with the audiotape. In fact, Susan was told that the induction exercise involved breathing that was the inverse of what she had learned on the audiotape and that it was designed to deliberately cause some autonomic activity in order to provoke a first-hand experience so that they could ascertain how she reacted to such sensations. The therapist explained that while this might initially be frightening to her, it would provide an account of what was going through her mind during her panic attacks and help to elucidate her response sequence. It was explained to Susan that, at the same time, it was still a controlled breathing exercise, but was designed to mimic a panic reaction as opposed to preventing one. Susan was assured that this was a safe exercise, particularly since her physician had cleared her based on her medical examination.* The induction exercise involved having Susan breathe in and out through her mouth in a staccato fashion as long as she could for the first few minutes. The significance of this was to produce a kind of overbreathing similar to that in which individuals sometimes engage during panic attacks. Susan recalled that she had told the therapist on several occasions that she felt as though she were out of breath and that in her attempts to restabilize her breathing, she would actually blow off too much carbon dioxide and inhale too much oxygen, which would cause her to hyperventilate. In a sense, this was what the exercise was deliberately trying to achieve in order to produce some of the main symptoms of panic so that a reconceptualization of their effect could be constructed in a less catastrophic manner.

Once Susan's consent was obtained, it was explained that the exercise was not mandatory and that there were other alternatives to treatment. Susan agreed to try the exercise in the interest of overcoming her attacks.

Induction Exercise

Susan then was informed that the therapist was going to be initiating an exercise with her in which she would overbreathe by inhaling and exhaling quickly through the mouth in a staccato-like fashion for as long as she could. The therapist would start the exercise with her, but

---

*It is essential, prior to this exercise, that medical clearance be obtained through a physician to ensure that the patient does not have any significant cardiovascular disorders (coronary artery disease, arrhythmia) or a seizure disorder, etc.

then discontinue his own breathing in order to watch the clock and monitor her behaviors. It was made clear to Susan that the idea was for her to continue breathing in this fashion until she could no longer breathe normally (due to excessive symptoms or hyperventilation). At that point, the physical sensations that Susan was experiencing would be assessed, as well as the thoughts that were going through her mind.

As the exercise began, Susan breathed according to the instructions for approximately a minute and a half. She was informed of the time limit and spontaneously discontinued, at which time she stated that her heart was beating rapidly. When asked what was going through her mind at that particular moment, she stated, "I can't breathe. I just can't get enough air." She also stated that she felt tingly in the arms and that they were weak and her hands were shaking. The thoughts accompanying these sensations apparently were still unclear and Susan abruptly stopped the exercise.

Once again it was difficult for Susan to fully convey her thoughts as they were only partial thoughts, and also had a tendency to mesh together in her mind.

At this point, Susan took a drink of water and the exercise was repeated in order to get completely through all of the thoughts and emotions that she experienced during the sensations.

The exercise began again, and Susan seemed to persist with her deliberate overbreathing for less than one minute. Since her autonomic activity had already escalated from the previous attack, it was likely that it didn't take long before she reached a respiratory climax, much like a pot of hot water that is reboiled.

Approximately 40 seconds into the exercise, Susan began to hyperventilate and the therapist intervened as she was now experiencing a full-blown panic attack. She was overbreathing to the point where she could not catch her breath.

The following excerpt provides a clear scenario of exactly what happened as Susan began to hyperventilate.

Therapist: Okay. Stop. Susan, look at me. Susan, look at me. What's going on? Tell me what is going on with you?

Susan: It's happening. It's starting to happen again.

Therapist: Look at me, Susan. Breathe through your nose. Close your eyes. Slowly breathe through your nose and exhale through your mouth. Try to concentrate on what I am telling you to do. Breathe through your nose slowly. Exhale through your mouth slowly as well. Take deep breaths through your nose and try to exhale slowly through your mouth. That's it. Slow. Okay. Let's focus again on that image of the piston that you shared with me in the previous session.*

Just imagine that your heart and respiration are functioning lika a piston. It was going real fast and now we are going to slow it down gradually. Just take a deep breath. Exhale through your mouth slowly and continuously—and let's just bring all of your body functions down to a normal level. Exhale slowly, take a deep breath—take it real slow. Very good. Exhale. Okay.

Now, before the point during your hyperventilation when I said, "Look at me, tell me what was going on," you got very upset. What was freaking you out?

Susan:	It was happening. It was an attack!
Therapist:	What was going on?
Susan:	Well, my heart started to race and I felt light-headed [Figure 10].
Therapist:	That must have been tough for you. What was the most frightening thing about the sensations you were experiencing?
Susan:	You mean the symptoms?
Therapist:	Yes.
Susan:	They were the same as before.
Therapist:	What were you telling yourself?
Susan:	I was telling myself that it is going to happen, it is going to happen, it is happening [crying].
Therapist:	What's happening?
Susan:	"I am going to have an attack."
Therapist:	And?
Susan:	I was afraid.
Therapist:	But nothing other than, "I am going to have an attack"?
Susan:	Maybe lose control. I knew I wasn't going to die.
Therapist:	So the worst thought you had was, "I may lose control"?
Susan:	Yes.
Therapist:	But you didn't lose control?

---

*The picture of a fast-running piston in a combustion engine is the image that Susan used to describe how her heart felt when beating out of control.

Susan:	No.
Therapist:	Okay. You want to keep that in mind since one of the things that we are going to begin to do is reprogram your thinking about what exactly happens to you when you experience these sensations. There is sort of an anticipation of how the sensations are going to affect you. But they never really seem to progress beyond the point of simply giving you the urge to extricate yourself from the situation or feeling that you need to leave.
	The fact is that all of the information that we have gathered so far doesn't support your anticipation of losing control. You have always responded to the anticipation of losing control, but never actually lose it, do you? The worst that you have done is either to leave the situation or to ride out the panic attack.
Susan:	Right.
Therapist:	As we look at the end results, it is nothing other than autonomic activity that, for one thing, is limited and benign—in the sense that it is short term and it does not really hurt you, and second, it always eventually subsides. Consequently, you need to begin to think about your symptoms in different terms as we begin to go over each sensation and restructure in your mind exactly how they affect you.
	In the case of your increased heart rate and difficulty in breathing, a great deal of what you tell yourself makes a difference in terms of how bad these symptoms become. Actually, the end result isn't really as terrible as you anticipated, is it?
Susan:	That's true!
Therapist:	Did you notice how quickly we brought your symptoms down when I simply coached you on the use of controlled breathing?
Susan:	Yeah!
Therapist:	That's also the tool that we are going to begin to use to deal with your panic symptoms, but much sooner during the panic sequence. The idea is never to let your panic symptoms escalate to the point where they are uncontrollable.
Susan:	So when the breathing starts, with the panic onset like that, should I just practice the controlled breathing?
Therapist:	Yes, practice controlled breathing and restructuring your interpretation of the bodily sensations. For example, instead of saying, "Oh, no, it is starting, I am not getting enough air," perhaps we

can come up with some alternative responses collaboratively that would serve as a more constructive and accurate response.

For example, something like, "Okay, I have a little increased heart rate, and I am having some difficulty breathing. But this may be nothing more than just a little stress period. I've experienced this before and didn't die or lose control." Just take a deep breath, close your eyes, inhale slowly, exhale, and slow down your breathing rate. As a result, you can see how curtailing your symptoms actually served to deescalate the attack.

So, as a homework assignment, I would like you to continue to fill out the panic diary as you have been doing thus far. Also, I would like you to try this exercise at home—not to the extent that you have done it in here, but just try a little overbreathing, enough to increase your autonomic symptoms to the point where they are uncomfortable and then utilize the breathing retraining to deescalate them. Just a little bit of escalation until you get the heart rate up and then do the breathing retraining as you have learned in our sessions.

Most important, we will talk a little bit more about how to restructure your thinking with regard to this entire sequence of panic. For example, the automatic thought that you had before was, "Oh, no, it's starting and I am not getting enough air," and so on and so forth.

During this next week, I'd like you to think about some alternative responses to the aforementioned statement of losing control, now that you know this really isn't as deadly as you anticipated it to be.

Now do you have some idea of how the principle works? It is a combination of restructuring your thinking and controlling your breathing in a fashion that deescalates your symptoms. The idea is that when you feel the trigger symptoms coming on, you cut them off at the beginning.

Susan: I can see how that would work.

Therapist: It can be very effective. And remember, the breathing that you learned is competitive with a state of anxiety. So you are using something that is not permitting your autonomic symptoms to escalate. You are using controlled breathing in a relaxing way to reduce your symptoms' intensity and eventually to eliminate them.

	This, combined with restructuring your thinking, will put us where we want to be. Okay?
Susan:	Okay.
Therapist:	All right. So unless you have any other questions, why don't we set up a time to meet next week. And we will try to go a little further in our treatment process.

Session 3

Susan said that she had had a fairly good week and had had only one attack. She presented the therapist with her panic diary in which she described how she had been in the kitchen putting the dishes in the dishwasher just after dinner one night when she started to experience some increase in her heart rate. She said that she couldn't get in touch with anything in her mind that preceded it and that soon after her initial symptom, she began to have difficulty breathing. She claimed that she started to get "that feeling again" and remembered to intervene with some of the cognitive self-talk and to initiate controlled breathing techniques, and was able to arrest the escalation process and felt pretty good about her accomplishment. Susan preferred to think of it as "applying logic" and practiced her breathing while utilizing a different method of interpretation for her sensations. She also reinforced the notion that she was not going to lose control and that she could get through her anxiety successfully.

The therapist informed Susan that this intervention was how she had to continue to address the autonomic activity and that it was best to "nip it in the bud." The analogy of a snowball rolling down the hill was used to emphasize the importance of intervening early in the panic sequence.

At this point, the therapist opted to focus on what was happening between Susan and her husband. She was reminded that in the last session, they had talked a little about the fact that there was tension in her marriage. Asked whether or not, she had further addressed the issue with her husband during the past week, she responded that things were much the same and that she felt very frustrated because the tension actually appeared to be increasing.

Susan was reminded of the importance of considering these underlying issues since they had much to do with her stress level, thus exacerbating her tendency toward panic attacks. She also stated that the tension at home, combined with the pressure at work and the uncertainty of the future, was very disturbing to her. It appeared that the primary tension, however, was related to the conflict in her relationship with her husband, and her desire to appease him, while fulfilling her own needs and long-term objectives. In essence, Susan felt somewhat trapped. It was decided that Susan should approach her husband with the idea of their seeing a marital therapist together to address their relationship issues. Susan promised to discuss it with him, although she was unsure as to how he would respond to her proposal. She was given the names of several marriage counselors from among whom she and her husband could choose. The therapist explained that it would be improper for him to conduct the marital therapy since he was already working individually with Susan, and if he were to see them together, it not only would be a conflict of interests, but would be unfair to her husband, as well as to himself. The therapist also explained that it was necessary for a therapist conducting conjoint therapy to be totally objective from the start, which seemed to make sense to Susan.

This is an extremely important aspect of treating panic disorder, one that many short-term therapists unfortunately overlook. Unless the underlying dynamics are addressed, or at least uncovered, the likelihood of the recurrence of some form of autonomic activity remains. In essence, the techniques demonstrated thus far in this case are excellent for helping one manage the symptoms of anxiety, however, they will not necessarily effect a complete cure. The cure lies in getting at the root of the problem, which, for Susan, appeared to be interpersonal conflict and the necessity to regulate the stress in her life. It was also recommended that Susan continue to keep her panic log and utilize the exercises that she was taught with regard to breathing retraining and cognitive restructuring. As a method of exposure, it was suggested that she review some of the situations in which she had experienced panic, such as driving home in the car and the route she took on the day that she had had the major attack. Susan was asked to consider revisiting the department store where she had left her packages and to attempt to reconstruct her negative cognitive-behavioral experiences by reexposing herself to the same stimuli. The therapist also warned Susan that she might have periodic relapses, which was not unusual. This is part of the inoculation procedure, which was then reviewed with reference to the strategies that she could utilize were she to panic again. Susan was reminded that she had been struggling with anxiety for 10 years and that it was not going to disappear overnight.

Session 5

The fifth session took place approximately two months after Susan's treatment began. These sessions were spread over time in order to give her the opportunity to utilize and implement some of the strategies she learned.

At this session, Susan informed the therapist that she hadn't had any real panic attacks since their previous meeting. She said that she had been using the tapes and practicing the exercises, which seemed to help considerably. She said that she also noticed a marked reduction in her level of anxiety. She stated that she believed that she had not had any panic attacks because of her ability to stave off the early signs by immediately using the breathing exercises and focusing on exactly what she was telling herself. She also stated that she realized that when her heart rate increases and her breathing becomes more rapid, that doesn't necessarily mean that anything catastrophic is happening.

It is interesting to note that at one time, her breathing pattern was the most threatening symptom to Susan, whereas now, via cognitive self-talk and simultaneously controlling her breathing, she also was able to control the escalation of her symptoms. She agreed that the more she utilized these exercises, the more confident she became with them, and so with even the slightest evidence of autonomic activity, she could automatically implement the techniques that control the escalation of her symptoms.

Susan added that she and her husband had entered into marital counseling, and that her husband had consented to it after they had a lengthy discussion about the future of their relationship. It was suggested to Susan that this was an important step, particularly if she and her husband were able to resolve some of their issues. At the same time, it was an exercise in assertiveness for Susan in her being able to talk to her husband and to do something about the conflict in their marriage. The notion was reinforced that what Susan was doing was actually confronting an underlying issue that was one of the main sources of her panic disorder. Other issues had to do with her level of self-esteem, her confidence in herself, and her stress level as a result of her tendency to overinvest herself in her work.

The therapist pointed out once again that anxiety is a warning signal that something is amiss, and that although it is important not to over-catastrophize the symptoms, it is equally important not to ignore them.

Follow-up

An additional four follow-up sessions with Susan were scheduled, to take place at one-month intervals. The ninth and tenth visits were conducted over the telephone. Susan continued to report feeling extremely good about her progress, and said that she had had no panic attacks during the four months. It was mutually decided that therapy would be relegated to an as-needed basis, with the provision that she continue in marital therapy and address some of the issues with which she was struggling in her marriage. Susan was also urged to continue utilizing the relaxation techniques and stress-management strategies that had been discussed. It was emphasized that even though she might be symptom-free, it was important that she continue to practice these techniques in order to keep her stress at a manageable level.

8

Conclusions and Future Directions

As with anything in life, maintaining a balanced perspective is the prudent way to approach a given situation, particularly when it is fraught with uncertainty. And nowhere is this statement more applicable than in the treatment of nervous and mental disorders. There is much controversy in the professional literature over the pros and cons of the various forms of treatment for panic, but we firmly believe that an integrated approach is the most effective and that this will be the treatment of the future. In fact, the most recent practice guidelines for the treatment of panic disorder as set forth by the American Psychiatric Association (APA, 1998) for the first time underscore the notion of using a combined treatment approach. Treatment options presented include psychiatric management, pharmacological interventions, and psychosocial treatment. This package also has a psychoeducational component, which has been found effective in defusing the mystique surrounding panic. The guidelines further note that patients may benefit from a combination of drug treatment and CBT. This is a major breakthrough and a significant departure from the former thinking in the field of medicine, which endorsed only a pharmacological approach to panic. It is also likely that, in time, researchers will turn to a more holistic approach to treating panic as further information about and interest in alternative interventions develop.

As we embark on a new millennium and our technology advances, it is hoped that we will pave the way for a more intense focus on using preventative measures to deal with anxiety disorder through early detection. The exciting research being conducted with DNA and brain imaging may unlock new data about the etiology of anxiety and panic and how individuals might avoid the onset of symptoms. Future psychosocial research, it is also hoped, will examine more carefully the role of multiple cognitive-behavioral moderators in the maintenance of panic and agoraphobic responses—particularly the use of subtle ways to avoid them (e.g., utilizing safety signals, changing one's attitude toward anxiety, learning to cope with life's demands, recognizing the need to control one's various fears, of emotions, of death, and so on). It will also be useful to study more of the interactions among these variables and cognitive variables, including attributions and the perceived consequences of panic, anxiety sensitivity, and the need to take responsibility for controlling panic symptoms. Another potentially important research issue concerns the capacity to process nonverbally mediated information; that is, automatic, conditioned, and nonconscious information processing that can account for some of the spontaneous features of certain panic attacks. Results of studies in these areas not only will help to clarify the mechanisms through which psychotherapy achieves its beneficial effects, but also will help us to understand how relapses can be prevented. For now, clinicians must remain cognizant of the treatment strategies currently available and ascertain which techniques work for their patients and which ones do not.

What is clear, however, is that the future holds great promise for our panic-disordered patients as research and education continue to progress.

References

Acierno, R., Tremont, G., Last, C., & Montgomery, D. (1994). Triparite assessment of the efficacy of eye-movement desensitization in a multi-phobic patient. *Journal of Anxiety Disorders, 8*(3), 259–276.

Adamec, R. (1978). Normal and abnormal limbic system mechanisms of emotive biasing (pp. 405–455). In K. E. Livingston & O. Hornykiewicz (Eds.), *Limbic mechanisms.* New York: Plenum.

Adams, G., Boies, L., & Paparella, M. (1978). *Boies' fundamentals of otolaryngology.* Philadelphia: Saunders.

Agras, W. S., Leitenberg, H., & Barlow, D. H. (1968). Social reinforcement in the modification of agoraphobia. *Archives of General Psychiatry, 19*, 423–427.

Aǧarǧün, M.Y., Kara, H., Algün, E., Sekerokǧlu, R., & Tarakçioǧlu, M. (1996). High cholesterol levels in patients with sleep panic. *Biological Psychiatry, 15*, 1064–1065.

Aguilera, D. C. (1990). *Crises intervention: Theory and methodology* St. Louis: Mosby.

Alford, B. A., Beck, A. T., Freeman, A., & Wright, F. (1990). Brief focused cognitive therapy of panic disorder. *Psychotherapy, 27*(2), 230–234.

Altemus, M. (1997). Effects of pregnancy and lactation on anxiety disorders. *ADAA Reporter, 8*(3), 2–22.

References

American Psychiatric Association (1952). *Diagnostic and statistical manual of mental disorders (1st ed.; DSM-I)*. Washington, DC: Author.

American Psychiatric Association (1968). *Diagnostic and statistical manual of mental disorders (2nd ed; DSM-II)*. Washington, DC: Author.

American Psychiatric Association (1980). *Diagnostic and statistical manual of mental disorders (3rd ed; DSM-III)*. Washington, DC: Author.

American Psychiatric Association (1987). *Diagnostic and statistical manual of mental disorders*; III-R (3rd ed). Washington, DC: APA.

American Psychiatric Association (1993). Anxiety disorders. DSM-IV draft criteria—Task Force on DSM-IV, p. K:1.

American Psychiatric Association (1994). *Diagnostic and statistical manual of mental disorders*; IV (4th ed.). Washington, DC: American Psychiatric Association.

American Psychiatric Association (1998). Practice guidelines for the treatment of patients with panic disorder. *American Journal of Psychiatry, 155*(5), S1–S34.

Amies, P. L., Gelder, M. G., & Shaw, P. M. (1983). Social phobia: A comparative clinical study. *British Journal of Psychiatry, 142*, 174–179.

Anderson, D. J., Noyes, R., Jr., & Crowe, R. R. (1984). A comparison of panic disorder and generalized anxiety disorder. *American Journal of Psychiatry, 141*, 572–575.

Andrews, G. (1982). A treatment outline for agoraphobia: The quality assurance project. *Australian and New Zealand Journal of Psychiatry, 16*, 25–233.

Antony, M. M., & Barlow, D. H. (1989). Emotion theory as a framework for explaining panic attacks and panic disorder. In R. M. Rapee (Ed.), *Current controversies in the anxiety disorders*. New York: Guilford.

Apfeldorf, W. L., Shear, M. K., Leon, A. C., & Portera, L. (1994). A brief screen for panic disorder. *Journal of Anxiety Disorders, 8*(1), 71–78.

Appleby, I. L., Klein, D. F., Sachar, E., & Levitt, M. (1981). Biochemical indices of lactate induced panic: A preliminary report. In D. F.

Klein & J. G. Rabkin (Eds.), *Anxiety: New research and changing concepts*. New York: Raven.

Argyle, N. (1988). The nature of cognitions in panic disorder. *Behavior Research and Therapy, 26*, 261–264.

Argyle, N., & Roth, M. (1989). The phenomenological study of 90 patients with panic disorder, part II. *Psychiatry Developments, 3*, 187–202.

Arnow, B. A., Taylor, C. B., & Agras, W. S. (1985). Enhancing agoraphobia treatment outcomes by changing couple communication patterns. *Behavior Therapy, 16*, 452–467.

Arntz, A., Krol, W., & van Rijsoort, M. (1993). One-session treatment of panic by information only. Presented at the 23rd Congress of the European Association of Behaviour and Cognitive Therapy, London.

Aronson, T. A., & Craig, T. J. (1986). Cocaine precipitation of panic disorder. *American Journal of Psychiatry, 143*, 643–645.

Aronson, T. A., & Logue, C. M. (1988). Phenomenology of panic attacks: A descriptive study of panic disorder patients' self-reports. *Journal of Clinical Psychiatry, 49*, 8–13.

Arrindell, W., & Emmelkamp, P. (1986). Marital quality and general life adjustment in relation to treatment outcome in agoraphobia. *Advances in Behavior Research and Therapy, 8*, 139–185.

Arrindell, W. A., Cox, B. J., Van Der Ende, J., & Kwee, M. G. T. (1995). Phobic dimensions—II. Cross-national confirmation of the multidimensional structure underlying the Mobility Inventory (MI). *Behaviour Research and Therapy, 33*(6), 711–724.

Ascher, M. (1984). Paradox in behavior therapy: Some data and some possibilities. *Journal of Behavior Therapy and Experimental Psychiatry, 15*(5), 187.

Ball, S. G., Otto, M. W., Pollack, M. H., Uccello, R., & Rosenbaum, J. F. (1995). Differentiating social phobia and panic disorder: A test of core beliefs. *Cognitive Therapy and Research, 19*(4), 473–481.

Ballenger, J. C. (1986). Biological aspects of panic disorder. *American Journal of Psychiatry, 143*, 516–518.

Ballenger, J. C., Burrows, G. D., DuPont, R. L., Lesser, I. M., Noyes, R., Pecknold, J. C., Rifkin, A., & Swinson, R. P. (1988). Alprazolam in panic disorder and agoraphobia: Results from a multicenter trial. I. Efficacy in short term treatment. *Archives of General Psychiatry, 45*, 413–422.

Bandelow, B. (1995). Assessing the efficacy of treatments for panic disorder and agoraphobia. II. The Panic and Agoraphobia Scale. *International Clinical Psychopharmacology, 10,* 73–81.

Bandelow, D., Hajak, G., Holzrichter, S., Kunerf, H. I., & Ruther, R. J. (1995). Assessing the efficacy of treatments for panic and agoraphobia. I. Methodological problems. *International Clinical Psychopharmacology, 10,* 83–93.

Bandura, A. (1977). Self-efficacy: Toward a unifying theory of behavioral change. *Psychological Review, 84,* 191–215.

Bandura, A., Adams, N. E., Hardy, A. B., & Howells, G. N. (1980). Test of the generality of self-efficacy theory. *Cognitive Therapy and Research, 4,* 39–66.

Barlow, D. H. (1988). *Anxiety and its disorders: The nature and treatment of anxiety and panic.* New York: Guilford.

Barlow, D. H., Brown, T. A., & Craske, M. G. (1994). Definition of panic attacks and panic disorder in DSM-IV: Implications for research. *Journal of Abnormal Psychology, 103,* 553–564.

Barlow, D. H., & Cerny, J. A. (1988). *Psychological treatment of panic: Treatment manuals for practitioners* New York: Guilford.

Barlow, D. H., Cohen, A. S., Waddell, M., Vermilyea, J A., Klosko, J. S., Blanchard, E. B., & DiNardo, P. A. (1984). Panic and generalized anxiety disorders: Nature and treatment. *Behavior Therapy, 15,* 431–449.

Barlow, D. H., & Craske, M. G. (1988). The phenomenology of panic. In S. Rachman & J. D. Maser (Eds.), *Panic: Psychological perspectives.* Hillsdale, NJ.: Erlbaum.

Barlow, D. H., & Craske, M. G. (1994). *Mastery of your anxiety and panic II.* Albany, NY: Graywind.

Barlow, D. H., Craske, M. G., Cerny, J. A., & Klosko, J. S. (1989). Behavioral treatment of panic disorder. *Behavior Therapy, 20,* 261–282.

Barlow, D. H., DiNardo, P. A., Vermilyea, B. B., Vermilyea, J. A., & Blanchard, E. B. (1986). Co-morbidity and depression among the anxiety disorders: Issues in diagnosis and classification. *Journal of Nervous and Mental Disease, 174,* 63–72.

Barlow, D. H., Hayes, S. C., & Nelson, R. O. (1984). *The scientist-practitioner: Research and accountability in clinical and educational settings.* New York: Pergamon.

Barlow, D. H., Mavissakalia, M. R., & Shofield, L. D. (1980). Patterns of desynchrony in agoraphobia: A preliminary report. *Behaviour Research and Therapy, 18*, 441–448.

Barlow, D. H., O'Brien, G. T., & Last, C. G. (1984a). Couples treatment of agoraphobia in relation to marital adjustment. *Archives of General Psychiatry, 36*, 807–811.

Barlow, D. H., O'Brien, G. T., & Last, C. G. (1984b). Couples treatment of agoraphobia. *Behavior Therapy, 15*, 41–58.

Barlow, D. H., Vermilyea, J., Blanchard, E., Vermilyea, B., DiNardo, P., & Cerny, J. A. (1985). The phenomenon of panic. *Journal of Abnormal Psychology, 94*, 320–328.

Barlow, D. H., Gorman, J. M., Shear, M. K., & Woods, S. W. (1998, November). Study design and pretreatment attrition. In D. H. Barlow (chair), *Results from the multicenter clinical trial on the treatment of panic disorder: Cognitive behavior treatment versus imipramine versus their combination.* Symposium presented at the 32nd annual convention of the Association for Advancement of Behavior Therapy, Washington, D.C.

Barraclough, B., Bunch, J., Nelson, B., & Sainsbury, P. (1974). A hundred cases of suicide: Clinical aspects. *British Journal of Psychiatry, 125*, 355–373.

Barsky, A. J., Barnett, M. C., & Cleary, P. D. (1994). Hypochondriasis and panic disorder: Boundary and overlap. *Archives of General Psychiatry, 51*(11), 918–925.

Beard, G. M. (1880). *Practical treatise on nervous exhaustion (neurastheria).* New York: William Wood.

Beck, A. T. (1987). *Anxiety inventory.* Philadelphia: Center for Cognitive Therapy.

Beck, A. T., Emery, G., & Greenberg, R. L. (1985). *Anxiety disorders and phobias.* New York: Guilford.

Beck, A. T., Epstein, N., Brown, G., & Steer, R. A. (1988). An inventory for measuring clinical anxiety: Psychometric properties. *Journal of Consulting and Clinical Psychology, 56*, 893–897.

Beck, A. T., Freeman, A., & Associates (1990). *Cognitive therapy of personality disorders.* New York: Guilford.

Beck, A. T., Laude, R., & Bohnert, M. (1974). Ideational components of anxiety neurosis. *Archives of General Psychiatry, 31*, 319–325.

Beck, A. T., Sokol, L., Clark, D. M., Berchick, B., & Wright, F. (1992).

A crossed over study of focussed cognitive therapy for panic disorder. *American Journal of Psychiatry, 149,* 778–783.

Beck, A. T., & Steer, R. A. (1990). *Beck anxiety inventory manual.* San Antonio, TX: Psychological Corp., Harcourt Brace Jovanovich.

Beck, A. T., Steer, R. A., Sanderson, W. C., & Madland-Skeie, T. (1991). Panic disorder and suicidal ideation and behavior: Discrepant findings in psychiatric outpatients. *American Journal of Psychiatry, 148*(9).

Beitman, B. D., DeRosear, L., Basha, I., Flaker, G., & Corcoran, C. (1987). Panic disorder with cardiology patients with atypical or non-anginal chest pain. *Journal of Anxiety Disorders, 1*(3), 277–282.

Bernstein, D. A., & Borkovec, T. D. (1973). Progressive relaxation training. A manual for helping professionals. Champaign, IL: Research Press.

Black, D. W., Wesner, R., Bowers, W., & Gabel, J. (1993) A comparison of fluvoxamine, cognitive therapy and placebo in the treatment of panic disorder. *Archives of General Psychiatry, 50,* 44–50.

Black, D. W., Wesner, R. B., Gabel, J., Bowers, W., et al. (1994). Predictors of short-term treatment response in 66 patients with panic disorder. *Journal of Affective Disorders, 30*(4), 233–241.

Borden, J. W., Clum, G. A., & Salmon, P. G. (1991). Mechanisms of change in the treatment of panic. *Cognitive Therapy and Research, 15*(4), 257–272.

Borkovec, T. D., & Grayson, J. B. (1980). Consequences of increasing the functional impact of emotional stimuli. In K. Blankstein, P. Pliner, & J. Polivy (Eds.), *Assessment and modification of emotional behavior.* New York: Plenum.

Borkovec, T. D., Grayson, J. B., & Cooper, K. M. (1978). Treatment of general tension: Subjective and physiological effects of progressive muscle relaxation. *Journal of Consulting and Clinical Psychology, 46*(3), 518–528.

Bouchard, S., Gauthier, J. G., Laberge, B., French, D., Pelletier, M. H., & Godbout, C. (1996). Exposure versus cognitive restructuring in the treatment of panic disorder with agoraphobia: Interim result. *Behaviour Research and Therapy, 34*(4), 224–234.

Boudewyns, P. A., Stwertka, S. A., Hyer, L. A., Albrecht, J. W., & Sperr, E. V. (1993). Eye movement desensitization and reprocessing: A pilot study. *Behavior Therapy, 16,* 30–33.

Boulenger, J., Uhde, T. W., Wolff, E. A., & Post, R. M. (1984). Increased sensitivity to caffeine in patients with panic disorders. *Archives of General Psychiatry, 41*, 1067–1071.

Boyd, J. H. (1986). Use of mental health services for the treatment of panic disorder. *American Journal of Psychiatry, 143*, 1569–1574.

Bradley, B. P., Mogg, K. M., Millar, N., & White, J. (1995). Selective processing of negative information: Effects of clinical anxiety, concurrent depression, and awareness. *Journal of Abnormal Psychology, 104*(3), 532–536.

Bradwejn, J., Koszycki, D., Payeur, R., Bourin, M., & Borthwick, H. (1992). Replication of action of cholecystokinin tetrapeptide in panic disorder: Clinical and behavioral findings. *American Journal of Psychiatry, 149*, 962–964.

Breggin, P. R. (1964). The psychophysiology of anxiety with a review of the literature concerning adrenaline. *Journal of Nervous and Mental Disease, 139*, 558–568.

Breier, A., Charney, D. S., & Heninger, G. B. (1984). Major depression in patients with agoraphobia and panic disorder. *Archives of General Psychiatry, 41*, 1129–1135.

Briggs, A. C., Strech, D. D., & Brandon, S. (1993). Subtyping panic disorder by symptom profile. *British Journal of Psychiatry, 163*, 201–209.

Brown, C. S., Rakel, R. E., Well, B. G., Downs, J. M., & Akiskal, H. S. (1991). A practical update on anxiety disorders and their pharmacologic treatment. *Archives of Internal Medicine, 151*, 873–884.

Brown, G. K., Beck, A. T., Newman, C. F., Beck, J. S., & Tran, G. Q. (1997). A comparison of focused and standard cognitive therapy for panic disorder. *Journal of Anxiety Disorder, 11*(3), 329–345.

Brown, T. A., Antony, M. M., & Barlow, D. H. (1995). Diagnostic comorbidity in panic disorder: Effect on treatment outcome and course of comorbid diagnoses following treatment. *Journal of Consulting and Clinical Psychology, 63*, 408–418.

Brown, T. A., & Cash, T. F. (1990). The phenomenon of nonclinical panic: Parameters of panic, fear and avoidance. *Journal of Anxiety Disorders, 4*(1), 15–29.

Brown, T. A., Chorpita, B. A., Korotisch, W., & Barlow, D. H. (1997). Psychometric properties of the Depression, Anxiety Stress Scales (DASS) in clinical samples. *Behaviour Research and Therapy, 35*(1), 79–89.

Brown, T. A., & Deagle, E. A. (1992). Structured interview assessment of nonclinical panic. *Behavior Therapy, 23,* 75–85.

Bryant, R. A., & Harvey, A. G. (1995). Processing threatening information in posttraumatic stress disorder. *Journal of Abnormal Psychology, 104*(3), 537–541.

Buglass, D., Clarke, J., Henderson, A. S., Kreitman, N., & Presley, A. S. (1977). A study of agoraphobic housewives. *Psychological Medicine, 7,* 73–86.

Burton, T. (1990/1624). *The anatomy of melancholy* (pp. 319–325). Oxford: Oxford University Press.

Busch, F. N., Cooper, A. M., Klerman, G. L., et al. (1991). Neurophysiological, cognitive-behavioral, and psychoanalytic approaches to panic disorder; Toward an integration. *Psychoanalytic Inquiry, 11,* 316–332.

Callahan, R., & Callahan, J. (1996). *Thought Field Therapy and Trauma.* Indian Wells, CA: Thought Field Therapy ™ Training Center.

Cameron, O. G., & Thyer, B. A. (1985). Treatment of pavor nocturnal with alprazolam. *Journal of Clinical Psychology, 46,* 405.

Canter, A., Kondo, C. Y., & Krott, J. R. (1975). A comparison of EMG feedback and progressive muscle relaxation training in anxiety neurosis. *British Journal of Psychiatry, 127,* 470–477.

Cantor, N., & Mischel, W. (1979). Prototypes in person perception. In L. Berkowitz (Ed.), *Advances in experimental social psychology* (Vol. 12). New York: Academic.

Carlson, J. G., Chemtob, C. M. Rusnak, K., Hedlund, N. L., & Muraoka, M. Y. (1998). Eye movement desenistization and reprocessing (EMDR) treatment for combat related posttraumatic stress disorder. *Journal of Traumatic Stress, 11*(1), 3–24.

Cassano, G. B., Perugi, G., Musetti, L., & Akiskal, H. S. (1989). Nature of anxiety presenting concomitantly with depression. *Comprehensive Psychiatry, 30,* 473–482.

Catalan, J., Gath, D., Edmonds, G., & Ennis, J. (1984). The effects of non-prescribing of anxiolytics in general practice: I. Controlled evaluation of psychiatric and social outcome. *British Journal of Psychiatry, 144,* 593–602.

Caughey, J. L. (1939). Cardiovascular neurosis—A review. *Psychosomatic Medicine, 1,* 311–324.

Cerny, J. A., Barlow, D. H., Craske, M., & Himadi, W. G. (1987). Couples treatment of agoraphobia: A two year follow-up. *Behavior Therapy, 18,* 401–415.

Chambers, C. D., Johnson, K. A., & Dick, L. M. (1996). Birth outcome in pregnant women taking fluoxetine. *New England Journal of Medicine, 335*, 1010–1015.

Chambless, D. L. (1985). The relationship between severity of agoraphobia and associated psychopathology. *Behaviour Research and Therapy, 23*, 305–310.

Chambless, D. L., Caputo, G. C., Bright, P., & Gallagher, R. (1984), Assessment of fear of fear in agoraphobia: The body sensations questionnaire and the agoraphobic questionnaire. *Journal of Consulting and Clinical Psychology, 52*, 1090–1097.

Chambless, D. L., Caputo, G. C., Jasin, S. E., Gracely, E. J., & Williams, C. (1985). The mobility inventory for agoraphobia. *Behaviour Research and Therapy, 23*, 35–44.

Chambless, D. L., & Gillis, M. M. (1996). Cognitive therapy of anxiety. In K. S. Dobson & K. D. Craig (Eds.), *Advances in cognitive-behavioral therapy*. Thousand Oaks, CA: Sage.

Chambless, D. L., Goldstein, A. J., Gallagher, R., & Bright, P. (1986). Integrating behavior therapy and psychotherapy in the treatment of agoraphobia. *Psychotherapy, 23*, 150–159.

Chambless, D. L., & Gracely, E. J. (1989). Fear of fear and the anxiety disorders. *Cognitive Therapy and Research, 13*, 9–20.

Charney, D. S., & Heninger, G. R. (1986a). Abnormal regulation of noradrenergic function in panic disorders. *Archives of General Psychiatry, 43*, 1042–1054.

Charney, D. S., & Heninger, G. R. (1986b). Noradrenergic function of panic anxiety: Effects of yohimbine in healthy subjects and patients with agoraphobia and panic disorder. *Archives of General Psychiatry, 41*, 751–763.

Charney, D. S., & Heninger, G. R. (1986c). Serotonin function in panic anxiety: Effects of intravenous tryptophan in healthy subjects and patients with panic disorder before and during alprazolam treatment. *Archives of General Psychiatry, 43*, 1059–1065.

Charney, D. S., Heninger, G. R., & Breier, A. (1984). Noradrenergic function of panic anxiety: Effects of yohimbine in healthy subjects and patients with agoraphobia and panic disorder. *Archives of General Psychiatry, 41*, 751–763.

Charney, D. S., Heninger, G. R., & Jatlow, P. I. (1985). Increased anxiogenic effects of caffeine in panic disorder. *Archives of General Psychiatry, 42*, 233–243.

Charney, D. S., & Woods, S. W. (1989). Benzodiazepine treatment of panic disorder: A comparison of alprazolam and lorazepam. *Journal of Clinical Psychiatry, 50*, 418–423.

Charney, D. S., Woods, S. W., Goodman, W. K., & Heninger, G. R. (1987). Serotonin function in anxiety II. Effects of serotonin antagonist MCPP in panic disorder patients and healthy subjects. *Psychopharmacology, 92*, 14–24.

Charney, D. S., Woods, S. W., Price, L. H., Goodman, W. K., Glazer, W. M., & Heninger, G. R. (1990). Noradrenergic dysregulation in panic disorder. In J. C. Ballenger (Ed.), *Neurobiology of panic disorder*. New York: Wiley-Liss.

Chiriboga, D. A. (1977). Life events weighting systems: A comparative analysis. *Journal of Psychosomatic Research, 21*, 415–422.

Clancy, J., & Noyes, R. (1976). Anxiety neurosis: A disease for the medical model. *Psychosomatics, 17*, 90–93.

Clancy, J., Noyes, R., Hoenk, P. R., & Slymen, D. J. (1978). Secondary depression in anxiety neuroses. *Journal of Nervous and Mental Disease, 166*, 846–850.

Clark, D. M. (1986). A cognitive approach to panic. *Behavior Research and Therapy, 24*, 461–470.

Clark, D. M. (1988). A cognitive model of panic attacks. In S. Rachman & J. D. Maser (Eds.), *Panic: Psychological perspective*. Hillsdale, NJ: Erlbaum

Clark, D. M. (1989). Anxiety states. In K. Hawton, P. Salkovskis, J. Kirk, & D. M. Clark (Eds.), *Cognitive behavior therapy for psychiatric problems*. Oxford: Oxford University Press.

Clark, D. M. (1993). Cognitive mediation of panic attacks induced by biological challenge tests. *Advances in Behavior Research and Therapy, 15*, 75–84.

Clark, D. M., & Ehlers, A. (1993). An overview of the theory and treatment of panic disorder. *Applied and Preventive Psychology, 2*, 131–139.

Clark, D. M., & Salkovskis, P. M. (1987). *Cognitive treatment for panic attacks: Therapist's manual*. Oxford: Warneford Hospital.

Clark, D. M., Salkovskis, P. M., & Chalkley, A. J. (1985). Respiratory control as a treatment for panic attacks. *Journal of Behavior Therapy and Experimental Psychiatry, 16*, 23–30.

Clark, D. M., Salkovskis, P. M., Gelder, M. G., Koehler, C., Martin, M., Anastasiades, P., Hackman, A., Middleton, H., & Jeavons, A. (1988). Test of a cognitive theory of panic. In I. Hand & H. U. Wittchen (Eds.), *Panic and phobias II*. New York: Springer-Verlag.

Clark, D. M., Salkovskis, P. M., Hackman, A., Middleton, H., Anastasiades, P., & Gelder, M. (1994). A comparison of cognitive therapy, applied relaxation and Imipramine in the treatment of panic disorder. *British Journal of Psychiatry, 164,* 759–769.

Clark, L. A., & Watson, D. (1991). Tripartite model of anxiety and depression: Psychometric evidence and taxonomic implications. *Journal of Abnormal Psychology, 100*(3), 316–336.

Clum, G. A. (1989). Psychological interventions vs drugs in the treatment of panic. *Behavior Therapy, 20,* 429–457.

Clum, G. A. (1990). *Coping with panic.* Pacific Grove, CA: Brooks/Cole.

Clum, G. A., Broyles, S., Borden, J., & Watkins, P. L. (1990). Validity and reliability of the panic attack symptoms and cognitions questionnaires. *Journal of Psychopathology and Behavioral Assessment, 12*(3), 233–245.

Clum, G. A., & Pendry, D. (1987). Depression symptomatology as non-requisite for successful treatment of panic with antidepressant medications. *Journal of Anxiety Disorders, 1*(4), 337–344.

Clum, G. A., & Surls, R. (1993). A meta-analysis of treatments for panic disorder. *Journal of Consulting and Clinical Psychology, 61*(2), 317–326.

Cohen, A. S., Barlow, D. H., & Blanchard, E. B. (1985). Psychophysiology of relaxation-associated panic attacks. *Journal of Abnormal Psychology, 94,* 96–101.

Cohen, L. S., Sichel, D. A., Faraone, S. V., Robertson, L. M., Dimmock, I. A., & Rosenbaum, J. F. (1996). Course of panic disorder during pregnancy and the puerperium: A preliminary study. *Biological Psychiatry, 39,* 950–954.

Cohen, M. E., Badal, D. W., Kilpatrick, A., Reed, R. W., & White, P. D. (1951). The high familial prevalence of neurocirculatory asthenia (anxiety neurosis, effort syndrome). *American Journal of Human Genetics, 3,* 126–158.

Cohen, M. E., & White, P. D. (1950). Life situations, emotions and neurocirculatory asthenia (anxiety neurosis, neurasthenia, effort syndrome). In H. G. Wolf (Ed.), *Life stress and bodily disease* (Nervous and Mental Disease, Research Publication no. 29). Baltimore: Williams & Wilkins.

Connor, K. M., & Vaughan, D. S. (1999). *Kava: Nature's stress relief.* New York: Avon.

Conttrux, J., Note, I. D., Cungi, C., Legeron, P., Heim, F., Chneiweiss, L., Bernard, G., & Bouvard, M. (1995). A controlled study of cognitive behavior therapy with buspirone or placebo in panic disorder with agoraphobia. *British Journal of Psychiatry, 167,* 635–641.

Coplan, J. D., Sharma, T., Rosenblum, L. A., Friedman, S., Bassofft, T. B., Barbour, R. L., & Gorman J. M. (1992). Effects of sodium lactate infusion on cisternal lactate and carbon dioxide levels in non-human primates. *American Journal of Psychiatry, 149,* 1369–1373.

Cowley, D. S., & Arana, G. W. (1990). The diagnostic utility of lactate sensitivity in panic disorder. *Archives of General Psychiatry, 47,* 277–284.

Cowley, D. S., Dager, S. R., McClellan, J., Roy-Byrne, P. P., & Dunner, D. L. (1988). Response to lactate infusion in generalized anxiety disorder. *Biological Psychiatry, 24,* 409–414.

Cowley, D. S., & Roy-Byrne, P. P. (1989). Panic disorder during pregnancy. *Journal of Psychosomatic Obstetrical Gynecology, 10,* 193–210.

Cowley, D. S., & Roy-Byrne, P. P. (1991). The biology of generalized anxiety disorder and chronic anxiety. In R. M. Rapee & D. H. Barlow (Eds.), *Chronic anxiety: Generalized anxiety disorder and mixed anxiety-depression.* New York: Guilford.

Cox, B. J., (1996). The nature and assessment of catastrophic thoughts in panic disorder. *Behaviour Research and Therapy, 34*(4), 363–374.

Cox, B. J., Cohen, E., Direnfeld, D. M., & Swinson, R. P. (1996). Does the Beck Anxiety Inventory measure anything beyond panic attack symptoms? *Behaviour Research and Therapy, 34*(11/12), 949–954.

Cox, B. J., Endler, B. S., & Swinson, R. P. (1995a). Anxiety sensitivity and panic attack symptomatology. *Behavior Research and Therapy, 33*(7), 833–836.

Cox, B. J., Endler, N. S., & Swinson, R. P. (1995b). An examination of levels of agoraphobic anxiety in panic disorder. *Behaviour Research and Therapy, 33,* 57–62.

Cox, B. J., Parker, J. D. A., & Swinson, R. P. (1996). Anxiety sensitivity: Confirmatory evidence for multidimensional construct. *Behaviour Research and Therapy, 34*(7), 591–598.

Cox B. J., Swinson, R. P., Endler, N. S., & Norton, G. R. (1994). The symptom structure of panic attacks. *Comprehensive Psychiatry, 35,* 349–353.

Craske, M. G. (1991). Models and treatment of panic: Behavioral therapy for panic. *Journal of Cognitive Psychotherapy: An International Quarterly, 5*(3), 199–214.

Craske, M. G., (1996a). Cognitive-behavioral approaches to panic and agoraphobia. In K. S. Dobson & K. D. Craig (Eds.), *Advances in cognitive-behavioral therapy.* Thousand Oaks, CA: Sage.

Craske, M. G. (1996b). An integrated treatment approach to panic disorder. *Bulletin of the Meninnger Clinic, 60* (2, suppl. A): A87–A104.

Craske, M. G., & Barlow, D. H. (1989). Nocturnal panic: Response to hyperventilation and CO_2 challenges. *Journal of Abnormal Psychology, 99,* 302–307.

Craske, M. G., & Barlow, D. H. (1990a). Nocturnal panic. *Journal of Nervous and Mental Diseases, 177,* 160–167.

Craske, M. G., & Barlow, D. H. (1990b). *Therapist guide for the mastery of anxiety and panic.* Albany, NY: State University of New York, Center for Stress and Anxiety Disorders.

Craske, M. G., & Barlow, D. H. (1994). *Agoraphobia. Supplement to the MAP II Program.* Albany, NY: Graywind.

Craske, M. G., Street, L. & Barlow, D. H. (1989). Instruction to focus upon or distract from internal cues during exposure treatment for agoraphobic avoidance. *Behavior Research and Therapy 27,* 663–672.

Craske, M., Brown, T. A., & Barlow, D. H. (1991). Behavioral treatment of panic disorder: A two-year follow up. *Behavior Therapy, 22,* 289–304.

Craske, M. G., Maidenberg, E., & Bytritsky, A. (1995). Brief cognitive-behavioral versus nondirective therapy for panic disorder. *Journal of Behavior Therapy and Experimental Psychiatry, 26,* 113–120.

Craske, M. G., Meadows, E. A., & Barlow, D. H. (1994). *Mastery of your anxiety and panic II and agoraphobia supplement.* Therapist guide. San Antonio, TX: Psychological Corp.

Craske, M. G., Rachman, S. J., & Tallman, K. (1986). Mobility, cognitions, and panic. *Journal of Psychopathology and Behavioral Assessment, 8,* 199–209.

Craske, M. G., Zarate, R., Burton, T., & Barlow, D. H. (1993). Specific fears and panic attacks: A survey of clinical and nonclinical samples. *Journal of Anxiety Disorders, 7*(1), 1–19.

Crowe, R. R., Noyes, R., Pauls, D. L., & Slymen, D. J. (1983). A family study of panic disorder. *Archives of General Psychiatry, 40,* 1065–1069.

Crowe, R. R., Noyes, R., Wilson, A. F., Elston, R. C., & Ward, L. J. (1987). A linkage study of panic disorder. *Archives of General Psychiatry, 44,* 933–937.

Coryell, W., Noyes, R., & Claucy, J. (1982) Excess mortality in panic disorder. *Archives of General Psychiatry, 39,* 701–703.

DaCosta, J. M. (1871). On irritable heart: A clinical study of a functional cardiac disorder and its consequences. *American Journal of Medical Science, 61,* 17–52.

Dager, S. R., Cowley, D. S., & Dunner, D. L. (1987). Biological markers in panic states: Lactate induced panic and mitral valve prolapse. *Biological Psychiatry, 22,* 339–359.

Darwin, C. R. (1872). *The expression of emotions in man and animals.* London: John Murray.

Dattilio, F. M. (1986). Differences in cognitive responses to fear among individuals diagnosed as panic disorder, generalized anxiety disorder, agoraphobia with panic attacks and simple phobia. Dissertation Abstracts, *University Microfilming International,* Pub. no. 8711320, 216 pp.

Dattilio, F. M. (1987). The use of paradoxical intention in the treatment of panic attacks. *Journal of Counseling and Development, 66,* 66–67.

Dattilio, F. M. (1988). Relation of experience during sex and panic: A preliminary note. *Cognitive-Behaviorist, 10*(3), 31–33.

Dattilio, F. M. (1989). Relation of sensations during sex and panic. Paper presented at the World Congress of Behaviour and Cognitive Therapy, Oxford University.

Dattilio, F. M. (1990). Symptom induction and de-escalation in the treatment of panic attacks. *Journal of Mental Health Counseling, 12*(4), 515–519.

Dattilio, F. M. (1992a). Interoceptive sensations during sexual arousal and panic. *Behavior Therapist, 15*(9), 231–233.

Dattilio, F. M. (1992b). "The SAEB system"—crises intervention techniques with panic. Symposium on Crisis Intervention presented at the

26th Annual Association for the Advancement of Behavior Therapy (AABT), Boston.

Dattilio, F. M. (1994a). Paradoxical intention as a proposed alternative in the treatment of panic disorder. *Journal of Cognitive Psychotherapy, 8*(1), 33–40.

Dattilio, F. M. (1994b). SAEB: A method of conceptualization in the treatment of panic. *Cognitive and Behavior Practice, 1*(1), 179–191.

Dattilio, F. M. (1994c). The use of the SAEB system and symptom induction in the treatment of panic (videotape). Bristol, PA: Taylor & Francis.

Dattilio, F. M. (1995). Non-pharmacological alternatives to the treatment of panic disorders in emergency settings. *Current Psychiatry, 2*(2), 236–253.

Dattilio, F. M. The use of kava extract as adjunct to the treatment of panic disorder (in progress).

Dattilio, F. M., & Berchick, R. M. (1992). Panic disorder with agoraphobia (pp. 89–98). In A. Freeman & F. M. Dattilio (Eds.), *Comprehensive casebook of cognitive therapy*, New York: Plenum.

Dattilio, F. M., & Freeman, A. (Eds.) (1994). *Cognitive-behavioral strategies in crisis intervention.* New York: Guilford.

Dattilio, F. M., Freeman, A., & Blue, J. (1998). The therapeutic relationship (pp. 229–249). In A. S. Bellack & M. Hersen (Eds.), *Comprehensive clinical psychology.* Oxford: Elsevier Science.

Dattilio, F. M., & Foa, E. B. (1988). *Fear of fear: A comparison of cognitive responses among panic disorders with and without agoraphobia, generalized anxiety disorders and simple phobia* (Unpublished manuscript).

Dattilio, F. M., & Salas, J. A. (1999). Heart attack or panic attack? *ADAA Reporter, 10*(3), 1–3.

Davanloo, H. (1990). *Unlocking the unconscious.* Chichester, England: Wiley.

Dealey, R. S., Ishiki, D. M., Avery, D. H., Wilson, L. G., & Dunner, D. L. (1981). Secondary depression in anxiety disorders. *Comprehensive Psychiatry, 22,* 612–617.

D'Aulaire, I., & D'Aulaire, E. P. (1962). *Book of Greek myths.* New York: Doubleday.

De Beurs, E., Lange, A., Van Dyck, R., Blonk, R., & Koele, P. (1991). Behavioral assessment of avoidance in agoraphobia. *Journal of Psychopathology and Behavioral Assessment, 13,* 285–300.

De Beurs, E., vanBalkom, A. J. K. L., Lange, A., Koele, P., & Van Dyck, R. (1995). Treatment of panic disorder with agoraphobia: Comparison of fluvoxamine, placebo and psychological panic management combined with exposure and of exposure in vivo alone. *American Journal of Psychiatry, 152,* 683–691.

Dell, P. F. (1981) Some irreverent thoughts on paradox. *Family Process, 20,* 37–42.

De Loof, C., Zandbergen, J., Lousberg, H., Pols, H., & Griez, E. (1989). The role of life events in the onset of panic disorder. *Behaviour Research and Therapy, 27*(4), 461–463.

Den Boer, J. A., & Westenberg, H. G. M. (1990). Serotonin function in panic disorder: A double blind placebo controlled study with fluvaxamine and ritanserin. *Psychopharmacology, 102,* 85–94.

De Ruiter, C., Rijken, H., Garssen, B., Van Schaik, A., & Kraaimaat, F. (1989). Comorbidity among the anxiety disorders. *Journal of Anxiety Disorders, 3,* 57–68.

Diaferia, G., Sciuto, G., Perna, G., Bernardeschi, L., Battaglia, M., Rusmini, S., & Bellodi, L. (1993). DSM-III-R personality disorders in panic disorder. *Journal of Anxiety Disorders, 7*(2), 153–161.

Diez, C., Gastó, C., & Vallejo, J. (1989). Desarrollo de conductas de evitación en un sujeto con crisis de angustia atipicas. *Revista de Psiquiatría de la Facultad de Medicina de Barcelona, 16,* (6), 329–332.

DiNardo, P. A., & Barlow, D. H. (1988). *Anxiety Disorders Interview Schedule—Revised (ADIS-R).* Albany, NY: Graywind.

DiNardo, P. A., Barlow, D. H., Cerny, J., Vermilyea, B. B., Vermilyea, J. A., Himadi, W., & Waddell, M. (1985). *Anxiety Disorders Interview Schedule—Revised (ADIS-R).* Albany, NY: Phobia and Anxiety Disorders Clinic, State University of New York.

DiNardo, P. A., Brown, T. A., & Barlow, D. H. (1995). *Anxiety Disorders Interview Schedule for DSM-IV (lifetime version).* San Antonio, TX: Psychological Corp.

DiNardo, P. A., Moras, K., Barlow, D. H., Rapee, R. M., & Brown, T. A. (1993). Reliability of DSM-III-R anxiety disorder categories using the Anxiety Disorders Interview Schedule—Revised (ADIS-R). *Archives of General Psychiatry, 50,* 251–256.

Doctor, R. M. (1982). Major results of a large-scale pre-treatment survey of agoraphobics. In R. L. DuPont (Ed.), *Phobia: A comprehensive survey of modern treatments.* New York: Brunner/Mazel.

Dowd, E. T., & Trutt, S. D. (1988). Paradoxical interventions in behavior modification (pp. 96–130). In Hersen, Eisler, & Miller (Eds.). *Progress in behavior modification* (Vol. 12). New York: Guilford.

Dubro, A. F., Wetzler, S., & Khan, M. W. (1988). A comparison of three self-report questionnaires for the diagnosis of DSM-III personality disorders. *Journal of Personality Disorders, 2*, 256–266.

Dunner, D. L. (1985). Anxiety and panic: Relationship to depression and cardiac disorders. *Psychosomatics, 26*, 18–21.

Edinger, J. D., & Jacobsen, R. (1982). Incidence and significance of relaxation treatment side effects. *Behavior Therapist, 5*, 137–138.

Efran, J. S., & Caputo, C. (1984). Paradox in psychotherapy: A cybernetic perspective. *Journal of Behavior Therapy and Experimental Psychiatry, 15*(3), 235–240.

Ehlers, A., & Breuer, P. (1992). Increased cardiac awareness in panic disorder. *Journal of Abnormal Psychology, 101*(3), 371–382.

Ehlers, A., & Margraf, J. (1989). The psychophysiological model of panic attacks. In P. Emmelkamp, W. T. Everaerd, F. W. Kraaimaat, & M. J. Van Son (Eds.), *Fresh perspectives on anxiety disorders*. Lisa, The Netherlands: Swets & Zettinger.

Elkin, I., Shea, T., Watkins, J., Imber, S., Sotsky, S., Collins, J., Glass, D., Pilkonis, P., Leber, W., Docherty, J., Fiester, S., & Perloff, M. (1989). National Institute of Mental Health Treatment of Depression Collaborative Research Program: General effectiveness of treatments. *Archives of General Psychiatry, 48*, 971–982.

Endicott, J., & Spitzer, R. L. (1978). A diagnostic interview: The Schedule for Affective Disorders and Schizophrenia. *Archives of General Psychiatry, 35*, 837–844.

Epstein, N. B., & Dutton, S. S. (1997). Relationship characteristics of agoraphobia and their partners. Presented at the 31st Annual Association of the Advancement of Behavior Therapy meeting, November, Miami, Fla.

Epstein, N. B., Dutton, S. S., Dattilio, F. M., & Vittore, B. An analysis of relationship characteristics of agoraphobics and their spouses. *Journal of Clinical and Consulting Psychology* (in review).

Evans, L. (1989). Some biological aspects of panic disorder. *International Journal of Clinical Pharmacology Research, 9*, 139–145.

Evans, L., Holt, C. & Oei, T. P. S. (1991). Long term follow-up of agoraphobics treated by brief intensive group cognitive-behavioral psychotherapy. *Australian and New Zealand Journal of Psychiatry,* 25, 343–349.

Everly, G. S. (1989). *A clinical guide to the treatment of the human stress response* (pp. 28–59). New York: Plenum.

Fairburn, C. G., Jones, R., Peveler, R. C., Carr, S. J., Solomon, R. A., O'Connor, M. E., Burton, J., & Hope, R. A. (1991). Three psychological treatments for bulimia nervosa: A comparative trial. *Archives of General Psychiatry, 48,* 463–469.

Faravelli, C. (1985). Life events preceding the onset of panic disorder. *Journal of Affective Disorders, 9,* 103–105.

Faravelli, C., & Pallanti, S. (1989). Recent life events and panic disorder. *American Journal of Psychiatry, 146,* 622–626.

Faravelli, C., Webb, T., Ambonetti, A., Fonnesu, F., & Sessarego, A. (1985). Prevalence of traumatic life events in 31 agoraphobic patients with panic attacks. *American Journal of Psychiatry, 412,* 12.

Fava, G. A., Grandi, S., & Canestrari, R. (1988). Prodromal symptoms in panic with agoraphobia. *American Journal of Psychiatry, 145,* 1564–1567.

Fava, G. A., Kellner, R., Zielezny, M., & Grandi, S. (1988). Hypochondriacal fears and beliefs in agoraphobia. *Journal of Affective Disorders, 14,* 239–244.

Fawcett, J., Marcus, R. N., Anton, S. F., et al. (1995). Response of anxiety and agitation symptoms during the nefazodone treatment of major depression. *Journal of Clinical Psychiatry, 56* (suppl. 6), 37–42.

Feske, U., & De Beurs, E. (1997). The panic appraisal inventory: Psychometric properties. *Behavior Research and Therapy, 35*(9), 875–882.

Feske, U., & Goldstein, A. J. (1997). Eye movement desensitization and reprocessing treatment for panic disorder: A controlled outcome and partial dismantling study. *Journal of Consulting and Clinical Psychology, 65*(6) 1–10.

Frank, S. D. (1990). *Remember everything you read.* New York: Random House.

Frankl, V. E. (1975), Paradoxical intention and de-reflection, Psychotherapy: Theory, research and practice, *12,* 226–237.

Frankl, V. E. (1984). Paradoxical intention. In G. R. Weeks (Ed.), *Promoting change through paradoxical therapy,* Homewood, IL: Dow Jones-Irwin.

Freud, S. (1894). On the grounds for detaching a particular syndrome from neurasthenia under the description "anxiety neurosis" (pp. 76–106). *Standard edition of the complete psychological works of Sigmund Freud*, Vol. 3 (1893–1899). London: Hogarth.

Friedman, C. J., Shear, M. K., & Frances, A. (1987). DSM-III personality disorders in panic patients. *Journal of Personality Disorders, 1*, 132–235.

Friedman, S., & Chernen, L. (1994). Discriminating the panic disorder patient from patients with borderline personality disorder. *Journal of Anxiety Disorders, 8*(1), 49–61.

Fydrich, T., Dowdall, D., & Chambless, D. L. (1990). Aspects of reliability and validity of the Beck Anxiety Inventory. Presented at the National Conference on Phobias and Related Anxiety Disorders. Bethesda, Md.

Fyer, A. J., Liebowitz, M. R., Gorman, J. R., Davies, S. O., & Klein, D. F. (1985). Lactate vulnerability of remitted patients. *Psychiatric Research, 14*, 143–148.

Gallo, T. (1998). *Energy psychology: Explorations at the interface of energy, cognition, behavior and health*. Minneapolis: CRC Press/St. Lucie Press.

Galynker, I., Ieronimo, C., Perez-Acquino, A., & Lee, Y. (1996). Panic attacks with psychotic features. *Journal of Clinical Psychiatry, 57*(9), 402–406.

Garssen, B., Van Veenendaal, W., & Bloemink, R. (1983). Agoraphobia and the hyperventilation syndrome. *Behavior Research and Therapy, 21*, 643–649.

Gauthier, J., Bouchard, S., Côte, G., Laberge, B., & French, D. (1993). Development of two scales measuring self-efficacy to control panic attacks. *Canadian Psychology, 30*(2) 305.

Gelder, M. G., Bancroft, J. H. J., Gath, D. H., Johnston, D. W., Mathews, A. M., & Shaw, P. M. (1973). Specific and non-specific factors in behaviour therapy. *British Journal of Psychiatry, 123*, 445–462.

George, D. T., & Anderson, P. (1989). Aggressive thoughts and behaviors: Another symptom of panic disorder. *Acta Psychiatric Scandinavia, 79*, 500–502.

George, D. T., Zerby, A., Noble, S., & Nutt, D. J. (1988). Panic attacks and alcohol withdrawal: Can subjects differentiate the symptoms. *Biological Psychiatry, 24*, 240–243.

Ghosh, A., & Marks, I. M. (1987). Self-treatment of agoraphobia by exposure. *Behavior Therapy, 18,* 3–16.

Ghosh, A., Marks, I. M., & Carr, A. C. (1988). Therapist contact and outcome of self-exposure treatement for phobias: A controlled study. *British Journal of Psychiatry, 152,* 234–238.

Gittelman, R., & Klein, D. F. (1984). Relationship between separation anxiety and panic and agoraphobic disorders. *Psychopathology, 17* (suppl. 1), 56–65.

Goetz, R. R., Klein, D. F., & Gorman, J. M. (1994). Consistencies between recalled panic and lactate-induced panic. *Anxiety, 1*(1), 31–36.

Goldberg, R. J. (1988). Clinical presentations of panic-related disorders. *Journal of Anxiety Disorders, 2,* 61–75.

Goldenberg, H. (1983). *Contemporary clinical psychology,* Monterey, CA: Brooks/Cole.

Goldsmith, H. H. (1983). Genetic influences on personality from infancy to adulthood. *Child Development, 54,* 331–355.

Goldstein, A. J., & Chambless, D. L. (1978). A reanalysis of agoraphobia. *Behavior Therapy, 9,* 47–59.

Goldstein, A. J., & Feske, U. (1994) Eye movement desensitization and reprocessing for panic disorder: A case series. *Journal of Anxiety Disorders, 8,* 351–362.

Goldstein, D. J. (1995). Effects of third trimester fluoxetine exposure on the newborn. *Journal of Clinical Psychopharmacology, 15,* 417–420.

Goldstein, R. B., Wickramaratne, P. J., Horwath, E., & Weissman, M. M. (1997). Familial aggregation and phenomenology of "early onset" (at or before age 20 years) panic disorder. *Archives of General Psychiatry, 54,* 271–278.

Gorman, J. M. (1988). Blood gas changes and hypophosphatemia in lactate-induced panic (in reply to letter to the editor). *Archives of General Psychiatry, 45,* 96.

Gorman, J. M., Davies, S. O., Steinman, R., Liebowitz, M. R., Fyer, A. J., Coromilas, J., & Klein, D. F. (1987). An objective marker of lactate induced panic. *Psychiatric Research, 22,* 341–348.

Gorman, J. M., Fyer, A. J., Gliklich, J., King, D., & Klein, D. F. (1981). Mitral valve prolapse and panic disorder: Effect of imipramine. In D. F. Klein & J. G. Rabkin (Eds.), *Anxiety revisited.* New York: Raven.

Gorman, J. M., Fyer, M. R., Goetz, R. R., Askanazi, J., Liebowitz, M. R., Fyer, A. J., Kinney, J., & Klein, D. F. (1988). Ventilatory physiology of patients with panic disorder. *Archives of General Psychiatry, 45,* 31–39.

Gorman, J. M., Goetz, R. R., Dillon, D., Liebowitz, M. R., Fyer, A. J., Davies, S., & Klein, D. F. (1990). Sodium D-lactate infusion of panic disorder patients. *Neuropsychopharmacology, 3,* 181–189.

Gorman, J. M., Liebowitz, M. R., Fyer, A. J., Dillon, D., Davies, S. O., Stein, J., & Klein, D. F. (1985). Lactate infusions with obsessive-compulsive disorder patients. *American Journal of Psychiatry, 142,* 864–866.

Gorman, J. M., Liebowitz, M. R., Fyer, A. J., & Stein, J. (1989). A neuroanatomical hypothesis for panic disorder. *American Journal of Psychiatry, 146,* 148–161.

Gorman, J. M., & Papp, L. A. (1990). Respiratory physiology of panic. In J. C. Ballenger (Ed.), *Neurobiology of panic disorder.* New York: Wiley-Liss.

Ghosh, A., & Marks, I. M. (1987). Self-directed exposure for agoraphobia: A controlled trial. *Behavior Therapy, 18,* 3–16.

Gould, R. A., Clum, G. A., & Shapiro, D. (1993). The use of bibliotherapy in the treatment of panic: A preliminary investigation. *Behavior Therapy, 24,* 241–252.

Gray, J. A. (1982). *The neuropsychology of anxiety.* Oxford: Clarendon.

Green, M. A., & Curtis, G. C. (1988). Personality disorders in panic patients: Response to termination of antipanic medication. *Journal of Personality Disorders, 2,* 303–314.

Greenberg, R. L. (1989). Panic disorder and agoraphobia (pp. 25–49). In J. Scott, J. M. G. Williams, & A. T. Beck (Eds.), *Cognitive therapy in clinical practice: An illustrative casebook.* London: Routledge & Kegan Paul.

Griez, E., Lousberg, H., van den Hout, M. A., & van der Molen, G. M. (1987). CO_2 vulnerability in panic disorder. *Psychiatry Research, 20,* 87–96.

Grunhaus, L., Pande, A. C., Brown, M. B., & Greden, J. F. (1994). Clinical characteristics of patients with concurrent major depressive disorder and panic disorder. *American Journal of Psychiatry, 151,* 541–546.

Guttmacher, L. B., & Nelles, C. (1984). In vivo desensitization alteration of lactate induced panic: A case study. *Behavior Therapy, 15*, 369–372.

Hafner, R. J., & Milton, F. (1977) The influence of propranolol on the exposure in vivo on agoraphohics. *Psychological Medicine, 7*, 419–425.

Haley, J. (1996). *Learning and teaching therapy.* New York: Guilford.

Hamilton, S. P., Heiman, G. A., Haghighi, F. G., Mick, S., Klein, D. F., Hodge, S. E., Weissman, M. M., Fyer, A. J., & Knowles, J. A. (1999). Lack of genetic linkage or association between functional serotonin transporter polymorphism and panic disorder. *Psychiatric Genetics, 9*, 1–6.

Hartman, N., Kramer, R., Brown, W. T., et al. (1982). Panic disorder in patients with mitral valve prolapse. *American Journal of Psychiatry, 139*, 669–670.

Harvey, J. M., Richards, J. C., Dziadosz, T., & Swindell, A. (1993). Misinterpretation of ambiguous stimuli in panic disorder. *Cognitive Therapy and Research, 17*, 235–247.

Hauri, P., Friedman, R., Ravaris, C., & Fisher, J. (1985). Sleep in agoraphobia with panic attacks. In M. Chafe, D. McGinty, & R. Wilder (Eds.), *Sleep research.* Los Angeles: BIS/BRS.

Hauri, P., Friedman, R., & Ravaris, C. (1989). Sleep in patients with spontaneous panic attacks. *Sleep, 2*, 323–337.

Hayward, P., & Wardle, J. (1989). Benzodiazepine research: Current findings and practical consequences. *British Journal of Clinical Psychology, 28*, 307–327.

Hegel, M. T., Ravaris, C. L., & Ahles, T. A. (1994). Combined cognitive-behavioral and time-limited alprazolam treatment of panic disorder. *Behavior Therapy, 25*, 183–195.

Heide, F. J., & Borkovec, T. D. (1983). Relaxation induced anxiety: Paradoxical anxiety enhancement due to relaxation training. *Journal of Consulting and Clinical Psychology, 51*, 171–182.

Hibbert, E., & Pilsbury, D. (1988). Hyperventilation in panic attacks: Ambulant monitoring of transcutaneous carbon dioxide. *British Journal of Psychiatry, 153*, 76–80.

Hibbert, G. A. (1984). Hyperventilation as a cause of panic attacks. *British Medical Journal, 288*, 263–264.

Hiller, W., Zaudig, M., & Mombour, W. (1990). Development of diagnostic checklists for use in routine clinical care. *Archives of General Psychiatry, 47,* 782–784.

Himadi, W. G., Boice, R., & Barlow, D. H. (1986) Assessment of agoraphobia—II. Measurement of clinical change. *Behaviour Research and Therapy, 24*(3), 321–332.

Himadi, W. G., Cerny, J. A., Barlow, D. M., Cohen, S. O., & O'Brien, G. T. (1986). The relationship of marital adjustment to agoraphobia treatment outcome. *Behavior Research and Therapy, 24,* 107–115.

Hoffart, A., Friis, S., & Martinsen, E. W. (1992). Assessment of fear among agoraphobic patients: The Agoraphobic Cognitions Scale. *Journal of Psychopathology and Behavioral Assessment, 14,* 175–187.

Hoffart, A., & Hedley, L. (1997). Personality traits among panic disorder with agoraphobia patients before and after symptom-focused treatment. *Journal of Anxiety Disorders, 11*(1), 77–87.

Hoffart, A., & Martinsen, E. W. (1990). Exposure-based integrated vs. pure psychodynamic treatment of agoraphobic inpatients. *Psychotherapy, 27,* 210–218.

Hoffenberg, R. (1981). Hyperthyroidism, hypothyroidism and thyroid function testing. *Medicine International* (U.K. edition), *1,* 256–266.

Holden, A. E. O., O'Brien, G. T., Barlow, D. H., Stetson, D., & Infantino, A. (1983). Self-help manual for agoraphobia: A preliminary report of effectiveness. *Behavior Therapy, 14,* 545–556.

Hollifield, M., Katon, W., Skipper, B., Chapman, T., Ballenger, J. C., Mannuzza, S., & Fyer, A. (1997). Panic disorder and quality of life: Variables predictive of functional impairment. *American Journal of Psychiatry, 154*(6), 766–772.

Holmes, T. H., & Rahe, R. H. (1967). The social readjustment scale rating scale. *Journal of Psychosomatic Research, 11,* 213–218.

Holt, P. E., & Andrews, G. (1989). Hyperventilation and anxiety in panic disorder, social phobias and normal controls. *Behaviour Research and Therapy, 27*(4), 453–460.

Hope, J. A. (1832). *A treatise on the disease of the heart and great vessels comprising a new view of the physiology of the heart's action according to which the physical signs are explained.* London: Churchill.

Horowitz, L. M., Post, D. L., French, R. de S., Wallis, K. D., & Siegelman, E. Y. (1981). The prototype as a construct in abnormal psychology: 2. Clarifying disagreement in psychiatric judgements. *Journal of Abnormal Psychology, 90,* 575–585.

Hurst, M. W. (1979). Life changes and psychiatric symptoms development: Issues of content, scoring, and clustering. In J. E. Barret, R. M. Rose, & G. L. Klerman (Eds.), *Stress and mental disorder.* New York: Raven.

Ivers, H., Bouchard, S., Gauthier, G., Laberge, B., & Cote, G. (1994). The final version of the self-efficacy to control panic attack scale. Presented at the 27th AABT Convention. San Diego, Calif., November.

Jacob, R. G., Moller, M. B., Turner, S. M., & Wall, C. (1985). Oto-neurological examination in panic disorder patients and agoraphobia with panic attacks: A pilot study. *American Journal of Psychiatry, 142,* 715–720.

Jacob, R. G., & Rapport, M. D. (1984). Panic disorder: Medical and psychological parameters. In S. M. Turner (Ed.), *Behavioral theories and treatment of anxiety.* New York: Plenum.

Jacobson, N. S. (1988). Defining clinically significant change: An introduction. *Behavioral Assessment, 10,* 131–132.

Jacobson, N. S., Follete, W. C., & Revenstorf, D. (1984). Psychotherapy outcome research: Methods for reporting variability and evaluating clinical significance. *Behavior Therapy, 15,* 336–352.

Jacobson, N. S., & Truax, P. (1991). Clinical significance: A statistical approach to defining meaningful change in psychotherapy research. *Journal of Consulting and Clinical Psychology, 59*(1), 12–19.

Jannoun, L., Oppenheimer, C., & Gelder, M. (1982). A self-help program for anxiety state patients. *Behavior Therapy, 13,* 103–111.

Johnson S. B., & Melamed, B. G. (1979). Assessment and treatment of children's fears. In B. B. Lashey & A. E. Kazdin (Eds.) *Advances in clinical child psychology* (Vol. 2). New York: Plenum.

Kalus, O., Asnis, G. M., Rubinson, E., Kahn, R., Friedman, J. M. H., Igbal, N., Grosz, D., Van Praag, H., & Cahn, W. (1991). Desipramine treatment in panic disorder. *Journal of Affective Disorders, 21,* 239–244.

Kamieniecki, G. W., Wade, T., & Tsourtos, G. (1997). Interpretative bias for benign sensations in panic disorder with agoraphobia. *Journal of Anxiety Disorders, 11*(2), 141–156.

Kantor, J. S., Zitrin, C. M., & Zeldis, S. (1980). Mitral valve prolapse syndrome in agoraphobic patients. *American Journal of Psychiatry, 137*(4), 467–469.

Kaplan, H. S. (1988). Intimacy disorders and sexual panic states. *Journal of Sex and Marital Therapy, 14*(1), 3–12.

Katerndahl, D. A. (1990). Panic is panic: Homogeneity of the panic experience. *Family Practice Research Journal, 9*(2), 147–155.

Katerndahl, D. A. (1996). Intrapatient agreement on phenomenology of panic attacks. *Psychological Reports, 79*(1), 219–224.

Katerndahl, D. A., & Realini, J. P. (1997). Comorbid psychiatric disorders in subjects with panic attacks. *Journal of Nervous and Mental Disease, 185*(11), 669–674.

Kathol, R. G., Noyes, R., Jr., Slymen, D. J., Crowe, R. R., Clancy, J., & Kerber, R. E. (1980). Propranolol in chronic anxiety disorders: A controlled study. *Archives of General Psychiatry, 37*, 1361–1365.

Katon, W. (1988). Panic disorder: The importance of phenomenology. *Journal of Family Practice, 26*(1), 23–24.

Katon, W. (1992). *Panic disorder in the medical setting*. Rockville, MD: National Institute of Mental Health.

Katon, W., Hall, M. L., Russo, J., Cormier, L., Hollifield, M., Vitaliano, P. P., & Beiman, B. (1988). Chest pain: Relationship of psychiatric illness to coronary arteriographic results. *American Journal of Medicine, 84*, 1–9.

Katon, W., & Kleinman, A. M. (1980). Doctor–patient negotiation and other social science strategies in patient care (pp. 253–259). In L. Eisenberg & A. M. Kleinman (Eds.), *The relevance of social science for medicine*, Datrecht, Holland: Reidel.

Katon, W., Vitaliano, P. P., Russo, J., Jones, M., & Anderson, K. (1987). Panic disorder: Spectrum of severity and somatization. *Journal of Nervous and Mental Disease, 175*, 12–19.

Kazdin, A. E. (1992). *Research design in clinical psychology*. Boston: Allyn & Bacon.

Kenardy, J., Evans, L., & Oei, T. P. S. (1988). The importance of cognitions in panic attacks. *Behavior Therapy, 19*, 471–483.

Kendall, P. C., Chansky, T. E., Kane, M. T., Kim, R. S., Kortlander, E., Ronan, K. R., Sessa, F. M., & Siqueland, L. (1992). *Anxiety disorders in youths: Cognitive-behavioral interventions*. Boston: Allyn & Bacon.

Kendall, P. C., & Norton-Ford, J. D. (1982). *Clinical psychology: Scientific and professional dimensions*. New York: Wiley.

Kendler, K. S., Heath, A., Martin, N. G., & Eaves, L. J. (1987). Symptoms of anxiety and symptoms of depression: Same genes, different environments? *Archives of General Psychiatry, 44*, 451–457.

Kendler, K. S., Walters, E. E., Neale, M. C., Kessler, R. C., et al. (1995). The structure of the genetic and environmental risk factors for six major psychiatric disorders in women: Phobia, generalized anxiety disorder, panic disorder, bulimia, major depression, and alcoholism. *Archives of General Psychiatry, 52*(5), 374–383, 457.

Kerr, W. J., Dalton, J. W., & Gliebe, P. A. (1937). Some physical phenomena associated with anxiety states and their relation to hyperventilation. *Annals of Internal Medicine, 11*, 961–992.

Khawaja, N. G., & Oei, T. P. S. (1992). Development of a catastrophic cognition questionnaire. *Journal of Anxiety Disorders, 6*, 305–318.

Khawaja, N. G., Oei, T. P. S., & Baglioni, A. J. (1994). Modification of the Catastrophic Cognition Questionnaire (CCQ-M) for normals and patients: Exploratory LISREL analyses. *Journal of Psychopathology and Behavioral Assessment, 16*, 325–342.

Kiselica, M. S., & Baker, S. B. (1992). Progressive muscle relaxation and cognitive restructuring: Potential problems and proposed solutions. *Journal of Mental Health Counseling, 14*(2), 149–165.

Klasko, J. S., Barlow, D. H., Tassinari, R., & Cerny, J. A. (1990). A comparison of alprazolam and behavior therapy in the treatment of panic disorder. *Journal of Clinical and Consulting Psychology, 58*, 77–84.

Klein, D. F. (1964). Delineation of two drug-responsive anxiety syndromes. *Psychopharmacologia, 3*, 397–408.

Klein, D. F. (1967) Importance of psychiatric diagnosis in prediction of clinical drug effects. *Archives of General Psychiatry, 16*, 118–126.

Klein, D. F. (1981). Anxiety reconceptualization. In D. F. Klein & J. Rabkin (Eds.), *Anxiety: New research and changing concepts*. New York: Raven.

Klein, D. F. (1993). False suffocation alarm, spontaneous panics, and related conditions: An integrative hypothesis. *Archives of General Psychiatry, 50*, 306–317.

Klein, D. F. (1994). A reply to Taylor and Rachman. *Archives of General Psychiatry, 510*, 506.

Klein, D. F., & Fink, M. (1962). Psychiatric reaction patterns to imipramine. *American Journal of Psychiatry, 119*, 432–438.

Klein, D. F., & Klein, H. M. (1989). The definition and psychopharmacology of spontaneous panic and phobia (pp. 135–162). In P.
Tyrer (Ed.), *Psychopharmacology of anxiety*. New York: Oxford University Press.

Klein, D. F., Skrobala, A. M., & Garfinkel, R. S. (1995). Preliminary
look at the effects of pregnancy on the cause of panic disorder. *Anxiety, 1*, 227–232.

Klein, D. F., Zitring, C. M., Woerner, M. G., & Ross, D. C. (1983).
Treatment of phobias: II. Behavior therapy and supportive psychotherapy. Are there any specific ingredients? *Archives of General Psychiatry, 40*, 139–145.

Klein, E., & Uhde, J. W. (1988). Controlled study of verapamil for
treatment of panic disorder. *American Journal of Psychiatry, 145*,
431–434.

Kleiner, L., & Marshall, W. L. (1987). The role of interpersonal problems in the development of agoraphobia with panic attacks. *Journal
of Anxiety Disorders, 1*(2), 313–323.

Klosko, J. S., Barlow, D. H., Tassinari, R. B., & Cerny, J. A. (1988).
Comparison of alprazolam and cognitive behavior therapy in the
treatment of panic disorder: A preliminary report. In I. Hand & H. U.
Wittchen (Eds.), *Panic and phobias 2: Treatment and variables affecting course and outcome*. Berlin: Springer-Verlag.

Klosko, J. S., Barlow, D. H., Tassinari, R. B., & Cerny, J. A. (1990). A
comparison of alprazolam and behavior therapy in the treatment of
panic disorder. *Journal of Consulting and Clinical Psychology, 58*,
77–84.

Knight, L. E. (1998 March/April). Melatonin: Sweet dreams. *Doctors'
Forum, 3*(2), 28–31.

Knowles, J. A., Fyer, A. J., Vieland, V. J., Weissman, M. M., Hodge,
S. E., Heiman, G. A., Haghighi, F., deJesus, G. M., Rassnick, H.,
Preud'homme-Rivelli, X., Austin, T., Cunjak, J., Mick, S., Fine, L. D.,
Woodley, K. A., Das, K., Maier, W., Adams, P. B., Freimer, N. B.,
Klein, D. F., & Gilliam, T. C. (1998). Results of a genome-wide ge-
netic screen for panic disorder. *American Journal of Genetics, 81*,
139–147.

Knowles, J. A., & Weissman, M. M. (1995). Panic disorder and agoraphobia. In J. M. Oldham & M. B. Riba (Eds.), *Review of psychiatry*,
Vol. 14 (pp. 383–404). Washington, DC: American Psychiatric Press.

Kocmur, M., & Zavasnik, A. (1991, April). Patients' experience of the therapeutic process in a crises intervention unit. *Crises, 12*(1), 69–81.

Kohut, H. (1972). Thoughts on narcissism and narcissistic rage. *Psychoanalytic Study of the Child, 27,* 360–400.

Laberge, B., Gauthier, J., Cote, G., Plamondon, J., & Cormier, H. J. (1992), The treatment of coexisting panic and depression: A review of the literature. *Journal of Anxiety Disorders, 6*(2), 169–180.

LaBoeuf, A., & Lodge, J. (1980). A comparison of frontalis EMG feedback training and progressive relaxation in the treatment of clinic anxiety. *British Journal of Psychiatry, 137,* 279–284.

Lange, A., & Van Dyck, R. (1992). The function of agoraphobia in the marital relationship. *Acta Psychiatrica Scandinavia, 85,* 89–93.

Last, C. G. (1993). Relationship between familial and childhood anxiety disorders. In C. Last (Ed.), *Anxiety across the life span: A developmental perspective.* New York: Springer.

Last, C. G., Barlow, D. H., & O'Brien, G. T. (1984a). Cognitive change during behavioral and cognitive-behavioral treatment of agoraphobia. *Behavior Modification, 8,* 181–210.

Last, C. G., Barlow, D. H., & O'Brien, G. T. (1984b). Precipitants of agoraphobia: The role of stressful life events. *Psychological Reports, 54,* 567–570.

Last, C. G., Francis, G., Hersen, M., Kazdin, A. E., & Strauss, C. C. (1987). Separation anxiety and school phobia: A comparison using the DSM-III criteria. *American Journal of Psychiatry, 144,* 653–657.

Last, C. G., & Strauss, C. C. (1989). Panic disorder in children and adolescents. *Journal of Anxiety Disorders, 3,* 87–95.

Last, C. G., & Strauss, C. C. (1990). School refusal in anxiety disordered children and adolescents. *Journal of the American Academy of Child and Adolescent Psychiatry, 29,* 31–35.

Lazarus, A. A. (1963). The results of behavior therapy in 126 cases of severe neurosis. *Behaviour Research and Therapy, 1,* 69–79.

Lazarus, A. A. (1964). Crucial procedural factors in disensitization therapy. *Behaviour Research and Therapy, 2,* 65–70.

Lazarus, A. A. (1976). *Multimodal behavior therapy.* New York: Springer.

Lazarus, A. A., & Mayne, T. J. (1990). Relaxation: Some limitations, side effects and proposed solutions. *Psychotherapy, 27*(2), 261–266.

Lazrove, S., Kite, L., Triffleman, E., McGlashan, T., & Rounsaville, B.

(in press). The use of EMDR as treatment for chronic PTSD—encouraging results of an open trial. *American Journal of Orthopsychiatry.*

Lee, Y. J., Curtis, G. C., Weg, J. G., Abelson, J. L., Modell, J. G., & Campbell, K. M. (1993). Panic attacks induced by doxapram. *Biological Psychiatry, 33,* 295–297.

Lehman, E., Kinzler, E., & Friederman, J. (1996). Efficacy of a special kava extract in patients with states of anxiety, tension and excitedness of nonmental origin. A double blind placebo-controlled study of four weeks' treatment. *Phytomedicine, 3*(2), 113–119.

Lesser, I. M. (1988). The relationship between panic disorder and depression. *Journal of Anxiety Disorders, 2*(1), 3–15.

Lesser, I. M., Poland, R., Holcomb, C., & Rose, D. (1985). Electroencephalographic study of nighttime panic attacks. *Journal of Nervous and Mental Diseases, 173,* 744–746.

Lesser, I. M., Rubin, R. T., Pecknold, J. C., Rifkin, A., Swinson, R. P., Lydiard, R. B., Burrrows, G. D., Noyes, R., Jr., & DuPont, R. L., Jr. (1988). Secondary depression in panic disorder and agoraphobia. *Archives of General Psychiatry, 45,* 437–443.

Lewinsohn, P. M., Hops, H., Roberts, R. E., Seeley, J. R., & Andrews, J. A. (1993). Adolescent psychopathology: I. Prevalence and incidents of depression and other DSM-III-R disorders in high school students. *Journal of Abnormal Psychology, 102,* 133–144.

Lewis, T. (1917). *Medical Research Committee: Report upon soldiers returned as cases of "disordered action of the heart" (D.A.H.) or "valvular disease of the heart" (V.D.H.).* London: His Majesty's Stationary Office.

Lewis, T. (1940). *The soldier's heart and effort syndrome.* London: Shaw.

Ley, R. A. (1985a). Agoraphobia, the panic attack and the hyperventilation syndrome. *Behavior Research and Therapy, 23,* 79–82.

Ley, R. A. (1985b). Blood, breath and fears: A hyperventilation theory of panic attacks and agoraphobia. *Clinical Psychology Review, 5,* 271–285.

Ley, R. A. (1986). Hyperventilation and lactate infusion in the production of panic attacks. *Clinical Psychology Review, 8,* 1–18.

Ley, R. A. (1987a). Panic disorder: A hyperventilation interpretation. In L. Michelson & L. M. Ascher (Eds.), *Anxiety and stress disorders: Cognitive behavioral assessment and treatment.* New York: Guilford.

References

Ley, R. A. (1987b). Panic attacks during sleep: A hyperventilation-probability model. Presented at the seventh International Symposium on Respiratory Psychophysiology, Karolinska Institute, Stockholm, Sweden.

Ley, R. A. (1988). Panic attacks during relaxation and relaxation-induced anxiety: A hyperventilation interpretation. *Journal of Behavior Therapy and Experimental Psychiatry, 19*, 253–259.

Ley, R. A. (1996), *Current controversies in the anxiety disorders.* New York: Guilford.

Liberthson, R., Sheehan, D. V., King, M. E., & Weyman, A. E. (1986). The prevalence of mitral valve prolapse with panic disorder. *American Journal of Psychiatry, 143*, 511–515.

Lidren, D. M., Watkins, P., Gould, R. A., Clum, G. A., Asterino, M., & Tulloch, H. L. (1994). A comparison of bibliotherapy and group therapy in the treatment of panic disorder. *Journal of Counseling and Clinical Psychology, 62*, 865–869.

Liebowitz, M. R., Fyer, A. B., & Gorman, J. M. (1986). Alprozolam in the treatment of panic disorder. *Journal of Clinical Psychopharmacology, 6*, 13–20.

Liebowitz, M. R., Gorman, J. M., Fyer, A. J., & Klein, D. F. (1985). Social phobia: Review of a neglected anxiety disorder. *Archives of General Psychiatry, 42*, 729–736.

Liebowitz, M. R., Gorman, J. M., Fyer, A. B., Levitt, M., Dillon, D., Levy, G., Appleby, I. L., Anderson, J., Oalij, M., Davies, S. O., & Klein, D. F. (1985). Lactate provocation of panic attacks: I. Biochemical and physiological findings. *Archives of General Psychiatry, 42*, 709–719.

Lisander, B. (1979). Somato-autonomic reactions and their higher control. In C. Brooks, K. Koizumi, & A. Sato (Eds.), *Integrative functions of the autonomic nervous system.* New York: Elsevier.

Lovibond, S. H., & Lovibond, P. F. (1993). *Manual for the Depression Anxiety and Stress Scales (DASS).* Psychology Foundation Monograph. New South Wales, Australia: University of New South Wales.

Lovibond, P. F., & Lovibond, S. H. (1995). The structure of negative emotional states: Comparison of the Depression Anxiety Stress Scales (DASS) with the Beck Depression and Anxiety Inventories. *Behaviour Research and Therapy, 33*, 335–342.

Lum, L. C. (1976). The syndrome of habitual chronic hyperventilation.

In O. W. Hill (Ed.), *Modern trends in psychosomatic medicine*, (Vol 3). London: Butterworth's.

Lum, L. C., (1981). Hyperventilation and anxiety state. *Journal of the Royal Society of Medicine, 74*, 1–4.

Lydiard, R. B. (1988). Panic disorder: Pharmacologic treatment. *Annals of Psychiatry, 18*, 468–472.

Lydiard, R. B., & Ballenger, T. C. (1987). Antidepressants in panic disorder and agoraphobia. *Journal of Affective Disorders, 13*, 153–168.

Lydiard, R. B., Howell, E. F., Laraia, M. T., Fossey, M. D., & Ballenger, J. C. (1989). Depression in patients receiving lorazepam for panic. *American Journal of Psychiatry, 146*, 1230–1231.

Mackenzie, T. B., & Popkin, M. K. (1983). Organic anxiety syndrome. *American Journal of Psychiatry, 140*, 342–344.

MacLeod, J. (1981). *Davidson's principles and practice of medicine.* Edinburgh: Churchill Livingstone.

Maller, R. G., & Reiss, S. (1992). Anxiety sensitivity in 1984 and panic attacks in 1987. *Journal of Anxiety Disorders, 6*, 241–247.

Mandel, J., & Klein, D. F. (1969). Anxiety attacks and subsequent agoraphobia. *Comprehensive Psychiatry, 10*, 476–478.

Mannuzza, S., Fyer, A. J., Liebowitz, M. R., & Klein, D. F. (1990), Delineating the boundaries of social phobia: Its relationship to panic disorder and agoraphobia. *Journal of Anxiety Disorders, 4*(1), 41–59.

Marcus, S., Marquis, P., & Sakai, C. (1997) Controlled study of treatment of PTSD using EMDR in an HMO setting. *Psychotherapy, 34*, 307–315.

Margraf, J., Barlow, D. H., Clark, D. M., & Telch, M. J. (1993). Psychological treatment of panic: Work in progress on outcome, active ingredients, and follow-up. *Behavior Research and Therapy, 31*, 1–8.

Margraf, J., & Ehlers, A. (1989). Etiology models of panic: Medical and biological aspects. In R. Baker (Ed.), *Panic disorder: Theory, research, and therapy.* Chihester, England: Wiley.

Margraf, J., Ehlers, A., & Roth, W. T. (1986a). Sodium lactate infusions and panic attacks: A review and critique. *Psychosomatic Medicine, 48*, 23–51.

Margraf, J., Ehlers, A., & Roth, W. T. (1986b). Expectancy effects and hyperventilation as laboratory stressor. In H. Weiner, I. Florin, R. Murrison, & D. Hellhammer (Eds.), *Frontiers of stress research.* Toronto: Huber.

Margraf, J., & Schneider, S. (1991, November). Outcome and active ingredients of cognitive-behavioral treatments for panic disorder. Presented at the annual meeting of the Association for the Advancement of Behavior Therapy, New York.

Margraf, J., Taylor, C. B., Ehlers, A., Roth, W. T., & Agras, W. T. (1987). Panic attacks in the natural environment. *Journal of Nervous and Mental Disease, 175,* 558–565.

Marks, I. M. (1969). *Fears and phobias.* London: Heinemann.

Marks, I. M. (1978). *Living with fear.* New York: McGraw-Hill.

Marks, I. M. (1987). *Fear, phobias, and rituals: Panic, anxiety and their disorders.* New York: Oxford University Press.

Marks, I. M., & Mathews, A. M. (1979). Brief standard self-rating for phobic patients. *Behaviour Research and Therapy, 17,* 263–267.

Marks, I. M., Swinson, R. P., Basoglu, M., Kuch, K., Noshirvani, H., O'Sullivan, G., Lelliot, P. T., Kirby, M., McNamee, G., Sengun, S., & Wickwire, K. (1993). Alprazolam and exposure alone and combined in panic disorder with agoraphobia: A controlled study in London and Toronto. *British Journal of Psychiatry, 162,* 776–787.

Marks, M. P., Basoglu, M., Alkubaisy, T., Sengun, S., & Marks, I. M. (1991). Are anxiety symptoms and catastrophic cognitions directly related? *Journal of Anxiety Disorders, 5,* 247–254.

Marquis, J. N. (1991). A report on 78 cases treated by eye movement desensitization. *Journal of Behavior Therapy and Experimental Psychiatry, 22*(3), 192–197.

Martin, N. G., Jardine, R., Andrews, G., & Heath, A. C. (1988). Anxiety disorders and neuroticism: Are there genetic factors specific to panic? *Acta Psychiatrica Scandinavica, 77,* 698–706.

Mathews, A. M., Gelder, M. G., & Johnston, D. W. (1981). *Agoraphobia: Nature and treatment.* New York: Guilford.

Mavissakalian, M. (1986a). The Fear Questionnaire: A validity study. *Behaviour Research and Therapy, 24,* 83–85.

Mavissakalian, M. (1986b). Clinically significant improvement in agoraphobia research. *Behaviour Research and Therapy, 24,* 369–370.

Mavissakalian, M., & Hamann, M. S. (1988). Correlates of DSM-III personality disorder in panic disorder and agoraphobia. *Comprehensive Psychiatry, 29,* 535–544.

Mavissakalian, M., & Michelson, L. (1983). Self-directed in vivo exposure practice in behavioral and pharmacological treatment of agoraphobia. *Behavior Therapy, 14,* 506–519.

Mavissakalian, M., Salerni, R., Thompson, M. E., & Michelson, L. (1983). Mitral valve prolapse and agoraphobia. *American Journal of Psychiatry, 140,* 1612–1614.

McCue, E. C., & McCue, P. A. (1984). Organic and hyperventilatory causes of anxiety-type symptoms. *Behavioral Psychotherapy, 12,* 308–317.

McNally, R. J. (1989). Is anxiety sensitivity distinguishable from trait anxiety?. A reply to Lilienfeld, Jacob, and Turner. *Journal of Abnormal Psychology, 98,* 193–194.

McNally, R. J. (1990). Psychological approaches to panic disorder: A review. *Psychological Bulletin, 108,* 403–419.

McNally, R. J. (1994). *Panic disorder: A critical analysis.* New York: Guilford.

McNally, R. J. (1995). Automaticity and anxiety disorders. *Behavior Research and Therapy, 33*(7), 747–754.

McNally, R. J., & Lorenz, M. (1987). Anxiety sensitivity in agoraphobics. *Journal of Behavior Therapy and Experimental Psychiatry, 18,* 3–11.

McNally, R. J., & Lukach, B. M. (1992). Are panic attacks traumatic stressors? *American Journal of Psychiatry, 149*(6), 824–826.

Meichenbaum, D. (1977). *Cognitive-behavior modification.* New York: Plenum.

Mellman, T. A., & Uhde, T. W. (1987) Obsessive compulsive symptoms in panic disorder. *American Journal of Psychiatry, 12,* 1573–1576.

Mellman, T., & Uhde, T. W. (1989). Electroencephalographic sleep in panic disorder: A focus on sleep-related panic attacks. *Archives of General Psychiatry, 46,* 178–184.

Mellman, T., & Uhde, T. W. (1990). Sleep in panic and generalized anxiety disorders. In J. C. Ballenger (Ed.), *Neurobiology of panic disorders.* New York: Wiley-Liss.

Michelson, L., Marchione, K., & Greenwald, M. (1989, November). Cognitive-behavioral treatments of agoraphobia. Presented at the annual meeting of the Association for the Advancement of Behavior Therapy, Washington, D.C.

Millon, T. (1991). Classification in psychpathology: Rationale, alternatives, and standards. *Journal of Abnormal Psychology, 100*(3), 245–261.

Mills, I., & Salkovskis, P. M. (1988). Mood and habituation to phobic stimuli. *Behaviour Research and Therapy, 26*(5), 435–439.

Milrod, B., Busch, F., Cooper, A., & Shapiro, T. (1997). *Manual of panic-focused psychodynamic psychotherapy.* Washington, DC: American Psychiatric Press.

Milrod, B. L., & Shear, M. K. (1991). Dynamic treatment of panic disorder: A review. *Journal of Nervous and Mental Disease, 179,* 741–743.

Mogg, K., Bradley, B. P., & Williams, R. (1995). Attentional bias in anxiety and depression: The role of awareness. *British Journal of Clinical Psychology, 34*(1), 17–36.

Müller, W. E. G., & Rossol, R. (1994). Effects of hypericum extract on the expression of serotonin receptors. *Journal of Geriatric Psychiatry and Neurology, 7*(suppl 1), 63–64.

Munjack, D., Brown, R. A., & McDowell, D. E. (1987). Comparison of social anxiety in patients with social anxiety and panic disorder. *Journal of Nervous and Mental Disease, 175,* 49–51.

Munjack, D., Brown, R. A., & McDowell, D. E. (1993). Existence of hyperventilation in panic disorder with and without agoraphobia, GAD and normals: Implications for the cognitive theory of panic. *Journal of Anxiety Disorders, 7,* 37–48.

Myers, A. B. R. (1870). *On the aetiology and prevalence of disease of the heart among soldiers.* London: Churchill.

Myers, J. K., Weissman, M. N., Tischler, G. E., Holzer, C. E., Leaf, P. J., Ovaschel, H., Anthony, J. C., Boyd, J. H., Burke, J. D., Kramer, M., & Stoltzman, R. (1984). Six-month prevalence of psychiatric disorders in three communities. *Archives of General Psychiatry. 41,* 959–970.

Nelles, W. B., & Barlow, D. H. (1988). Do children panic? *Clinical Psychology in Review, 8,* 359–372.

Nelson, R. O., & Barlow, D. H. (1981). Behavioral assessment: Basic strategies and initial procedures. In D. H. Barlow (Ed.), *Behavioral assessment of adult disorders.* New York: Guilford.

Norton, G. R., Block, G., & Malan, J. (1991). The psychopathology of panicking and non-panicking male alcoholics. *Alcoholism Treatment Quarterly, 83*(3), 67–75.

Norton, G. R., Dorwards, J., & Cox, B. J. (1986). Factors associated with panic attacks in nonclinical subjects. *Behavior Therapy, 17,* 239–252.

Norton, G. R., Harrison, B., Hauch, J., & Rhodes, L. (1985). Characteristics of people with infrequent panic attacks. *Journal of Abnormal Psychology, 94,* 216–221.

Norton, G. R., McLeod, L., Guerin, J., Hewitt, P. L., et al. (1996). Panic disorder or social phobia: Which is worse? *Behavior Research and Therapy, 34*(3), 273–276.

Noyes, R., Jr., Anderson, D. J., Clancy, J., Crowe, R. R., Slymen, D. J., Ghoneim, M. M., & Hinnicks, J. E. (1984). Diazepam and propranolol in panic disorder and agoraphobia. *Archives of General Psychiatry, 41,* 287–292.

Noyes, R., Jr., Hafner, J., & Milton, F. (1977). The influence of propranolol on the exposure in vivo of agoraphobics. *Psychological Medicine, 7,* 419–425.

Noyes, R., Reich, J., Clancy, J., & O'Gorman, T. W. (1986). Reduction in hypochondriasis with treatment of panic disorder. *British Journal of Psychiatry, 149,* 631–635.

Noyes, R., Jr., Woodman, C. L., Holt, C. S., Reich, J. H., & Zimmerman, B. M. (1995). Avoidant personality traits distinguish social phobic and panic disorder subjects. *Journal of Nervous and Mental Disease, 183*(3), 145–153.

Noyes, R., Jr., Woodman, C., Garvey, M. J., Cook, D. L., Suelzer, M., Clancy, J., & Anderson, D. J. (1992). Generalized anxiety disorder vs. panic disorder: Distinguishing characteristics and patterns of comorbidity. *Journal of Nervous and Mental Disease, 180,* 369–379.

Nutt, D. J., Glue, P., Lawson, C., & Wilson, S. (1990). Flumanzenil provocation of panic attacks: Evidence for altered benzodiazepine receptor sensitivity in panic disorder. *Archives of General Psychiatry, 47,* 917–925.

Oehrberg, S., Christiansen, P. E., & Behnke, K. (1995). Paroxetine in the treatment of panic disorder: A randomized double-blind placebo-controlled study. *British Journal of Psychiatry, 167,* 374–379.

Okel, B., & Hurst, J. (1961). Prolonged hyperventilation in man: Associated electrolyte changes and subjective symptoms. *Archives of Internal Medicine, 108,* 157–162.

References

Ollendick, T. H., Mattis, S. G., & King, N. J. (1994). Panic in children and adolescents: A review. *Journal of Child Psychology and Psychiatry, 35*, 113–134.

Oppenheimer, B. S. (1918). Report on neurocirculatory asthenia and its management. *Military Surgeon, 42*, 711–744.

Oppenheimer, B. S., & Rothschild, M. A. (1918) The psychoneurotic factor in irritable heart of soldiers. *Journal of the American Medical Association, 70*, 1919–1922.

Orwin, A. (1973). The running treatment: A preliminary communication on a new use for an old therapy (physical activity) in the agoraphobic syndrome. *British Journal of Psychiatry, 122*, 175–179.

Öst, L. G. (1987). Applied relaxation: Description of a coping technique and review of controlled studies. *Behaviour Research and Therapy, 25*, 397–409.

Öst, L. G. (1988). Applied relaxation vs. progressive relaxation in the treatment of panic disorder. *Behavior Research and Therapy, 26*(1), 13–22.

Öst, L. G., & Hugdahl, K. (1983). Acquisition of agoraphobia, mode of onset and anxiety response patterns. *Behavior Research and Therapy, 21*, 623–631.

Ottaviani, R., & Beck, A. T. (1987). Cognitive aspects of panic disorders. *Journal of Anxiety Disorders, 1*, 15–28.

Otto, M. W., Pollack, M. H., Sachs, G. S., Reiter, S. R., Meltzer-Brody, S., & Rosenbaum, J. F. (1993). Discontinuation of benzodiazepine treatment: Efficacy of cognitive-behavior therapy for patients with panic disorder. *American Journal of Psychiatry, 150*, 1485–1490.

Page, A. C. (1994). Distinguishing panic disorder and agoraphobia from social phobia. *Journal of Nervous and Mental Disease, 182*(11), 611–617.

Papp, L. A., Klein, D. F., & Gorman, J. M. (1993) Carbon dioxide hypersensitivity, hyperventilation and panic disorder. *American Journal of Psychiatry, 150*, 1149–1157.

Papp, L. A., Klein, D. F., Martinez, J., Schneier, F., Cole, R. Liebowitz, M. R., Hollander, E., Fyer, A. J., Jordan, F., & Gorman, J. M. (1993). Diagnostic and substance specificity of carbon-dioxide-induced panic. *American Journal of Psychiatry, 150*, 250–257.

Paykel, E. S., & Hollyman, J. (1984). Life events and depression—a psychiatric view. *Trends in Neuroscience*, 478–481.

Peterson, R. A., & Heilbronner, R. L. (1987). The anxiety sensitivity index: Construct validity and factor analytic structure. *Journal of Anxiety Disorders, 1,* 117–121.

Pierpaoli, M. D., & Regelson, M. D. (1995). *The melatonin miracle.* New York: Simon & Schuster.

Pitts, F. N., & McClure, J. N. (1967). Lactate metabolism in anxiety neurosis. *New England Journal of Medicine, 277,* 1329–1336.

Pollard, C. A., Tait, R. C., Meldrum, D., Dubinsky, I., et al. (1996). Agoraphobia without panic: Case illustration of an overlooked syndrome. *Journal of Nervous and Mental Disease, 184*(1), 61–62.

Prince, M., & Putnam, J. J. (1912). A clinical study of a case of phobia: A symposium. *Journal of Abnormal Social Psychology, 7,* 259–292.

Quitkin, F. M., Rifkin, A., Kaplan, J., & Klein, D. F. (1972). Phobic anxiety syndrome complicated by drug dependence and addiction. A treatable form of drug abuse. *Archives of General Psychiatry, 27,* 159–162.

Rachman, S. (1984). Agoraphobia: A safety-signal perspective. *Behaviour Research and Therapy, 22,* 59–70.

Rachman, S. J. (1990). *Fear and courage* (2nd ed.). New York: Freeman.

Rapee, R. M. (1985a). Distinctions between panic disorder and generalized anxiety disorder: Clinical presentation. *Australian and New Zealand Journal of Psychiatry, 19,* 227–232.

Rapee, R. M. (1985b). A case of panic disorder treated with breathing retraining. *Journal of Behavior Therapy and Experimental Psychiatry, 16*(1), 63–65.

Rapee, R. M. (1986). Differential response to hyperventilation in panic disorder and generalized anxiety disorder. *Journal of Abnormal Psychology, 95*(1), 24–28.

Rapee, R. M. (1993). Psychological factors in panic disorder. *Advances in Behavior Research and Therapy, 15,* 85–102.

Rapee, R. M. (1995). Psychological factors influencing the affective response to biological challenge procedures in panic disorder. *Journal of Anxiety Disorders, 9,* 59–74.

Rapee, R. M. (1996). Information-processing view of panic disorder. In R. M. Rapee (Ed.), *Current controversies in the anxiety disorders.* New York: Guilford.

Rapee, R. M., Ancis, J., & Barlow, D. H. (1988). Emotional reactions to physiological sensations: Comparison of panic disorder and non-clinical subjects. *Behavior Research and Therapy, 26,* 265–269.

Rapee, R. M., Craske, M. G., & Barlow, D. H. (1990). Subject-described features of panic attacks using self-monitoring. *Journal of Anxiety Disorders, 4,* 171–181.

Rapee, R. M., Mattick, R., & Murrell, E. (1986). Cognitive mediation in the affective component of spontaneous panic attacks. *Journal of Behavior Therapy and Experimental Psychiatry, 17,* 245–253.

Raskin, M., Bali, L. R., & Peeke, H. V. (1980). Muscle biofeedback and transcendental meditation. *Archives of General Psychiatry, 37,* 93–97.

Raskin, M., Peeke, H. V., Dickman, W., & Pinsker, H. (1982). Panic and generalized anxiety disorders: Developmental antecedents and precipitants. *Archives of General Psychiatry, 39,* 687–689.

Rasmussen, S. A., & Tsuang, M. T. (1986). Epidemiological and clinical findings of significance to the design of neuropharmacologic studies of obsessive-compulsive disorder. *Psychopharmacological Bulletin, 22,* 723–733.

Regier, D. A., Boyd, J. H., Burke, J. D., Rae, D. S., Myers, J. K., Kramer, M., Robins, L. N., Karno, M., & Locke, B. Z. (1988). One-month prevalence of mental disorders in the United States: Based on five epidemiologic catchment area sites. *Archives of General Psychiatry, 45,* 977–986.

Reich, J., Noyes, R., Jr., & Troughton, E. (1987). Dependent personality disorder associated with phobic avoidance in patients with panic disorder. *American Journal of Psychiatry, 144,* 323–326.

Reich, J., Noyes, R., & Yates, W. (1988). Anxiety symptoms distinguishing social phobia from panic and generalized anxiety disorders. *Journal of Nervous and Mental Diseases, 176,* 510–513.

Reiss, S. (1987). Theoretical perspective on the fear of anxiety. *Clinical Psychology Review, 7,* 585–596.

Reiss, S. (1991). Expectancy model of fear, anxiety and panic. *Clinical Psychology Review, 11,* 141–153.

Reiss, S., & McNally, R. J. (1985). Expectancy model of fear. In S. Reiss & R. R. Bootzin (Eds.), *Theoretical issues in behavior therapy.* San Diego: Academic Press.

Reiss, S., Peterson, R. A., Gursky, D. M., & McNally, R. J. (1986). Anxiety sensitivity, anxiety frequency and the prediction of fearfulness. *Behavior Research and Therapy, 24,* 1–8.

Renneberg, B., Chambless, D. L., & Gracely, E. J. (1992). Prevalence of SCID-diagnosed personality disorders in agoraphobic outpatients. *Journal of Anxiety Disorders, 6*(2), 111–118.

Reschke, A. H., Mannuzza, S., Chapman, T. F., Lipsitz, J. D., et al. (1995). Sodium lactate response and familial risk for panic disorder. *American Journal of Psychiatry, 152*(2), 277–279.

Roberts, A. R. (Ed.) (1990). *Crises intervention handbook: Assessment, treatment and research.* Belmont, CA: Wadsworth.

Robinson, D. S., Shrotriya, R. C., Alms, D. R., Messina, M., & Andary, J. (1989). Treatment of panic disorder: Non-benzodiazepine anxiolytics, including buspirone. *Psychopharmacology Bulletin, 25,* 21–26.

Rosen, J. E., Hamerman, E., Sitcoske, M., Glowa, J. R., & Schulkin, J. (1996). Hyperexcitability: Exaggerated fear-potentiated startle produced by partial amygdala kindling. *Behavioral Neuroscience, 110*(1), 43–50.

Rosenman, R. H. (1985). The impact of anxiety on the cardiovascular system. *Psychosomatics, 26,* 6–17.

Roth, M. (1959). The phobic anxiety-depersonalization syndrome. *Proceedings of the Royal Society of Medicine, 52,* 587–596.

Rothbaum, B. O. (1997). A controlled study of eye movement desensitization and reprocessing for posttraumatic stress disordered sexual assault victims. *Bulletin of the Menninger Clinic, 61,* 317–334.

Rothbaum, B. O., Hodges, L. F., Kooper, R., Opdyke, D., Williford, J., & North, M. M. (1995). Effectiveness of virtual reality graded exposure in the treatment of agoraphobia. *American Journal of Psychiatry, 152,* 626–628.

Rothbaum, B. O., Hodges, L., Watson, B. A., Kessler, G. D., & Opdyke, D. (1996). Virtual reality exposure therapy in the treatment of fear of flying: A case report. *Behaviour Research and Therapy, 34*(8/6), 477–481.

Roy-Byrne, P. P., Cowley, D. S., & Katon, W. (in press). Pharmacotherapy of anxiety disorders. In *Textbook of therapeutic medicine for practicing physicians.*

Roy-Byrne, P. P., Geraci, M., & Uhde, T. (1986a). Life events and the onset of panic disorder. *American Journal of Psychiatry, 43,* 1424–1427

Roy-Byrne, P. P., Geraci, M., & Uhde, T. (1986b). Life events and the course of an illness in patients with panic disorder. *American Journal of Psychiatry, 143*, 1033–1035.

Roy-Byrne, P. P., & Katon, W. (1987). An update on treatment of the anxiety disorders. *Hospital and Community Psychiatry, 38*, 835–843.

Roy-Byrne, P. P., Mellman, T., & Uhde, T. (1988). Biological findings in panic disorder: Neuroendocrine and sleep-related abnormalities. *Journal of Anxiety Disorders, 2*, 17–29.

Rupert, P. A., & Holmes, D. S. (1978). Effects of multiple sessions of true and placebo heart rate biofeedback training on the heart rates and anxiety levels of anxious patients during and following treatment. *Psychophysiology, 15*, 582–589.

Said, T., Rossi, J., Van Oyen, M., & Wint, S. (1998). The treatment of hyperventilation and panic disorder with Davanloo's intensive short term dynamic psychotherapy: Part I to III. *International Journal of Intensive Short-Term Dynamic Psychotherapy, 12*(1), 3–25.

Said, T., & Schubmehl, J. Q. (1998). Editorial comment. *International Journal of Intensive Short-Term Dynamic Psychotherapy, 12* (1), 1–2.

Salas, J. A., & Dattilio, F. M. (1997). Biofeedback. *Doctors' Forum, 2*(4), 8–11.

Salkovskis, P. M. (1988). Phenomenology, assessment, and the cognitive model of panic. In S. Rachman & J. D. Maser (Eds.), *Panic: Psychological perspectives*. Hillsdale, NJ: Erlbaum.

Salkovskis, P. M. (1995a). Safety seeking behaviours in agoraphobia: An experimental investigation. Presented at the World Congress of Behavioural and Cognitive Psychotherapies, Copenhagen, Denmark.

Salkovskis, P. M. (1995b). Cognitive approaches to health anxiety and obsessional problems: Some unique features and how this affects treatment. Presented at the World Congress of Behavioural and Cognitive Psychotherapies, Copenhagen, Denmark.

Salkovskis, P. M., & Clark, D. M. (1989). Affective responses to hyperventilation: A test of the cognitive model of panic. In S. Rachman & J. C. Maser (Eds.), *Panic: Psychological perspectives*. Hillsdale, NJ: Erlbaum.

Salkovskis, P. M., & Clark, D. M. (1993). Panic disorder and hypochondriasis. *Advances in Behavior Research and Therapy, 15*, 23–48.

Salkovskis, P. M., Clark, D. M., & Gelder, M. G. (1996). Cognition-behaviour links in the persistence of panic. *Behaviour Research and Therapy, 34*(5/6), 453–458.

Salkovskis, P. M., Clark, D. M., & Hackmann, A. (1991). Treatment of panic attacks using cognitive therapy without exposure or breathing retraining. *Behaviour Research and Therapy, 29*, 161–166.

Salkovskis, P. M., Jones, D. R. O., & Clark, D. M. (1986). Respiratory control in the treatment of panic attacks: Replication and extension with concurrent measurement of behaviour and pCO_2. *British Journal of Psychiatry, 148*, 526–532.

Salkovskis, P. M., Warwick, H. M. C., Clark, D. M., & Vessels, D. J. (1986). A demonstration of acute hyperventilation during naturally occurring panic attacks. *Behaviour Research and Therapy, 24*, 91–94.

Sandberg, D. P., & Liebowitz, M. R. (1990). Potential mechanisms for sodium lactate's induction of panic. In J. C. Ballenger (Ed.), *Neurobiology of panic disorder*. New York: Wiley-Liss.

Sanderson, A., & Carpenter, R. (1992). Eye movement desensitization versus image confrontation: A single-session crossover study of 58 phobic subjects. *Journal of Behavior Therapy and Experimental Psychiatry, 23*(4), 269–275.

Sanderson, W. C., DiNardo, P. A., Rapee, R. M., & Barlow, D. H. (1990). Syndrome comorbidity in patients diagnosed with DSM-III-R anxiety disorders. *Journal of Abnormal Psychology, 99*, 308–312.

Sanderson, W. C., Rapee, R. M., & Barlow, D. H. (1989). The influence of an illusion of control on panic attacks induced via inhalation of 5.5% carbon dioxide-enriched air. *Archives of General Psychiatry, 46*, 157–162.

Sanderson, W. C., & Wetzler, S. (1993). Observations on the cognitive-behavioral treatment of panic disorder: Impact of benzodiazepines. *Psychotherapy, 30*(1), 125–132.

Scheck, M. M., Schaeffer, J. A., & Gillette, C. S. (1998). Brief psychological intervention with traumatized young women: The efficacy of eye movement desensitization and reprocessing. *Journal of Traumatic Stress, 11*, 25–44.

Schmidt, N. B., Lerew, D. R., & Jackson, R. J. (1997). The role of anxiety sensitivity in the pathogenesis of panic: Prospective evaluation of spontaneous panic attacks during acute stress. *Journal of Abnormal Psychology, 106*(3), 355–364.

Schmidt, N. B., & Telch, M. J. (1994). The role of safety information and fear of bodily sensations in moderating responses to hyperventilation challenge. *Behavior Therapy, 25*, 197–208.

Schmidt, N. B., & Telch, M. J. (1997). Non-psychiatric medical co-morbidity, health perceptions and treatment outcome in patients with panic disorders. *Health Psychology, 16*, 114–122.

Schneier, F. R., Liebowitz, M. R., Davies, S. O., Fairbanks, J., Hollander, E., Campeas, R., & Klein, D. F. (1990). Fluoxetine in panic disorder. *Journal of Clinical Psychopharmacology, 10*(2), 119–121.

Schwartz, M. S., & Olson, R. P., (1995). A historical perspective on the field of biofeedback and applied psychophysiology. In M. S. Schwartz (Ed.), *Biofeedback*. New York: Guilford.

Scupi, B. S., Maser, J. D., & Uhde, T. W. (1992). The National Institute of Mental Health Panic Questionnaire. An instrument for assessing clinical characteristics of panic disorder. *Journal of Nervous and Mental Disease, 180*, 566–572.

Sexton, T. L., Montgomery, D., Goff, K., & Nugent, W. (1993). Ethical, therapeutic and legal considerations in the use of paradoxical techniques: The emerging debate. *Journal of Mental Health Counseling, 15*(3), 260–277.

Shapiro, A. K., Struening, E. L., Shapiro, E., & Milcarek, B. I. (1983). Diazepam: How much better than placebo? *Journal of Psychiatric Research, 17*, 15–73.

Shapiro, F. (1989a) Efficacy of the eye movement desensitization procedure in the treatment of traumatic memories. *Journal of Traumatic Stress, 2*(2), 199–275.

Shapiro, F. (1989b). Eye movement desensitization: A new treatment for posttraumatic stress disorder. *Journal of Behavior Therapy and Experimental Psychiatry, 20*(3), 211–217.

Shapiro, F. (1991). Eye movement desensitization and reprocessing procedure. From EMD to EMDR—a new treatment model for anxiety related trauma. *Behavior Therapist, 14*, 128, 133–135.

Shapiro, F. (1995). *Eye movement desensitization and reprocessing: Basic principles, protocols and procedures*. New York: Guilford.

Shapiro, F. (1996). Eye movement desensitization and reprocessing (EMDR): Evaluation of controlled PTSD research. *Journal of Behavior Therapy and Experimental Psychiatry, 27*, 209–218.

Shapiro, F. (1998a). Eye movement desensitization and reprocessing

(EMDR): Historical context, recent research, and future directions. In L. Vandercreek & T. Jackson (Eds.), *Innovations in clinical practice: A source book* (Vol. 16). Sarasota, FL: Professional Resource Press.

Shapiro, F. (1998b). Personal communication.

Shapiro, F., & Forrest, M. S. (1997). *EMDR: The breakthrough therapy.* New York: Basic Books.

Sharp, D. M., Power, K., Simpson, R. J., Swanson, V., Moodie, E., Anstee, J. A., & Ashford, J. J. (1996). Fluvoxamine, placebo and cognitive behaviour therapy used alone and in combination in the treatment of panic disorder and agoraphobia. *Journal of Anxiety Disorders, 10,* 19–242.

Shear, M. K., Devereaux, R. B., Kramer-Fox, R., Mann, J. J., & Frances, A. (1984). Low prevalence of mitral valve prolapse in patients with panic disorder. *American Journal of Psychiatry, 141,* 302–303.

Shear, M. K., Fyer, A. J., Ball, G., Josephson, S., Fitzpatrick, M., Gitlin, B., Frances, A., Gorman, J., Liebowitz, M., & Klein, D. F.(1991). Vulnerability to sodium lactate in panic disorder patients given cognitive-behavioral therapy. *American Journal of Psychiatry, 148,* 795–797.

Shear, M. K., Pilkonis, P. A., Cloitre, M., & Leon, A. C. (1994). Cognitive behavioral treatment compared with nonprescriptive treatment of panic disorder. *Archives of General Psychiatry, 51,* 395–401.

Sheehan, D. V. (1982). Panic attacks and phobias. *New England Journal of Medicine, 307,* 156–158.

Sheehan, D. V. (1983). *The anxiety disease.* New York: Scribner's.

Sheehan, D. V., Ballenger, J., & Jacobsen, G. (1980). Treatment of endogenous anxiety with phobic, hysterical, and hypochondriacal symptoms. *Archives of General Psychiatry, 37,* 51–59.

Sheehan, D. V., Carr, D. B., Fishman, S. M., Walsh, M. M., & Peltier-Saxe, D. (1985). Lactate infusion in anxiety research: Its evolution and practice. *Journal of Clinical Psychiatry, 46,* 158–165.

Sheehan, D. V., Sheehan, K. F., & Minichiello, E. (1981). Age of onset of phobic disorders: A re-evaluation. *Comprehensive Psychiatry, 22,* 544–553.

Sholomskas, D. E., Wickamaratne, P. J., Dologo, L., O'Brien, D. W., Leaf, P. J., & Woods, S. W. (1993). Postpartum onset of panic disorder: A coincidental event? *Journal of Clinical Psychiatry, 54,* 476–480.

Singh, Y. N., & Blumenthal, M. (1997). Kava: An overview. *Herbalgram, 39,* 33–55.

Skerrit, P. W. (1983). Anxiety and the heart—a historical review. *Psychological Medicine, 13,* 17–25.

Skolnick, P., & Paul, S. M. (1983). New concepts in the neurobiology of anxiety. *Journal of Clinical Psychiatry, 44,* 12–19.

Snaith, R. P. (1968). A clinical investigation of phobia. *British Journal of Psychiatry, 117,* 673–697.

Solkol, L., Beck, A. T., Greenberg, R. L., Wright, F. D., & Berchick, R. J. (1989). Cognitive therapy of panic disorder: A non-pharmacological alternative. *Journal of Nervous and Mental Disease, 177,* 711–716.

Solymon, L., Beck, P., Solymon, C., & Hugel, R. (1974). Some etiological factors in phobic neurosis. *Canadian Journal of Psychiatry, 19,* 69–78.

Spiegel, D. A., & Bruce, T. J. (1997). Benzodiazepines and exposure-based cognitive-behavior therapies for panic disorder: Conclusions from combined treatment trials. *American Journal of Psychiatry, 154*(6), 788–789.

Spiegel, D. A., Bruce, T. J., Gregg, S. F., & Nuzzarello, A. (1994). Does cognitive behavior therapy assist slow-taper alprazolam discontinuation in panic disorder? *American Journal of Psychiatry, 151,* 876–881.

Spielberger, C. D. (1983). *Manual for the state-trait anxiety inventory (STAI Form Y).* Palo Alto, CA: Consulting Psychologists Press.

Spielberger, C. D., Gorsuch, R. E., & Lushene, R. E. (1970). *Manual for the state-trait anxiety inventory (STAI Form Y).* Palo Alto, CA: Consulting Psychologists Press.

Spitzer, R. L., & Williams, J. B. W. (1986). *Structured clinical interview for DSM-III-R, Upjohn Version (SCID-UP-R).* New York: Biometrics Research Dept., New York State Psychiatric Institute.

Spitzer, R. L., Williams, J. B. W., & Gibbon, M. (1987). *Instructional manual for the Structured Clinical Interview Schedule for DSM-III (SCID, 7/1/85 revision).* New York: Biometrics Research Dept., New York State Psychiatric Institute.

Stacevic, V., Uhlenhuth, E. H., Kellner, R., & Pathak, D. (1993). Co-morbidity in panic disorder. *Psychiatry Research, 46,* 285–293.

Stampler, F. M. (1982). Panic disorder: Description, conceptualization and implications for treatment *Clinical Psychology Review, 2*(1), 469–486.

Starkman, M. N., Zelnik, T. C., Nesse, R. M., & Cameron, O. G. (1985). Anxiety in patients with pheochromocytomas. *Archives of Internal Medicine, 145,* 248–252.

Starr, C. G. (1991). *A history of the ancient world* (4th ed.). New York: Oxford University Press.

Steer, R., & Beck, A. T. (1996). Generalized anxiety and panic disorders: Response to Cox, Cohen, Direnfeld, and Swinson. *Behavior Research and Therapy, 34*(11–12), 955–957.

Stein, M. B., & Uhde, T. W. (1990). Panic disorder and major depression: Lifetime relationship and biological markers. In J. C. Ballenger (Ed.), *Clinical aspects of panic disorder.* New York: Wiley-Liss.

Svensson, T. H. (1987). Peripheral, autonomic regulation of locus coeruleus noradrenergic neurons in brain: Putative implications for psychiatry and psychopharmacology. *Psychopharmacology, 92,* 1–7.

Swinson, R. P., Soulios, C., Cox, B. J., & Kuch, K. (1992). Brief treatment of emergency room patients with panic attacks. *American Journal of Psychiatry, 149,* 944–946.

Taylor, C. B., Sheikh, J., Agras, W. S., Roth, W. T., Margraf, J., Ehlers, A., Maddock, R. J., & Gossard, D. (1986). Self report of panic attacks: Agreement with heart rate changes. *American Journal of Psychiatry, 143,* 478–482.

Taylor, M. A. (1987). DSM-III organic mental disorders. In G. L. Tischler (Ed.), *Diagnosis and classification in psychiatry: A critical appraisal of DSM-III.* Cambridge, England: Cambridge University Press.

Taylor, S. (1994). Comment on Otto et al. (1992): Hypochondriacal concerns, anxiety sensitivity and panic disorder. *Journal of Anxiety Disorders, 6,* 93–104.

Taylor, S. (1995). Panic disorder and hypochondriacal concerns: Reply to Otto and Pollack (1994). *Journal of Anxiety Disorders, 9*(1), 87–88.

Taylor, S., Koch, W. J., & McNally, R. J. (1992). How does anxiety sensitivity vary across the anxiety disorders? *Journal of Anxiety Disorders, 6,* 249–259.

Taylor, S., Koch, W. J., McNally, R. J., & Crockett, D. J. (1992). Conceptualization of anxiety sensitivity. *Psychological Assessment, 4,* 245–250.

Taylor, S., & Rachman, S. J. (1992). Fear and avoidance of aversive affective states: Dimension and causal relations. *Journal of Anxiety Disorders, 6,* 15–25.

Taylor, S., & Rachman, S. (1994). Klein's suffocation theory of panic. *Archives of General Psychiatry, 51,* 505–506.

Taylor, S., Woody, S., Koch, W. J., McLean, P. D., & Anderson, K. W. (1996). Suffocation false alarms and efficacy of cognitive behavioral therapy for panic disorder. *Behavior Therapy, 27*(1), 115–126.

Telch, M. J. (1988). Combined pharmacological and psychological treatment for panic sufferers. In S. Rachman & J. D. Maser (Eds.), *Panic: Psychological perspectives.* Hillsdale, NJ: Erlbaum.

Telch, M. J., Brouillard, M., Telch, C. F., Agras, W. S., & Taylor, C. B. (1989). The role of cognitive appraisal in panic-related avoidance. *Behavior Research and Therapy, 27,* 373–383.

Telch, M. J., & Harrington, P. J. (1992, November). The role of anxiety sensitivity and expectedness of arousal in mediating affective response to 35% carbon dioxide. Presented at meeting of the Association for the Advancement of Behavior Therapy, Boston.

Telch, M. J., & Lucas, R. A. (1994). Combined pharmacological and psychological treatment of panic disorder: Current status and future direction (pp. 117–197). In B. E. Wolf & J. D. Masser (Eds.), *Treatment of panic disorder: A consensus development conference.* Washington, DC: American Psychiatric Press.

Telch, M. J., Lucas, J. A., Schmidt, N. B., Hanna, H. H., Jaimez, T. L., & Lucas, R. A. (1993). Group cognitive-behavioral treatment of panic disorder. *Behavior Research and Therapy, 31*(3), 279–287.

Telch, M. J., Shermis, M. D., & Lucas, J. A. (1989). Anxiety sensitivity: Unitary personality trait or domain-specific appraisals? *Journal of Anxiety Disorders, 3,* 25–32.

Telch, M. J., Silverman, A., & Schmidt, N. B. (1996). The relationship between anxiety sensitivity and perceived control in a caffeine challenge. *Journal of Anxiety Disorders, 10,* 21–35.

Tellegen, A. (1985). Structures of mood and personality and their relevance to assessing anxiety, with an emphasis on self-report. In A. H. Tuma & J. D. Maser (Eds.), *Anxiety and the anxiety disorders.* Hillsdale, NJ: Erlbaum.

Thomas, A., Chess, S., Birch, H. G., Hertzig, M., & Korn, J. S. (1963). *Behavioral individuality in early childhood*. New York: Universities Press.

Thorpe, G. L., & Burns, L. E. (1983). *The agoraphobic syndrome*. New York: Wiley.

Thyer, B. A. (1993). Childhood separation anxiety disorder and adult-onset agoraphobia: Review of evidence. In C. G. Last (Ed.), *Anxiety across life span: A developmental perspective*. New York: Springer.

Thyer, B. A., Himle, J., & Fischer, D. (1988). Is parental death a selective precursor to either panic disorder or agoraphobia? A test of the separation anxiety hypothesis. *Journal of Anxiety Disorders, 2*, 333–338.

Thyer, B. A., Himle, J., & Miller-Gogoleski, M. A. (1989). The relationship of parental death to panic disorder: A community-based replication. *Phobia Practice and Research Journal, 2*, 29–36.

Thyer, B. A., Nesse, R. M., Cameron, O. G., & Curtis, G. C. (1985). Agoraphobia: A test for the separation anxiety hypothesis. *Behavior Research and Therapy, 23*, 75–78.

Thyer, B. A., Nesse, R. M., Curtis, G. C., & Cameron, O. G. (1986). Panic disorder: A test for the separation anxiety hypothesis. *Behavior Research and Therapy, 24*, 209–211.

Torgersen, A. M. (1981). Genetic factors in temperamental individuality. *Journal of the American Academy of Child Psychiatry, 20*, 702–711.

Torgersen, A. M. (1987). Longitudinal research on temperament in twins. *Acta Geneticae Medicae et Gemellologiae, 36*, 145–154.

Torgersen, A. M. (1989). Genetic and environmental influences on temperamental development: A longitudinal study of twins from infancy to adolescence. In S. Doxiadis (Ed.), *Early influences shaping the individual*. New York: Plenum.

Torgersen, S. (1983). Genetic factors in anxiety disorder. *Archives of General Psychiatry, 40*, 1085–1089.

Torgersen, S. (1985). Hereditary differentiation of anxiety and affective neuroses. *British Journal of Psychiatry, 146*, 530–534.

Torgersen, S. (1993). Relationship between adult and childhood anxiety disorders: A genetic hypothesis. In C. G. Last (Ed.), *Anxiety across life span: A developmental perspective*. New York: Springer.

Toseland, R. W., & Siporin, M. (1986). When to recommend group treatment: A review of the clinical and the research literature. *International Journal of Group Psychotherapy, 36*(2), 171–201.

Trull, T. J., Nietzel, M. T., & Main, A. (1988). The use of meta-analysis to assess the clinical significance of behavior therapy for agoraphobia. *Behavior Therapy, 19,* 527–538.

Tucker, W. I. (1956). Diagnosis and treatment of the phobic reaction. *American Journal of Psychiatry, 112,* 825–830.

Uhde, J. W. (1990). Caffeine provocation of panic: A focus on biological mechanisms. In J. C. Ballenger (Ed.), *Neurobiology of panic.* New York: Wiley-Liss.

Uhde, J. W., Boulenger, J., Roy-Byrne, P. P., Vittone, B. J., Geraci, M., & Post, R. M. (1985). Longitudinal course of panic disorder: Clinical and psychological considerations. *Progress in Neuropsychopharmacology and Biological Psychiatry, 9,* 39–51.

Uhde, T. W., & Mellman, T. W. (1987). Commentary on "relaxation induced panic (RIP): When resting isn't peaceful." *Integrative Psychiatry, 5,* 101–104.

Van Balkom, A. J. L. M., Bakker, A., Spinhoven, P., Blaauw, B. M. J. W., Smeenk, S., & Ruesink, B. (1997). A meta-analysis of the treatment of panic disorder with or without agoraphobia: A comparison of psychopharmacological, cognitive-behavioral, and combination treatments. *Journal of Nervous and Mental Diseases, 185* (8), 510–516.

Van den Hout, M. (1988). The explanation of experimental panic. In J. Rachman & J. D. Maser (Eds.), *Panic: Psychological perspectives.* Hilsdale, NJ: Erlbaum.

Van den Hout, M. A., & Griez, E. (1985). Peripheral panic symptoms occur during changes in alveolar carbon dioxide. *Comprehensive Psychiatry, 26,* 381–387.

Van den Hout, M., Van der Molen, G., Griez, E., & Lousberg, H. (1987). Specificity of interoceptive fear to panic disorder. *Journal of Psychopathology and Behavioral Assessment, 9,* 99–109.

Van Hout, W. J. P. J., Emmelkamp, P. M. G., & Scholing, A. (1994). The role of negative self-statements during exposure in vivo: A process study of eight panic disorder patients with agoraphobia. *Behavior Modification, 18*(4), 389–410.

Van Rijsoort, M., & Arntz, A. (1997). Interpersonal therapy as a treatment for panic disorder. Paper presented at the 27th Congress of the

European Association for Behavioural and Cognitive Psychotherapies, September 24–27, Venice, Italy.

Villeponteaux, V. A., Lydiard, R. B., Laraia, M. T., Stuart, G. W., & Ballenger, J. C. (1992). The effects of pregnancy on preexisting panic disorder. *Journal of Clinical Psychiatry, 53*, 210–203.

Volz, H. P., & Kieser, M. (1997). Kava-kava extract WS 1490 versus placebo in anxiety disorders: A randomized placebo controlled 25-week outpatient trial. *Pharmacopsychiatry, 30*, 1–5.

Von Korff, M., Shapiro, S., Burke, J. D., Teitelbaum, M., Skinner, E. A., German, P., Turner, R. W., Klein, L., & Burns, B. (1987). Anxiety and depression in a primary care clinic: Comparison of diagnostic interview schedule, general health questionnaire, and practitioner assessments. *Archives of General Psychiatry, 44*, 152–156.

Wardle, J. (1990). Behavior therapy and benzodiazepines: Allies or antagonists? *British Journal of Psychiatry, 156*, 163–168.

Wardle, J., Hayward, P., Higgitt, A., Stabl, M., Blizard, R., & Gray, J. (1994). Effects of concurrent diazepam treatment on the outcome of exposure therapy in agoraphobia. *Behaviour Research and Therapy, 32*, 203–215.

Ware, J. E., & Sherbourne, C. D. (1992). The MOS 36-item Short-Form Health Survey (SF-36), I: conceptual framework and item selection. *Medical Care, 30*, 473–483.

Warwick, H. M. C., & Salokovskis, P. M. (1990). Hypochondriasis. *Behavior Research and Therapy, 28*, 105–117.

Wayne, G. J. (1966). The psychiatric emergency: An overview. In G. J. Wayne & R. R. Koegler (Eds.), *Emergency psychiatric and brief therapy* (p. 321). Boston: Little, Brown.

Weiss, S. R. B., & Uhde, T. W. (1990). Annual models of anxiety (pp. 3–27). In J. C. Ballenger (Ed.), *Neurobiology of panic disorder*. New York: Wiley-Liss.

Weissman, M. M. (1993). Family genetic studies of panic disorder. *Journal of Psychiatric Research, 27*(suppl. 1), 69–78.

Weissman, M. M., Klerman, G. L., Markowitz, J. S., & Oullette, R. (1989). Suicidal ideation and suicide attempts in panic disorder and attacks. *New England Journal of Medicine, 321*, 1209–1214.

Weissman, M. M., Leckman, J. F., Merikangas, K. R., Gammon, G. D., & Prusoff, B. A. (1984). Depression and anxiety disorders in parents and children. *Archives of General Psychiatry, 41*, 845–852.

Weissman, M. M., & Merikangas, K. R. (1986, June). The epidemiology of anxiety and panic disorders: An update. *Journal of Clinical Psychiatry, 47*(suppl. 1), 1–7.

Weissman, M. M., Myers, J. K., Tischler, G. L., et al. (1985). Psychiatric disorders (DSM-III) and cognitive impairment among elderly in a U.S. urban community. *Acta Psychiatrica Scandinavica, 71,* 366–379.

Wells, A., & Dattilio, F. M. (1992). Negative outcome in cognitive-behavior therapy: A case study. *Behavioural Psychotherapy, 20,* 291–294.

Westling, B. E., & Ost, L., (1995). Cognitive bias in panic disorder patients and changes after cognitive-behavioral treatments. *Behavior Research and Therapy, 33*(5), 585–588.

White, J. (in press). "Stress control" large group therapy for generalized anxiety disorder: Two year follow-up. *Journal of Mental Health.*

White, J., Brooks, N., & Keenan, M. (1995). "Stress control." A controlled comparative investigation of large group therapy for generalized anxiety disorder: Progress of change. *Clinical Psychology/ Psychotherapy, 2,* 86–97.

White, J., Keenan, M., & Brooks, N. (1992). Stress control: A controlled comparative investigation of large group therapy for generalized anxiety disorder. *Behavioral Psychotherapy, 20,* 97–114.

Williams, J. C. (1836). *Practical observations on nervous and sympathetic palpitations of the heart, as well as on palpitations, the result of organic disease.* London: Churchill.

Williams, K. E., Chambless, D. L., & Ahrens, A. (1997). Are emotions frightening? An extension of the fear of fear construct. *Behaviour Research and Therapy, 35*(3), 239–248.

Williams, S. L. (1990). Guided mastery treatment of agoraphobia: Beyond stimulus exposure. *Progress in Behavior Modification, 26,* 89–121.

Williams, S. L., & Zane, G. (1989). Guided mastery and stimulus exposure treatment for severe performance anxiety in agoraphobics. *Behaviour Research and Therapy, 27*(3), 237–245.

Wilson, D., Silver, S. M, Covi, W., & Foster, S. (1996). Eye movement desensitization and reprocessing: Effectiveness and autonomic correlates. *Journal of Behavior Therapy and Experimental Psychiatry, 27,* 219–229.

References

Wilson, R. (1986). *Don't panic: Taking control of anxiety attacks.* New York: Rawson.

Wilson, S. A., Becker, L. A., & Tinker, R. H. (1995). Eye movement desensitization and reprocessing (EMDR) treatment for psychologically traumatized individuals. *Journal of Consulting and Clinical Psychology, 63,* 928–937.

Wilson, S. A., Becker, L. A., & Tinker, R. H. (1997). Fifteen-month follow-up of eye movement desensitization and reprocessing (EMDR) treatment for PTSD and psychological trauma. *Journal of Consulting and Clinical Psychology, 65,* 1047–1056.

Witchen, H. U. (1988). Natural course and spontaneous remissions of untreated anxiety disorders. Results of the Munich follow-up study (MFS). In I. Hand & H. U. Wittchen (Eds.), *Panic and phobias 2: Treatment and variables affecting course and outcome.* Berlin: Springer-Verlag.

Wolf, M. E., & Mosnaim, A. D. (1983). Phenylethylamine in neuro-psychiatric disorders. *General Pharmacology, 14*(4), 385–390.

Wolf, S. (1947). Sustained contraction of the diaphragm, the mechanism of a common type of dyspnea and precordial pain. *Journal of Clinical Investigation. 26,* 1201.

Wolpe, J., (1958). *Psychotherapy by reciprocal inhibition.* Stanford, CA: Stanford University Press.

Wolpe, J. (1970). Identifying the antecedents of an agoraphobic reaction: A transcript. *Journal of Behavior Therapy and Experimental Psychiatry, 1,* 299–304.

Wolpe, J. (1982). *The practice of behavior therapy* (3rd ed.). New York: Pergamon.

Wolpe, J., & Abrams, J. (1991). Posttraumatic stress disorder overcome by eye movement desensitization: A case report. *Journal of Behavior Therapy and Experimental Psychiatry, 22,* 39–43.

Woods, S. W., Charney, D. S., Goodman, W. K., Redmond, D. E., & Heninger, G. R. (1987). Carbon dioxide-induced anxiety: Behavioral, physiological, and biochemical effects of carbon dioxide in patients with panic disorders and healthy subjects. *Archives of General Psychiatry, 45,* 43–52.

Zarate, R., Rapee, R. M., Craske, M. G., & Barolw, D. H. (1988). Response-norms for symptom induction procedures. Presented at the

22nd annual convention of the Association for the Advancement of Behavior Therapy, New York.

Zegans, L. S. (1982). Stress and development of somatic disorders. In L. Goldberger & S. Breznitz (Eds.), *Handbook of stress*. New York: Free Press.

Zinborg, R. E., & Barlow, D. H. (1996). Structure of anxiety and anxiety disorders: A hierarchical model. *Journal of Abnormal Psychology, 105*(2), 181–193.

Zitrin, C. M., Klein, D. F., & Woerner, M. G. (1978). Behavior therapy, supportive psychotherapy, imipramine and phobias. *Archives of General Psychiatry, 35*, 107–116.

Zitrin, C. M., Klein, D. F., Woerner, M. G., & Ross, D. C. (1978). Treatment of phobias: 1. Comparison of imipramine hydrochloride and placebo. *Archives of General Psychiatry, 40*, 125–138.

Zoellner, L. A., Craske, M., & Rapee, R. (1996). Stability of catastrophic cognitions in panic disorder. *Behavior Research and Therapy, 34*(5/6), 399–402.

Zuercher-White, E. (1997). *Treating panic disorder and agoraphobia: A step-by-step clinical guide*. Oakland, CA: New Harbinger.

Zung, W. W. K. (1975). A rating instrument for anxiety disorders. *Psychosomatics, 12*, 371–379.

Appendix A

Suggested Professional Readings

The following are suggested professional readings for clinicians and practitioners. The asterisks indicate that the work in question is one we particularly recommend.

*Ballenger, J. C. (1990). *Neurobiology of panic disorder*. New York: Wiley-Liss.
Exclusively addresses the psychobiology of panic disorder. Individuals who want an in-depth look at the biochemistry and etiology of panic will find this an excellent source.
*Barlow, D. H. (1988). *Anxiety and its disorders: The nature and treatment of anxiety and panic*. New York: Guilford.
Covers the full spectrum of anxiety disorders, including a superb chapter on panic. Although more than 10 years old, it is still to be considered by many researchers and clinicians in the field to be the Bible on anxiety disorders.
*Barlow, D. H., & Cerny, J. A. (1988). *Psychological treatment of panic: Treatment manuals for practitioners*. New York: Guilford.
Another book that focuses exclusively on panic disorder, it addresses the nature and consequences of panic, and includes a thorough discussion of the treatments used.

Beck, A. T., & Emery, G. (1985). *Anxiety disorders and phobias: A cognitive perspective.* New York: Basic Books.

A section on panic disorder specifically underscores the cognitive-behavioral approach.

Hecker, J. E., & Thorpe, G. L. (1991). *Agoraphobia and panic: A guide to psychological treatment.* Needham Heights, MA: Allyn & Bacon.

*Katon, W. (1992). *Panic disorder in the medical setting.* Rockville, MD: National Institute of Mental Health.

Full of information on the treatment of panic disorder, it spans the spectrum from psychobiology to cognitive-behavioral treatments, and also includes a detailed history of panic.

*Kendall, P. C., Chansky, T. E., Kane, M. T., Kim, R. S. Kortlander, E., Ronan, K. R., Sessa, F. M., & Siqueland, L. (1992). *Anxiety disorders in youths: Cognitive-behavioral interventions.* Boston: Allyn & Bacon.

This text on anxiety disorders addresses issues with children and adolescents. It has a strong chapter on panic disorder and specific treatment modalities.

Klerman, G. L. (Ed.) (1993). *Panic, anxiety and its treatments.* Washington, DC: American Psychiatric Press.

Rachman, S., & Maser, J. D. (1988). *Panic: Psychological perspectives.* Hillsdale, NJ: Erlbaum.

*Rapee, R. M. (Ed.) (1996). *Current controversies in the anxiety disorders.* New York: Guilford.

Several chapters on panic address issues of classification, etiology, and treatment.

Zal, H. M. (1990). *Panic disorder: The great pretender.* New York: Plenum Press.

*Zuercher-White, E. (1997). *Treating panic disorder and agoraphobia: A step-by-step clinical guide.* Oakland, CA: New Harbinger.

A comprehensive treatment-focused text that would be of interest to both clinicians and patients.

Appendix B

Suggested Readings for Patients

As most clinicians know, it is extremely important for patients to be exposed to resources, particularly through the use of bibliotherapy. The following references may prove helpful. Once again, those sources preceded by an asterisk are ones that we feel are particularly useful.

Aisbett, B. (1993). *Living with it: A survivor's guide to panic attacks.* Sydney, Australia: Harper Collins.

Babior, S., & Goldman, C. (1990). *Overcoming panic attacks: Strategies to free yourself from the anxiety trap.* Minneapolis: Compcare.

*Barlow, D. H., & Craske, M. G. (1988). *Mastery of your anxiety and panic.* Albany, NY: Graywind.

Bourne, E. J. (1990). *The anxiety and phobia workbook: A step-by-step program for curing yourself of extreme anxiety, panic attacks and phobias.* New York: M.J.F. Books.

*Clum, G. A. (1990). *Coping with panic: A drug-free approach to dealing with anxiety attacks.* Belmont, CA: Wadsworth.

Fox, B. (1997). *Power over panic: Freedom from panic/anxiety related disorders.* South Melbourne, Australia: Addison, Wesley, Longman.

Gold, M. S. (1989). *The good news about panic anxiety and phobias.* New York: Bantam Books.

Greist, J., Jefferson, J., & Marks, I. (1986). *Anxiety and its treatment:*

Help is available. Washington, DC: American Psychiatric Association Press.

Handly, R., & Neff, P. (1985). *Anxiety and panic attacks: Their cause and cure*. New York: Rawson.

Kernodle, W. D. (1991). *Panic disorder*. Richmond, VA: William Byrd.

Marks, I. (1978). *Living with fear*. New York: McGraw-Hill.

Otto, M. W., Pollack, M. H., & Barlow, D. H. (1995). *Stopping anxiety medication: A workbook for patients wanting to discontinue benzodiazepine treatment for panic disorder*. San Antonio, TX: Graywind/Psychological Corp.

Peurifoy, R. Z. (1995). *Anxiety, phobias, and panic: A step-by-step program for regaining control of your life*. New York: Warner Books.

*Rachman, S., & DeSilva, P. (1996). *Panic disorder: The facts*. Oxford: Oxford University Press.

Sheehan, D. (1983). *The anxiety disease*. Toronto: Bantam Books.

Trickett, S. (1996). *Panic attacks: A natural approach*. Berkeley, CA: Ulysses.

Weekes, C. (1969). *A simple effective cure for agoraphobia*. New York: Bantam Books.

Weekes, C. (1976). *Peace from nervous suffering*. New York: Bantam Books.

Weekes, C. (1976). *Simple, effective treatment of agoraphobia*. New York: Hawthorne.

*Wilson, R. (1986). *Don't panic: Taking control of anxiety attacks*. New York: Rawson.

*Zuercher-White, E. (1995). *An end to panic: Breakthrough techniques for overcoming panic disorder*. Oakland, CA: New Harbinger.

Appendix C

Referral Sources of Information

The following are referral sources that clinicians or patients may contact in order to receive more information with regard to panic disorder and its treatments. Many of these organizations also provide free literature and phamphlets.

American Academy of Family
Physicians
(AAFP)
8880 Ward Parkway
Kansas City, MO 64114
(816) 333-9700

American Psychiatric Association
(APA)
1400 K St., N.W.
Washington, DC 20005
(202) 682-6324

American Counseling Association
(ACA)
5999 Stevenson Ave.
Alexandria, VA 22304
(703) 823-9800

American Psychological
Association
(APA)
750 1st St., NE
Washington, DC 20002
(202) 336-5500

Anxiety Disorders Association of America
(ADAA)
6000 Executive Blvd., Suite 513
Rockville, MD 20852-4004
1-900-737-3400 ($2 per minute)

Association for the Advancement of Behavior Therapy (AABT)
15 West 36th St.
New York, NY 10018
(212) 279-7970

Freedom from Fear
308 Seaview Ave.
South Beach, Staten Island, NY 10305
(718) 351-1717

National Alliance for the Mentally Ill
(NAMI)
2101 Wilson Blvd., Suite 302
Arlington, VA 22201
1-800-950-NAMI

National Anxiety Foundation
(NAF)
3135 Custer Drive
Lexington, KY 40517-4001
1-800-755-1576

National Institute of Mental Health
(NIMH)
5600 Fishers Lane
Rockville, MD 20857
(301) 443-4513
1-800-64-PANIC

National Mental Health Association
(NHMA)
1021 Prince St.
Alexandria, VA 22314-2971
1-800-969-NMHA

National Panic/Anxiety Disorder Newsletter
1718 Burgandy Place
Santa Rosa, CA 95403
(707) 527-5738

Pathway Systems
P.O. Box 269
Chapel Hill, NC 27514
1-800-394-2299

Science and Medicine
79 Madison Ave.
New York, NY 10016-7880
(212) 213-714

This list was prepared by the Panic Disorder Education Program, National Institute of Mental Health, Parklawn Building, Room 7-99, 5600 Fishers Lane, Rockville, MD 20857.

Appendix D

Model of Treatment Plan for Panic Disorder

This treatment model represents a general plan of strategies, goals, and interventions that can be implemented in the treatment of panic disorder. In following the guidelines described below, both clinical judgment and flexibility must be considered. The treatment plan should be adjusted to each patient's individual characteristics and circumstances. In addition, since panic-disordered individuals frequently present with co-existing disorders, clinicians must decide the priority of disorders to target. A general rule to follow is that, unless the other disorder is causing most of the patient's dysfunction and distress, panic disorder should be a priority.

Overall Aims of Treatment

1. Establishing a strong therapeutic alliance based on trust, respect, effective communication, and collaborative work.
2. Facilitating patients' reconceptualizations of their disorders in a more objective and optimistic manner and providing them with an adequate rationale for the treatment approach to be implemented.
3. Helping patients to become active participants in their own recovery process.

4. Encouraging patients to take credit for the changes they accomplish in order to increase their self-esteem and internal locus of control.
5. Preventing premature termination of treatment by utilizing careful planning.

Overall Intervention Strategy

The treatment plan as outlined uses a cognitive-behavioral approach, however, it also may be adapted to a combination of other modalities. In this version, we have conceptualized the treatment of panic disorder in three phases: (I) panic control, (II) agoraphobia control, and (III) reduction of vulnerability to panic disorder. Phases I and II are standard components of CBT protocols (e.g., Barlow, Craske, Cerny, & Klosko, 1989; Clark & Salkovskis, 1987; Craske, Brown, & Barlow, 1991; Telch, Lucas, Schmidt, et al. 1993). The usefulness of adding a third phase to the treatment strategy has not yet been explored in controlled-outcome studies. However, in our clinical experiences, many panic cases suggest that interpersonal conflicts serve as an important predisposing factor for panic. Furthermore, patients seem to reduce their chances for relapse when interventions targeting such risk factors are employed.

Finally, since not all panic-disordered individuals experience agoraphobia or are significantly vulnerable to panic after the panic-control phase, their treatment may be limited to the initial phase.

Treatment Format

The panic-control phase requires from 12 to 14 50-minute individual sessions, conducted on a weekly basis. The combined lengths of the other two phases will vary depending on the extent of the individual's fear/avoidance, the nature of the patient's resources and conflicts, and coexisting disorders.

Goals and Specific Interventions

Phase I: Panic-Control Phase

Goal 1:

To correct patients' misinterpretations of bodily sensations accompanying emotional experiences, naturalistic activities, and stress responses.

Intervention Techniques

- Self-monitoring to help patients identify antecedents of panic attacks.
- Socratic questioning to facilitate patients' perceptions of the sequential and reciprocal influences among their thoughts, feelings, bodily changes, and behavior.
- Educating patients about (a) the nature of panic disorder, (b) the adaptive nature of anxiety, (c) the effect of chronic/acute distress on their bodily changes, and (d) the impact of hyperventilation on their physical state. Several means can be used: bibliotherapy, didactic presentations, and multimedia education (i.e., audiotapes, videotapes).
- Cognitive restructuring of relevant distorted beliefs and distorted information processing, particularly, "emotional reasoning," "catastrophization," "black-and-white thinking," and "probability overestimation of negative events."

Goal 2:

To reduce hyperarousal and to change hyperventilatory breathing patterns before and/or during panic.

Intervention Techniques

- Brief progressive muscle-relaxation training.
- Diaphragmatic breathing training.
- Biofeedback-assisted relaxation and diaphragmatic breathing.
- Homework: Patients are asked to practice relaxation and diaphragmatic breathing once a day and to keep a log of their

daily practice indicating the maximum relaxation achieved on a scale ranging from 0 to 10 (maximum relaxation).

Goal 3.1:

To extinguish patients' conditioned fear of bodily changes (interoceptive phobic reactions) in controlled situations; that is, situations designed by the therapist or used in panic treatment protocols to evoke feared bodily changes.

Intervention Techniques

- Gradual interoceptive exposure coupled initially with participant modeling.
- Guided self-dialogue in which the therapist models the patient how to substitute catastrophic thoughts/images with more adaptive and objective self-statements/images.
- Autonomic control through respiratory control training and noncatastrophic self-statements.
- Homework: Patients are required to practice the interoceptive exposure exercises (e.g., hyperventilating) at home twice a day for a specific period of time. During the exercises, patients are also asked to monitor their negative automatic thoughts and to challenge them.

Goal 3.2:

To extinguish patients' conditioned fear of bodily changes (interoceptive phobic reactions) in naturalistic situations; that is, in daily activities (e.g., physical exercise, sexual activity) and stimuli (e.g., caffeine ingestion) that involve bodily changes associated with arousal. This goal also includes eliminating the fear of emotions given the bodily changes associated with the emotional experience.

Intervention Techniques

- Education about the concept of fear of emotions (e.g., fear of fear, fear of anger).
- Imaginal rehearsal/covert self-modeling in which patients are

taught to imagine themselves engaged in the activity and coping effectively with the situations.

- Homework assignments involving gradual and systematic in vivo exposure to relevant stimuli/situations. During the exercises, patients are also asked to monitor their negative automatic thoughts and to challenge them.
- Autonomic control through respiratory control training.
- Cognitive restructuring.

Goal 4:
To reduce the use of avoidance as a coping skill.

Intervention Techniques

- Education about the concepts of safety behaviors and safety objects/signals and their role in maintaining patients' fears.
- Self-monitoring to identify subtle avoidance techniques, safety behaviors, and safety objects/signals.
- Homework: Patients are instructed to expose themselves to the bodily changes induced by the interoceptive exposure exercises and naturally occurring fear reactions without the display of such avoidance behavior or without the use of safety signals. Most important, the therapist must check that patients are not using the new coping tools, such as relaxation, diaphragmatic breathing, and cognitive challenge and self-statements, as subtle avoidance behaviors.

Phase II: Agoraphobia Control

Goal:
To eliminate patients' phobic avoidance of and distress concerning phobic places and situations.

Intervention Techniques

- Education about the role of avoidance in maintaining the fear and phobic behavior.

- Education about the role of exposure in the elimination of agoraphobic avoidance.
- Homework: Patients are instructed to expose themselves in vivo to phobic situations in a gradual manner (in terms of the intensity of the evoked fear). Specifically, patients are instructed to use two-hour or three-hour exposure periods three times per week.
- Coaching on the proper use of the new coping skills.

Phase III: Panic-Vulnerability Reduction

Goal:
To reduce vulnerability to panic. To reduce the risk factors for anxiety and panic and to help patients to diminish the chances for relapse and to improve their quality of life.

Intervention Techniques Techniques vary according to the type of factors identified. To move into this stage, core schemata and core conflicts must be identified during the previous treatment phases.

For intrapersonal conflicts (e.g., fear of sexual or hostile impulses, fear of dying, attachment, loss of control)

- Cognitive restructuring.
- Emotional skills training.

Brief case example: Charles discovered that he underwent apparently spontaneous panic attacks whenever he experienced unaccepted—not fully symbolized—homosexual impulses. This conflict became part of the treatment in this phase.

For interpersonal conflicts (e.g., dependence, lack of individuation, marital conflicts)

- Assertiveness and social skills training.
- Marital /family therapy.
- Therapeutic relationship/therapeutic alliance.

Brief case example: Christine realized that her unpredictable panic attacks were associated with thoughts about her husband. He recently had confessed to having an affair, and Christine was not sure that his relationship with the other woman was over. Through self-monitoring, she became aware of a particular thought that often crossed her mind ("He might be with her right now"), which triggered intense fear. Since previously she had not been aware of such a thought, the bodily changes associated with her fear reactions were interpreted as a heart attack.

Note 1: Psychotropic medications can be incorporated at any point in the treatment process. The object is to help patients reduce excessive anxiety levels that are interfering with the psychosocial learning process during treatment.

Note 2: It is always useful, when conceptualizing a case, to identify any potential problem(s) that you anticipate during the course of treatment. This awareness may help you to prevent a lack of progress or the interruption of treatment.

Index